PRAISE FOR *E-CC*

WEBSITE OPTIMIZATION

A must-have for any e-commerce business, this book captures technical expertise and the methodologies required to run very successful optimization programmes.
John Donnellan, Director, E-Commerce EMEA, Canon Europe

At last, a practical guide dedicated to Conversion Rate Optimization (CRO) for online retail.
Dave Chaffey, Co-Founder, SmartInsights.com

This book explores how to understand people, their behaviour, their feedback, their testing choices and win bigger revenues.
Avinash Kaushik, Digital Marketing Evangelist, Google, and author of *Web Analytics 2.0* and *Web Analytics: An hour a day*

Highly recommended for anyone who's looking to optimize their online store.
Paras Chopra, Founder and Chairman, VWO

Dan and Johann draw from their own in-the-trenches experience to craft an essential read for the developing CRO practitioner. From their strategic approach down to targeted tactics, they provide the playbook on how to uncover insights for e-commerce growth. This is just the kind of guide I'd want all of our team and customers to read.
Bratt Wittwer, former CEO, Qualaroo

Second Edition

E-Commerce Website Optimization

Why 95% of your website visitors don't buy, and what you can do about it

Johann van Tonder
Dan Croxen-John

KoganPage

Publisher's note

Every possible effort has been made to ensure that the information contained in this book is accurate at the time of going to press, and the publishers and authors cannot accept responsibility for any errors or omissions, however caused. No responsibility for loss or damage occasioned to any person acting, or refraining from action, as a result of the material in this publication can be accepted by the publisher or the authors.

First published in Great Britain and the United States in 2016 by Kogan Page Limited
Second edition 2021

Apart from any fair dealing for the purposes of research or private study, or criticism or review, as permitted under the Copyright, Designs and Patents Act 1988, this publication may only be reproduced, stored or transmitted, in any form or by any means, with the prior permission in writing of the publishers, or in the case of reprographic reproduction in accordance with the terms and licences issued by the CLA. Enquiries concerning reproduction outside these terms should be sent to the publishers at the undermentioned addresses:

2nd Floor, 45 Gee Street	122 W 27th St, 10th Floor	4737/23 Ansari Road
London	New York, NY 10001	Daryaganj
EC1V 3RS	USA	New Delhi 110002
United Kingdom		India

www.koganpage.com

Kogan Page books are printed on paper from sustainable forests.

© Johann van Tonder and Dan Croxen-John 2016, 2021

The right of Johann van Tonder and Dan Croxen-John to be identified as the authors of this work has been asserted by them in accordance with the Copyright, Designs and Patents Act 1988.

ISBNs

Hardback   978 1 78966 445 4
Paperback 978 1 78966 442 3
Ebook   978 1 78966 443 0

British Library Cataloguing-in-Publication Data

A CIP record for this book is available from the British Library.

Library of Congress Control Number

2020948477

Typeset by Integra
Print production managed by Jellyfish
Printed and bound by CPI Group (UK) Ltd, Croydon CR0 4YY

CONTENTS

LIST OF FIGURES AND TABLES

Figures

Tables

PREFACE

We wrote this book for our younger selves. In the past we have both run online businesses where our challenge was to massively increase sales. At the time we were working on two different continents, but both of us were under intense pressure to find some way of growing our businesses.

A book like this did not exist at the time, and if it had we would have devoured it. If you are the person we were then, we have written this for you. Our vision was to write a step-by-step guide, with clear guidance on how to increase your online sales.

Our decision raised eyebrows. Some warned us that writing a book that gives away our knowledge, reveals our secret sauce and expertise, would hurt our agency by enabling potential clients to do it for themselves.

That never worried us. Every day we see how frustrated people get when using e-commerce websites, not only in terms of their experience of using the site, but also the thought processes they go through when making a purchase. Solving these problems is what drives us. At our agency, we have developed an e-commerce optimization process, refined over many years – and it works. This is what we share with you.

Follow our structured programme and watch your revenue curve go up. We routinely see our clients achieving double-digit revenue increases within 12 months. Implement the process and see your businesses grow this year, next year and into the future.

A note about the second edition

This second edition presents a major revision and comprehensive update of the successful first edition. Tools have changed, the industry keeps evolving, and so has our framework. That is the nature of what we do. Always learning. Always adapting. Always optimizing.

Everything you're about to read, we had to learn the hard way. We know this book can make your own challenge to increase online sales easier than it was for us. If you have any questions, or would like to share how this book has benefited your business, please e-mail either of us, dan.croxen-john@awa-digital.com or johann.vantonder@awa-digital.com. We would be happy to hear from you and help you in any way we can.

ACKNOWLEDGEMENTS

We owe thanks to the team at Kogan Page, Lachean Humphreys and Jenny Volich. Thank you for telling us that we needed to write a second edition, and thanks for all your support.

Nicole Major from AWA has acted as our editor, researcher, proofreader and general fixer. She has been invaluable to the process.

This book has featured more work from respected practitioners and experts from the world of business experimentation. We would like to especially thank Professor Stefan Thomke (Harvard Business School) and Ron Kohavi (Microsoft) for sharing their research and knowledge. It has informed many of our thought processes.

Johann: Thank you Andrea, Brandt, Mickey and Silke for your patience. Working on the second edition meant spending many evenings and weekends away from home.

Dan: Thank you to my co-author, Johann. Your persistence in completing this second edition while doing a demanding day job has been inspiring.

Introduction to e-commerce optimization 01

This book is about growing your e-commerce business.

You won't find a list of tactics ready to copy and paste. What worked for others in the past may not work for you today.

What you need more than another menu of conversion tactics is a strategy relevant to you – and guaranteed to grow your business.

That's the purpose of this book. A step-by-step guide to a proven approach used all over the world. One not based on the latest fads, but on time-tested scientific principles.

CRO (conversion rate optimization) is only part of it. We find CRO, as it has come to be practised, too shallow. It may surprise you to hear this from the authors, who run a leading CRO agency. However, we haven't allowed ourselves to be constrained by those shackles.

By definition, CRO is focused on improving online conversion rates: turn more website visitors into paying customers. That's important and you will find ways to do just that in this book. But obsessing over conversion rate at the expense of other metrics can be detrimental to your business.

To illustrate that, Scenario A in Table 1.1 has double the conversion rate of Scenario B. Which of the two scenarios would you prefer? Hint: you can't bank conversion rate. You can't use it to pay salaries or rent.

E-commerce website optimization

To be clear, we don't dismiss CRO outright. On the contrary, you could argue that the framework in this book is simply a broader interpretation of CRO. Semantic nuances aside, below are some key pillars of e-commerce website optimization.

Table 1.1 Scenario A has the better conversion rate, but produces less revenue. A narrow focus on conversion rate can be detrimental to your business.

	Number of visitors	Total transactions	Conversion rate	Average order value	Total revenue
Scenario A	1,000	100	10%	20	2,000
Scenario B	1,000	50	5%	50	2,500

Customer profitability

$$Profit = Revenue\ less\ Cost$$

That accounting view of profit doesn't do a great job of explaining where profit comes from. It's high level and backward-looking, which means it's not actionable.

Let's break it down through a different lens. Revenue comes from individual customers. No customers, no revenue.

$$Customers$$
$$\times$$
$$Average\ order\ value\ (AOV)$$
$$\times$$
$$Number\ of\ transactions$$
$$=$$
$$Revenue$$

To arrive at profit, we have to bring costs into the equation. A large portion of your cost base can be attributed directly to customers.

The cost of acquiring a new customer, for example, is often expressed as CAC (see the box 'Customer profitability metrics'). It's a fact that many e-commerce businesses do not break even on that first transaction.

There are also costs associated with retaining and serving customers. The net effect is that some customers – the frequent purchasers and/or big spenders – are profitable. On the other side of the spectrum, some customers frankly deserve to be fired. They cost more to have around as customers than the revenue they contribute.

Customer profitability metrics

These two popular e-commerce metrics are usually applied to a segment, cohort or channel. Making comparisons between them is more insightful than knowing the respective individual values.

Customer acquisition cost (CAC)

Bad joke alert: Where's the best place to hide a dead body? Page two of Google search results.[1]

Making it to the first page of search results can be tough. You're at the mercy of a secret and ever-changing algorithm. Paying your way to the top involves bidding against competitors, perpetuating the upward cost spiral.

CAC is a measure of the average cost to acquire one new customer. Start with a sum of all the costs associated with gaining new customers in a year, or any other period. Include marketing and advertising expenses, but also relevant personnel and tools costs. To calculate CAC, divide this value by the number of new customers acquired over that same period.

Lifetime value (LTV)

Also known as customer lifetime value (CLV), this is a measure of how much a customer is worth to you over time.

One method is to discount future cash flows attributable to a customer (or segment) to net present value (NPV), using an appropriate discount factor.

An easier alternative is to calculate the total gross profit of all transactions for a given customer (or segment) over a certain period, typically one year.

CAC < LTV

LTV gives you the upper limit of what you can spend to acquire a new customer.

Growth triangle

The view of profit set out above helps to identify high-impact growth levers. You can grow your business in three ways:

- Increase the number of people who buy from you.

- Get them to spend more when they buy.
- Persuade them to come back and buy from you again.

By definition, CRO pulls the first lever. It makes better sense to spread your efforts. Squeezing growth out of just one area is hard work. Attack all three areas, and all you need is a 26 per cent increase in each to deliver 100 per cent overall return (not 33.3 per cent because of the compound effect). That sounds infinitely more attainable than pursuing 2× growth in one single domain.

Optimize the sales conversation

CRO has been reduced to UI (user interface) tweaks and implementing 'best practice' conversion gimmicks. That doesn't address what is, in our view, the real opportunity.

When a potential customer is on your site, think of it as a sales conversation happening with your business. Your site acts like a shop assistant in a physical store. Customers have questions, either about the product itself or about some other aspect such as fulfilment. They have concerns about things like delivery, price and trust.

How likely you are to close that deal depends on how well your site answers those questions and concerns. It depends on whether your site is able to persuade the customer to do business with you, as opposed to Amazon or a competitor.

You can only do that if you know what's going on inside the mind of your customers. You are not your customer; don't make assumptions on their behalf. In Chapters 3, 4 and 5 we show you the techniques for learning more about your customers than you thought possible. Chapter 13 is devoted to understanding the sales conversation, so that you can make it more effective.

Test and learn

When you look at the health of your business in a year from now, you see the effect of each decision made between now and then. Make more profitable decisions than bad ones, and your bottom line will reflect that. That's why you need evidence informing your decisions, instead of hunches.

Yet, despite the prevalence of big data, *Harvard Business Review* concluded that 'most managers must operate in a world where they lack sufficient data to inform their decisions'.[2] To establish whether an idea will be successful, test it on actual visitors in real time. This is called experimentation (see the box 'Optimization vs experimentation').

Experimentation is like having insurance against decisions that can hurt your sales. Actually it's better than insurance, because you remove the risk rather than merely compensate for it. With experimentation, you keep only the winners.

As part of the process, you also identify those ideas that didn't go the way you expected – the negative ones that would have become permanent features had you not tested them. Not only do you save yourself from them, you also learn from them. This gives you insight into customer preferences and behaviour that you can build on.

Optimization vs experimentation

In this book, we talk a lot about the concepts optimization and experimentation.

Optimization refers to the concept of weighing up alternative approaches in order to select the best one. For example, you could compare two variations of a mobile basket page. The final decision is based on performance against a key metric, such as conversion rate or revenue.

Experimentation is a mechanism by which a variation is compared against the original. The most common type in e-commerce optimization is an A/B test, also called a split test, where half the audience see the original and the rest see the variation. This all happens without the knowledge of visitors in the test, so they are not primed to behave in a certain way.

Experimentation is covered in detail in Chapter 9.

The scientific method

For centuries, scientists have used experimentation to find answers to questions of importance. The scientific method has helped scientists in fields as diverse as social sciences, geology and chemistry come up with new ways of understanding the world, and ultimately improving aspects of our life.

It's an empirical approach, so decisions are based on evidence rather than gut feel. It relies on the ability to validate hypotheses,[3] as illustrated in Figure 1.1.

Figure 1.1 The scientific method

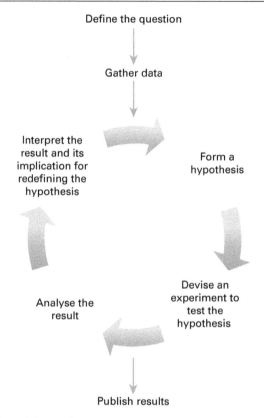

Define the question

Gather data

Interpret the result and its implication for redefining the hypothesis

Form a hypothesis

Analyse the result

Devise an experiment to test the hypothesis

Publish results

SOURCE Adapted from Christensen[4]

Step 1: Define the question

'A problem well stated is half solved', said the head of research at General Motors, serial inventor Charles Kettering.[5]

To come up with potential solutions to business problems, first understand the scope, impact and context of the problem. Building on that, we can formulate specific questions that can be answered with data. This is referred to as problem framing.

In e-commerce website optimization, sometimes a problem will be nominated by management. Other times, you may discover problems by doing explorative research.

Step 2: Gather data

Once you know the questions to ask, start gathering data and digging for insights. Much of the book is devoted to this topic.

Relying on guesswork, opinions and even so-called best practice is like playing the lottery. You may win a bit of money here and there, but it's all down to chance. By following an evidence-led approach, you remove luck from the scene and bet only on things that you know are likely to make a difference.

Step 3: Formulate a hypothesis

As you gather data pertaining to the business question, ideas about improvements and solutions will inevitably start forming.

Until you've actually tested an idea, you can't be sure that it will have the desired effect. A crucially important part of this process is being receptive to the reality that your theory is false. Companies with strong experimentation cultures, like Amazon, Facebook, Booking.com and Netflix, find that most of their ideas don't deliver expected results. Those ideas have been generated by the brightest people from top universities. Why should you be any different?

That's why each idea or proposed solution is treated as a theory until it has been validated. The hypothesis is a way of expressing an idea that makes it testable. This process is explained in detail in Chapter 8.

Step 4: Experiment

You may be spot-on with your idea, or totally wide of the mark. No one knows until you put it to the test by running an experiment. The results will either validate or refute your hypothesis – but either way, you'll learn something about your customers, their preferences and behaviour.

The most common form of experiment is an A/B test. Half your visitors see the current experience and half see the new variation, which incorporates changes that you predict will improve a certain metric. The test group has no idea that they are seeing something different.

Yet behind the scenes, the technology is carefully monitoring who has seen which version, how they are behaving, and the effect on various predefined metrics. After a short period of time, you compare results to see how the variation has altered the behaviour of the test group.

Step 5: Analyse the result

The experiment could have one of three outcomes:

- The variation is a 'winner' and your hypothesis is validated.
- The variation does not 'win' and the hypothesis is refuted.
- There is no difference between the variation and control; it is inconclusive.

On face value, it looks like you should have your fingers crossed for a win all the time. Yay! Crack open the Champagne, roll out the variation and watch all those visitors start spending. Ker-ching!

In fact, this kind of 'triumph and disaster' thinking is counter-productive. Long-term success comes out of being truly scientific. Hoping for a positive result means you're emotionally invested in it, which introduces a form of bias. Whatever the outcome, make it your aim to bank the learning and move forward.

A win can often point the way to further tests around the same hypothesis that could give you even bigger uplifts. Tests that don't win are also valuable. There is usually a lot you can learn from them – insight you can use to design another variation that really rakes in the cash. We've seen many big wins born out of insights that could only have been obtained by running a test and getting a negative result.

Step 6: Interpret the result

The purpose of a scientific study is usually to contribute new knowledge; this is no different. Whether you have validated or rejected the hypothesis, with every concluded test you know more about your customers than you did before. Gradually, you will learn vast amounts about what works for your customers and what doesn't.

Step 7: Document the result

In the scientific community, the contribution of new knowledge is formalized by publishing the details of the experiment. Similarly, your work is not complete until you have documented your result. This includes recording the insights from each experiment to share with your colleagues in other parts of the business.

With each experiment you collect new knowledge about your customers. Over time, this leads you to make long-term improvements in all areas of the business.

You'll be able to tie all the strands together to create a roadmap for the months ahead. The detailed process of prioritizing what to work on first – and what to ignore – and then creating an optimization roadmap is covered in Chapter 7.

The rest of this book tells you exactly how to implement those seven steps into your own organization, with practical examples, step-by-step instructions and case studies.

Summary

This book walks you through a proven system to help you to grow your e-commerce business. You can do that in one of three ways:

- Increase the number of people who buy from you.
- Get them to spend more when they buy.
- Persuade them to come back and buy from you again.

The system in this book is rooted in the scientific method, which has been used for years by scientists to find answers to important questions. In e-commerce website optimization, those are business questions related to the three growth pillars listed above.

You start with research to form a vivid picture about where the biggest opportunities for growth are. There will be no shortage of ideas about how to unlock the potential.

Until those ideas have been validated, they are theories. In a scientific experiment, the theories are then tested in real time on the visitors to your website, mobile app and other channels.

Some ideas may not give you the results you expected. This happens when the new variation performs worse than the original. This is not a failure! You have been able to catch and prevent an idea from going into production and hurting sales. More importantly, a negative test gives you unique insights that could not have been obtained in any other way. Often, that is the start of the next big winner.

Finally, the scientific method, since it aims to generate new knowledge, is continuous. If the world were to stop turning and things remained as they are, then perhaps optimization would be a one-off project. We all know that everything is changing all the time. Buckle up and enjoy the ride!

Notes

1 Pollit, C (2014) The best place to hide a dead body is page two of Google, *Huffpost* www.huffpost.com/entry/the-best-place-to-hide-a-_b_5168714 (archived at https://perma.cc/RTW6-KWD3)

2 Thomke, S and Manzi, J (2014) The discipline of business experimentation, *Harvard Business Review*, 92 (12), pp 70–79

3 Gauch, H G (2012) *Scientific Method in Brief*, Cambridge University Press, Cambridge

4 Christensen, L L (2007) *The Hands-On Guide for Science Communicators*, Springer, New York

5 LeFevre, M (2019) *Managing Design: Conversations, project controls, and best practices for commercial design and construction projects*, John Wiley & Sons, Hoboken, NJ

The kick-off　02

If you're a key decision-maker, getting started is easy.

A reader of the first edition of this book, who enjoyed good success from implementing our system, offers this advice:

- Give your team a copy of this book and have them read it.
- After a week, have a kick-off meeting.
- Install Hotjar (see later), activate heatmaps and session recordings.
- Do journey analysis and unmoderated usability testing (Chapter 4).
- After two weeks, review preliminary findings for quick wins.
- Run your first experiment (they used Google Optimize).
- Report the results and insights to the wider organization to build excitement.

Be an evangelist

What if you're not in that decision-making position? You don't have to be the CEO to introduce optimization and experimentation at your organization.

'You can't start a fire without a spark.' You're the spark in that line from Bruce Springsteen's hit song, *Dancing in the Dark*. Every optimization programme started with someone lighting a spark. Be that someone!

How you frame the conversations around it can make all the difference. Instead of trying to sell the idea, the trick is to build positive networks by 'discovering what you can do for someone else'.[1]

You are likely to find that optimization brings people together and breaks down silos between departments as everyone works together for a common goal.[2]

Initially, however, not everyone in your organization will be equally supportive of your plans. The brain is hard-wired to resist change. Also, don't underestimate how emotionally connected some of your co-workers may feel to 'their' website.

Invite ideas

Inviting your colleagues to contribute ideas can help to spread excitement and promote buy-in. Good ideas can come from anywhere, especially from those at the sharp edge of dealing with customers.

Some companies even offer prizes for the most impactful ideas. Create a test idea submission form in Google Forms, with these fields:

- Name.
- Description. What is the problem or opportunity?
- Rationale. What led to the idea? What data or insights can be offered in support?

Be open and receptive to any ideas that are generated in this way, no matter how unconvincing or unsubstantiated they seem at first glance. You will have a chance to filter out the subjective opinions and wild guesses later.

To set expectations, make sure your contributors know that everything will be filtered by a robust and objective prioritization process (Chapter 7). Their ideas might not be next in line just yet.

Get top-level support

No matter how conclusive your evidence, good luck with implementing that big win if the organization is not aligned. David Vismans, Chief Product Officer at Booking.com, stresses the importance of this element: 'If I had any advice for CEOs, it's this: large-scale testing is not a technical thing; it's a cultural thing that you need to fully embrace.'[3]

What do you think will be the outcome if you ask a co-worker to do something, backed by data, if your request is in conflict with instructions from their boss? This is what Matt LeMay, a highly accomplished product manager, calls the 'First Law of Organizational Gravity: individuals in an organization will avoid customer-facing work if it is not aligned with their day-to-day responsibilities and incentives.'[4]

That's one reason you need an executive sponsor in senior management – a 'key requirement for success' according to *Harvard Business Review*.[5] In that article, the role of the executive sponsor is summarized as:

- aligning goals with corporate strategy;

- gathering support from senior managers;
- providing ongoing direction.

The ideal candidate has a direct interest in online sales or the overall performance of digital channels. And, of course, control of the budget.

One more thing: if you can, avoid the HIPPO (Highest Paid Person's Opinion). It's that manager whose personal opinion wins the argument by virtue of their rank in the hierarchy. Optimization heaven is where your executive sponsor is open to data shaping everyday decisions.

The conversion rate of the Intuit website has gone up by 50 per cent since they started a disciplined experimentation programme. Founder Scott Cook has the right attitude, which has enabled this enormous success: 'Instead of focusing on the boss's vote... the emphasis is on getting real people to really behave in real experiments, and basing your decisions on that.'[6]

Still, the idea of 'experimenting' on a live site can be a scary thought. Explain it in terms that matter to the executive sponsor (see 'How to deal with resistance' at the end of this chapter for handling specific objections). Here are some ideas:

- It's the best way to separate the successful ideas from the bad ones – you only have to keep the winners.
- Rely on scientific rigour, instead of personal intuition.
- Increase return on investment (ROI) on development resources as only winning ideas make it on to their roadmap.
- Companies that do experimentation are more likely to push the boundaries of innovation and find breakthrough innovations.
- Don't just pay lip service to customer-centricity, put the customer at the centre of important decisions.

Get the team in place

Optimization is a team effort.

That team doesn't have to be big, nor does it have to be all in-house. Smaller organizations usually start with one internal person taking ownership of the testing roadmap. Specialist activities such as UX (user experience) research and A/B test coding are outsourced to subcontractors or an optimization agency.

In our own agency, we see this approach even with large enterprises that could afford to recruit their own internal teams. A major attraction is the broad exposure that agency staff have to similar programmes at other companies.

A small optimization team is typically made up of these roles:

- strategist/analyst;
- UX designer;
- front-end developer.

As you scale, your team might expand into a range of roles briefly outlined below. In practice, one or more of these roles may be performed by one individual.

Project manager

Responsible for keeping the process on track, coordinating team efforts and getting things done on time and on spec.

Researcher

Improving customer experience assumes a thorough understanding of their world. In Chapters 3, 4 and 5 we explain how to get into their hearts and minds with various research methodologies. These include surveys, usability testing, interviews, heatmaps, store visits, customer immersion and competitor audits. On larger programmes the work could be shared by several researchers, overseen by one person who brings it all together.

Data analyst

Research unleashes data. Raw data are useless until they are processed and turned into insights. Even small websites generate mountains of quantitative data that can be turned into actionable insights in the hands of a skilled data analyst.

UX designer

Creates wireframes and/or prototypes based on research findings. Depending on the scope of an experiment, they may also help developers integrate a split test elegantly into the website. UX designers are usually skilled at user research and can either assist with that component or take complete responsibility for it.

It is worth pointing out that this role demands empathy with the user rather than artistic talent. Therefore, the role may not be best suited to a graphic designer or visual designer. It has to do with translating research into wireframes, not making things look pretty.

Developer

Some experimentation platforms offer a drag-and-drop interface style so that anyone can build a test. Our advice is to avoid using that facility as far as possible. If you don't know your HTML from your JavaScript, having access to a front-end developer is essential.

Copywriter

Small copy changes can bring about big results for reasons we'll explore in later chapters. At Booking.com, where up to 1,000 experiments are live at any one time, some of the highest uplifts have been down to words alone.[7]

Much of this is microcopy: tiny phrases that guide the customer at key points. With so few words available to achieve so much, each one counts.

In the early stages the copywriter may review all the copy on the website, assessing its strengths and weaknesses against established copywriting principles.

Gathering evidence

Imagine starting your optimization programme with a blank canvas. How do you generate good ideas?

Remember the scientific method from Chapter 1. Start by asking questions. Next, gather evidence that can help you find answers and formulate theories about how to improve things.

We'll recommend certain software tools which act like X-ray machines that you hook up to your business. They help you to diagnose issues and identify opportunities.

Some of these tools will be embedded in your website by placing a tag in the site code. These tags are typically no more than a few lines of JavaScript that you'll get from the tool provider. In most cases, you can do this with limited technical knowledge, using a tag container. See the box 'Implementing tools without IT' for more information on this.

Implementing tools without IT

To add some tools to your site, you may need to install code on your website. This can cause delays if you have to rely on your IT department or developers.

A better solution is to have your developer do a one-off installation of a tag manager, such as Google Tag Manager (GTM). This is like a holder for software tags so that in future you can quickly add them without any IT input.

The only tool you can't put into a tag manager is the experimentation platform. Place the tag directly in your website code, exactly as instructed by the vendor.

In Chapters 4 and 5, we introduce you to a range of tools that allows you to gather valuable intelligence about your users and customers. Hotjar bundles many of them into one single package.

As a generalist tool, it lacks some of the advanced features you might find in specialist alternatives. However, it comes at an attractive price point and gives you basic access to the following:

- heatmaps and scrollmaps
- session recording
- funnel analysis
- forms analysis
- on-site polls
- live recruitment

We'll cover each of these in Chapters 4 and 5.

Experimentation platform

The workhorse of your experimentation programme, it takes care of the following:

- It serves an alternative experience to a selection of visitors by allowing you to make changes to a webpage.
- It splits traffic so that half of target visitors see the variation and the other half still see the original. For the visitor, it's a seamless experience, so they have no idea they are in a test.

- It calculates how the variation performs against the control and presents the results in an easy-to-read dashboard with graphs, tables and reports.
- It applies mathematical formulae to determine whether any difference in performance is statistically significant and not just down to chance.

Client-side vs server-side

The installation of your experimentation platform depends on whether you opt for a client-side or server-side testing tool. Most likely it's the former, unless you have a specific reason to go server-side.

With client-side testing, the changes in the experiment are made in the user's browser. The code base on your site remains completely unchanged. Server-side testing sends a different version to the user's browser directly from the server.

Installing client-side testing is relatively easy. Ask your developers or IT to insert a few lines of JavaScript on the site as directed by the vendor. Once the tag is in place, you can launch A/B tests without your back-end developers or IT getting involved.

That is a major advantage of client-side testing: speed and ease. Speed is very important, as we'll discuss in later chapters. The disadvantages, compared to server-side testing, are scope of testing and performance. Neither is serious if you follow the advice in this book.

With server-side tools you can test beyond the look and feel of your web and mobile sites. For example, you can make modifications to algorithms or product prices. Because they require server calls, the change can't be made in the user's browser. It enables experimentation on your full stack, including IoT (Internet of Things) and conversational tech. Building server-side tests requires the involvement of your back-end developers and slots into your code release schedules.

Overview of experimentation platforms

Table 2.1 has brief summaries of the most popular experimentation platforms. Other excellent enterprise solutions are, in alphabetical order:

- Maxymiser
- Monetate
- Qubit
- Sitespect

Table 2.1 A list of popular experimentation platforms

Experimentation platform	Notes
Google Optimize	<ul><li>Free! A premium version is available as Optimize 360</li><li>Built on Google Analytics, which enables deep post-test analysis in a familiar interface</li><li>At the time of writing, limited to five tests at a time</li><li>Great way to get started, especially if budget is a concern</li><li>Use it to embed experimentation and build a business case for investing in another tool, if necessary</li></ul>
Optimizely	<ul><li>An industry favourite, best suited for large enterprises</li><li>Founded by ex-Googlers who managed experimentation on the Obama campaign</li><li>Integrates well with third-party tools such as Google Analytics, Crazy Egg, Qualaroo and others</li><li>Offers an advanced personalization module integrating machine learning and NLP (natural language processing) for superior targeting</li><li>Offers server-side testing in addition to client-side</li><li>Suitable for product experiments, feature flagging, mobile apps, TV apps, IoT and voice apps</li></ul>
VWO	<ul><li>Popular with medium-sized businesses</li><li>Easy integration with popular e-commerce platforms, such as Magento, Shopify and BigCommerce</li><li>Built-in research tools, including heatmaps, session recording and on-site polling (similar to Hotjar)</li><li>Full-stack version available, enabling server-side testing and mobile app experimentation</li></ul>
ABTasty	<ul><li>Popular in French-speaking countries, but growing fast in the UK and elsewhere</li><li>Visual editor and widget library make test building more accessible to non-coders</li><li>Personalization made possible with advanced targeting and AI</li></ul>
Convert.com	<ul><li>Great tool at very attractive price point</li><li>Claims to be less susceptible to flicker, discussed in Chapter 9</li><li>Solid A/B testing tool, built on robust infrastructure, without the bells and whistles that tend to drive up the price tag</li></ul>

(continued)

Table 2.1 (Continued)

Experimentation platform	Notes
Conductrics	• WYSIWYG editor and browser extension let you make simple changes without coding • Machine learning helps you to discover valuable audience segments • Server-side API available
Adobe Target	• Best suited for large enterprises • Good choice if your organization already uses Adobe Analytics • Offers 'personalized experiences at scale'

The best option for you depends on various factors, for example:

- Available budget. Tools come at different price points. Expect to pay more for advanced features. Google Optimize is free, but may not be the best option for you.

- Your organization. Some tools are best suited for large enterprises, others are designed with SMEs in mind. Some focus on certain sectors, for example travel, media etc.

- Scope of testing. To do website optimization, you don't need a platform that caters for IoT.

- Existing ecosystem. If you are already using Adobe Analytics, then Adobe Target may be the best choice for you. If Oracle is deeply integrated into your organization, consider Maxymiser.

Some e-commerce platforms and CMS (content management systems) have their own A/B-testing functionality built in. Our experience is that these testing solutions rarely offer the level of complexity that the dedicated versions do.

How to deal with resistance

Experimentation is the ultimate business decision-making mechanism; few other decisions can be made with the same level of confidence.

You can make rational business decisions underpinned by the weight and certainty of data. When do you normally get to make a business decision with 95 per cent confidence that it will give you a good result?

Yet, despite the clear benefits of testing, some business executives and owners are reluctant to test. You may have some convincing to do to overcome their misplaced beliefs, such as the myths below.

Myth 1: 'Most test results are negative so you lose money'

Okay, it's true that many tests don't beat the current variation. But it's not true to say that business stands to lose money from negative tests. You can refute this with basic maths. There's always a time limit on a test, so any decline in sales attributable to it will be short-lived. By contrast, every win keeps on adding revenue for many months to come, far outweighing any losses.

Here's an illustration. To keep things simple, let's say that over a period of 10 months you run 10 tests, one a month. Six turn out to be negative, down on the control by £1,000 each. You're out of pocket by £6,000 in lost sales.

Imagine if you'd made those six changes live on the site permanently, letting 100 per cent of visitors see them. (A surprising number of companies do that, based on nothing more than liking the way it looks.)

In that scenario, you would have lost £6,000 every month until you somehow realized that those changes weren't working as well as before. You'd then get rid of them and be back to square one, with no clue as to what to do next. Instead, testing ensured that your loss was capped at £6,000 and gave you a wealth of knowledge on how to turn more visitors into customers.

The remaining four tests give you a healthy £1,000 of extra sales each, making a total of £4,000 during the test period. Unlike the tests where sales went down, these you'll keep on running. Over the next year, those four winning tests will continue to bring in that extra £4,000 every month. That's £48,000 over the course of a year. Take away the £6,000 for the negative tests, and you're still up £42,000 in the first 12 months.

But consider this too. Without running those six negative tests, you would never have got to the four winning ones. Negative tests are part of the process. You can't have one and not the other. It's the learnings from the tests that don't perform as you would like that let you crack the puzzle.

Myth 2: 'Other priorities are more urgent'

Some managers like the idea of testing, but let other priorities come first. Replatforming, bug fixing and addressing operational issues are the ones we most commonly hear about.

Of course these need to be dealt with, but it's a question of deciding what's important and what's urgent. Whatever the reasons for delaying testing, the impact is the same – losing valuable time and falling further behind the competition. Talk about leaving money on the table!

It's actually an argument for bumping testing higher up the agenda. It can give you vital insights that could inform those very initiatives that are causing the delay.

Myth 3: 'It's too expensive'

Saying that testing is too dear is like saying that you can't afford to do any marketing. What else should you be investing your money in, if not activities to help you generate more money?

How much is it costing your company to make changes to the live site that have no impact, or worse, actually hurt sales? With experimentation, you validate each change before it hits your development backlog.

As Lacy Rhoades from Etsy explains: 'Experimentation at Etsy comes from a desire to make informed decisions, and ensure that when we launch features for our millions of members, they work. Too often, we had features that took a lot of time and had to be maintained without any proof of their success or any popularity among users. A/B testing allows us to… say a feature is worth working on as soon as it's underway.'[8]

When you consider the cost of the lost opportunities, it's really the absence of testing that's expensive.

Myth 4: 'It wastes time'

E-commerce managers want results fast, but tests take time to run. However, it's a false economy to view this as slowing down the business. As long as you put a ceiling on test duration, as explained in later chapters, testing won't hold you back and your developers will only implement changes on the site that have proved their worth.

Myth 5: 'We want to invest in getting more traffic first'

A bit of a chicken and egg situation, as you can't improve conversion rates if there aren't any visitors to convert. But if you already have an existing flow of traffic, why not tune up your site so that more of the visitors you already have will turn into customers and actually spend money when they get there?

Shelling out to shovel ever-greater numbers of visitors to a site that doesn't convert is like scattering ever-bigger sacks of seed onto barren land. If you want a bumper harvest, get the soil fertile first.

Myth 6 'We don't have enough traffic'

It's true that if your site is small, it can be a challenge to run tests that are statistically significant. However, it may still be possible. In some ways, experimentation is even more important for a small site, because it really does have to focus on extracting value from the few visitors. There is more on this topic in Chapter 9.

Myth 7: 'Our technology is too unstable'

You'd like to test, but you're concerned that your ancient platform is too rickety. Don't let it get in the way of making improvements to your site that can potentially fund the required upgrade. By delaying it, you're being left further and further behind. When you finally get around to updating the old technology, it won't magically optimize the site for buying.

Myth 8: 'You can never trust the results of a test'

It's true that if you break the rules, results are not to be trusted. However, if you follow the basic principles outlined in this book, you'll have data you can rely on more than most other situations you'll ever be in.

Summary

Start small. Go for quick wins. Use that as a basis on which to evangelize the programme.

Your team can be as small as one person, aided by access to key resources – research, UX design and front-end development.

Google Optimize is a free experimentation platform. If budget is an issue, use it to build a business case for expanding the programme.

Have an executive sponsor on board from the start. That should be someone from senior management to align with corporate objectives, secure budget and win over support from other stakeholders.

Notes

1 Rezac, D with Hallgren, G and Thomson, J (2003) *The Frog and Prince: Secrets of positive networking to change your life*, Frog and Prince Networking Corporation, Vancouver

2 Econsultancy (2014) *The Past, Present and Future of Website Optimization*, Econsultancy, London

3 Thomke, S and Beyersdorfer D (2018) Booking.com, Harvard Business School Case 619-015, October

4 LeMay, M (2018) *Agile for Everybody: Creating fast, flexible, and customer-first organizations*, O'Reilly Media, Farnham, Surrey

5 Ashkenas, R (2015) How to be an effective executive sponsor, *Harvard Business Review*, 18 May

6 Kim, G *et al* (2016) *The DevOps Handbook: How to create world-class agility, reliability, and security in technology organizations*, IT Revolution Press, Portland, OR

7 Dreyer, I and Scerbikova, M (2017) *99 Failed Experiments in 30 Days?!* [Talk] 27 September, ProductTank, Cape Town, South Africa

8 Kim, G *et al* (2016) *The DevOps Handbook: How to Create World-Class Agility, Reliability, and Security in Technology Organizations*, IT Revolution Press, Portland, OR

Gather data   03

The e-commerce manager at a prominent retailer was telling us about their website optimization plans. 'We know exactly what to do,' they said confidently. Asked where that knowledge came from, they replied: 'Years of experience.'

Like this manager, you may feel that you know what needs to be done and that no further investigation is required. But nobody can be expected to know all the answers or, for that matter, all the questions.

You act on knowledge available to you at the time. That means going after opportunities you know to be real, presumably using solutions you know to be valid (*known knowns*). In e-commerce website optimization, you get to this point by validating ideas with A/B testing.

You may have ideas about how to address a particular opportunity, but until they've been tested, you can't be certain that they are going to be effective. These are *known unknowns*.

The e-commerce manager in the opening story above is relying on *unknown knowns* – intuition and experience. This is risky territory, because the human brain is prone to a range of cognitive biases (see Chapter 12). Even the best teams get it wrong most of the time.[1]

Finally, we don't know what we don't know. These are total blind spots – our *unknown unknowns* – that can be surfaced by looking at data. The biggest growth opportunities and insights may be hidden here.

It's an exciting journey, full of discovery and surprise. Don't be put off by terms like 'analysis' and 'research', which probably don't sell it well!

Here is a little taste of the types of research, based on a framework outlined in *Just Enough Research*,[2] that you'll be doing throughout the lifecycle of your optimization programme:

- **Generative/exploratory research**: uncover problems and opportunities; explore the *unknown unknown*.

- **Descriptive/explanatory research**: targeted analysis into the *known unknown*; understand the opportunity better; also post-test analysis to explain the outcome of experimentation and document those insights.

- **Evaluative research**: peer review and usability testing of proposed treatments and solutions.

- Causal research: the path from *unknown known* to *known known*, establish cause-and-effect relationship with experimentation (Chapters 8 and 9).

The role of previous research

If you have previously done research, you may wonder whether another round is really necessary. The enterprise clients we work with in our agency usually have a plethora of research reports, often done at great cost.

In our experience, research conducted for other purposes seldom offers the insights needed to power an optimization programme. It's not meant as criticism; objectives are different. For example, there are fundamental differences between typical marketing research and what you might need to do in optimization.

For our purposes, research is not done for the sake of creating reports and graphs and tables. Your task is to generate **actionable insights**. That's what the next few chapters are about.

Existing research can offer you a valuable foundation, though. It can aid your analysis; you can compare, confirm, extend or refute earlier findings. That is how new knowledge is generated, by layering new research on earlier studies.

Also, social scientists accept that different researchers will generate different insights from the same data. In fact, even the same researcher looking at the same data set at another time may have different interpretations!

From data to insights

Getting from data to meaningful insights can be intimidating.

Many managers we speak to find all the data overwhelming. They don't know what to do with them so they don't do anything. Others waste hours trying to find something in a data rabbit hole, with no idea of what it is that they're looking for.

Data are just raw information stored as numbers and/or text. In that state they are of little practical use. You give meaning to data through **analysis**. That simply means documenting your **observations** – what you saw and heard. **Insights** are your interpretation of those observations in the context of other findings.

Extract insights like the CIA

If you feel overwhelmed by data, spare a thought for intelligence analysts. Not only must they sift through tons of data, they must find information relevant to national security – like preventing the next bomb attack. We could probably learn a thing or two from them.

Sensemaking

There's a wonderfully descriptive term for the process of extracting meaning and insights from information – *sensemaking*.[3] The process, used by many intelligence agents, has been studied and codified. One widely cited study explained the flow from raw data into insights thus:[4]

> Data sources > Shoebox > Evidence file > Schema > Hypotheses > Stories

These are not steps in a linear process. Rather, it is a way of thinking about the transformation of data. Let's explore each of these six areas in more detail, to see how to make sense of your data.

Data sources

Over the next few chapters you'll learn about various data-gathering tools and methods used in e-commerce optimization. Each one gives you a different piece of the puzzle.

Data can be **quantitative** or **qualitative**. In broad terms, qualitative is what people say (text or speech) and quantitative is numbers. Quantitative data tell you *what* is happening, whereas qualitative data help you understand *why* it is happening. Some data have elements of both.

Suppose you observe an 80 per cent exit rate on your basket page. That means 8 out of 10 potential customers are leaving the site at this point in their journey. This is quantitative data telling you what is happening.

However, you can't treat that problem without knowing what might be causing it. So you fire up a quick survey on that page, asking abandoning users why they are leaving. Most of the comments talk about uncertainty about the delivery time frame. Now that's something you can act on in solving the problem.

Qualitative research can be a rich source of new insights into the world of your customers, their motivations, needs and pain points. The advantage of quantitative research is that you can express in numbers the observations underpinning those insights. A new dimension is added to it by counting, ordering, ranking, making comparisons and so on. It makes for a perfect marriage between qualitative and quantitative data. Use the strengths of each to shine a light on your observation from different angles. This is referred to as **triangulation** of data, and it is a cornerstone of the approach taken in this book.

There is a difference between what people say (**attitudinal data**) and what they do (**behavioural data**). It's important to cover both perspectives in your research.

Interviews and surveys are examples of attitudinal research. Behavioural insights are obtained by observing people. A/B testing is a good example of that because it measures changes in behaviour.

Humans are notoriously bad at predicting their own behaviour. Steve Jobs famously said: 'A lot of times, people don't know what they want until you show it to them.'[5] But what they can tell you about is the teeth-gnashing frustration they feel when they can't do something quickly and easily on your site. Instead of asking users how to improve a page, ask them why they left without taking any action. Then make a change based on that feedback and see if people behave differently.

Figure 3.1 shows some of the most common data sources used in e-commerce optimization, mapped out based on the above overview.

Figure 3.1 The e-commerce optimization research landscape

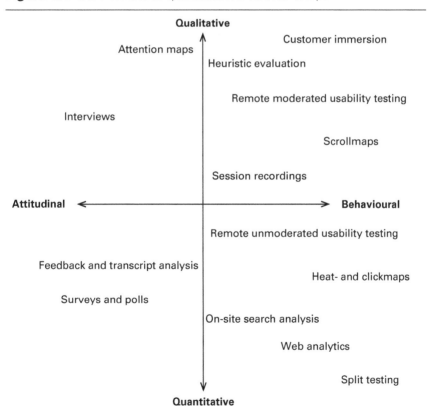

SOURCE Adapted from Steve Mulder[6]

Shoebox

Your task is not to squeeze every last drop of intelligence out of every tiny bit of data. At some point, the additional gain doesn't justify the additional effort. You don't need to chain yourself to a huge pile of reports and consume every number and every word.

When working with a big data set, start the analysis on a random sample. That initial selection of data is your proverbial shoebox.

Suppose for example that you have collected thousands of free-text responses as part of an e-mail survey. There's no need to put every single response under the microscope, not just yet. Start with 200 randomly selected responses. That will give you a good overview of what this particular source has to offer. If you feel you are still getting surprised by some of the responses after processing the initial batch, process another sample. If not, move to the next data source and loop back to this one later.

Limit your time on each data source. Make Parkinson's Law, 'work expands so as to fill the time available for its completion',[7] work in your favour. By limiting the scope of your analysis, you can avoid analysis paralysis.

You can come back to a data set later, by which time you'll have more context from having seen a wider range of data. You'll be better informed and have new perspectives when you loop back to it later. The journey from data to insights is non-linear. Avoid the rabbit hole, keep moving forward.

Evidence file

The evidence file is a collection of all your annotated observations in Google Docs or similar.

When social scientists do analysis, writing **theoretical memos** is part of their process. It's almost like a journal, where you keep track of theories, ideas and questions as they come to you. There's no need to do it in any formal way, as long as you diligently log those ideas and interpretations. It's been described as a 'conversation with ourselves about our data'.[8]

If that is the output of your analysis, then how is the act of analysis itself performed? Many people struggle with this. Partly it depends on whether the data are quantitative or qualitative. We cover the analytical methods for each data source in relevant sections throughout this book.

Don't try to overcomplicate it; to make observations is to record what you see and hear. Engage with the data, constantly asking questions, looking for patterns and making comparisons:

- What do you find interesting? Why?

- What patterns are emerging, in this data set as well as between this and other data sets? (See the box 'Patterns in data'.)

- What differences or similarities do you see between groupings of information?

- Any anomalies? Any outliers?

- Is there any information that helps to confirm or challenge some assumptions or insights previously obtained?

- Ask *what if*, *what now* and *so what* questions.

To make sense of qualitative information, break the haystack into meaning-ful heaps, creating virtual piles around themes. Scientists refer to this as **coding**. Start by sorting the individual items into categories, using a word or short phrase as labels.[9]

Categories of themes will reveal themselves to you as you progress. It's how you start to see links and connections, which is a key part of analysis. It also lets you identify the bigger issues and rank them in order of importance.

Five Whys analysis is a popular technique that can be used to explore and evolve ideas. It comes under the umbrella of 'root cause analysis', a way of identifying the core of a problem.

State the observation or problem, then ask why this is the case. Repeat until you get to a possible root cause.

As you ask the next question, you may realize that you need further data in order to give an informed response. This could be a prompt to access a different data source or even revisit an old one, with fresh per-spective. Even if you lack relevant data on which to base your answers, it can be the start of a hypothesis or it can be flagged for further research and analysis.

As an example, let's say you're investigating low mobile conversion rates. The process could develop as illustrated in Table 3.1.

Table 3.1 The Five Whys technique applied to an investigation into low mobile conversion rates

Iteration	Answer	Data source
First Why	Our mobile visitors don't buy as frequently as desktop visitors.	Web analytics
Second Why	Customers tend to browse on a mobile device; they may not be ready to buy yet.	Web analytics; mobile poll
Third Why	Many customers buy on desktop after browsing on mobile.	Cross-device analytics; customer survey, segmented by device type
Fourth Why	They find it more convenient to browse on mobile, but still prefer doing the transaction on desktop.	Usability testing; clickmaps; customer interviews
Fifth Why	Product images are an important part of the purchase cycle and it's easier to examine these on a bigger screen.	Usability testing; clickmaps; mobile poll

Patterns in data

Identifying patterns is an important analytical technique. In fact, for some it is the very definition of analysis – 'the search for patterns in data and for ideas that help explain why those patterns are there in the first place'.[10]

Hatch (2002) lists the following types of patterns to look out for in qualitative data sets,[11] which equally applies to quantitative analysis:

- Similarity: things are the same or happen in the same way.
- Difference: things are decidedly and predictably dissimilar.
- Frequency: how often or seldom an event occurs.
- Sequence: one event follows another in a given order.
- Correspondence: something occurs in relation to another event.
- Causation: something causes another event to occur.

Schema

Schematizing means organizing information so that relationships and patterns in the data, as well as gaps in your understanding, become apparent.

Data visualization is one of the best ways to make sense of data. It's also effective at communicating your insights to others.

The MIT Media Lab has a program to teach non-technical people how to work with data. The approach of Dr Rahul Bhargava is to have students draw sketches to tell stories with data.[12] As you do your analysis, ask yourself if there is anything you can represent visually.

Quantitative data lend themselves naturally to visual representation, such as graphs and charts:

- **Pie charts** are best for comparing the parts of a whole, such as new vs returning visitors.

- **Bar charts** are good for comparing different groups of data, such as themed survey answers or page templates in a customer journey map.

- **Line graphs** are the best way of plotting and comparing trends over time, such as how your conversion rate and revenue have changed over 12 months.

Qualitative data can also be visualized, for example:

- **Mind maps** show relationships between different pieces of information. If you read through a list of 200 customer comments, it's hard to keep track in your mind of how it all ties together.

- **Word clouds** help you see patterns in text data, by varying the visual prominence of words depending on how frequently they appear.

- **Experience maps** plot the experience customers have when they interact with your business.

Hypotheses

Ultimately, the objective of your research is to come up with hypotheses to test. Though it is a separate step later in the process (Chapter 8), it is firmly grounded in the work you are doing now. Hypotheses start brewing as soon as you start engaging with the data.

As you do the analysis, inevitably theories form in your head. These could be rough ideas about problems or opportunities, based on what you've observed. It could include thoughts about solutions, but it doesn't have to. It could be an assumption or question that needs further analysis.

Every theory, idea and assumption should be kept in your evidence file, with links to the insights that triggered it.

Stories

At the end of each day, review what you've learnt up until that point. List your three most interesting observations or insights for the day.

Harvard Business Review recommends expressing analysis in narratives: 'Although good business arguments are developed through the use of numbers, they are typically approved on the basis of a story... Storytelling can translate those dry and abstract numbers into compelling pictures of a leader's goals.'[13]

What is the story that's taking shape from your research? Dr Rahul Bhargava from the MIT Media Lab has proposed five data story genres:[14]

- Changes over time: a narrative describing how something has changed over a period of time.

- Interesting factoids: the most interesting, strange or thought-provoking observation in a data set.

- Surprising connections: the human brain responds well to patterns; when a connection is unexpected it raises the story value.

- Personal experiences: the protagonist in your story represents a trend or interesting observation found in the data; you could even relate it to your own experience.

- Revealing comparisons: intriguing juxtapositions can be created by exposing similarities or differences between things.

You are looking for actionable insights, so your story should contain a twist of how things can be better in the future. Don't worry about proposing a solution just yet; the task is to set up a problem or opportunity and create excitement about making that better. Like a cliff-hanger in fiction stories, leave your audience on the edge of their seats about the potential.

Problem framing

So far we've looked at research mainly from a broad diagnostic perspective, casting the net wide and being open to any and all opportunities.

Sometimes you might feel that there are known opportunities or problems to attack. They may have arisen from a diagnostic sweep or from previous analysis in other areas. It could be a strategic theme for your company with no specific data to back it up.

For example, a big-brand client of our agency has two websites. One is set up to act as a traffic magnet, optimized for organic search. The second site is a pure online shop, optimized for sales. Visitors are funnelled there, seamlessly, after landing on the first site. However, web analytics data suggest that those visitors perform poorly relative to other segments. Optimizing this underperforming customer segment was a strategic focus area for the business.

The key difference between the two approaches is that an open diagnostic starts with data, which leads to hypotheses; focusing on a specific opportunity starts with a hypothesis that gets enriched with data.

The essence of problem framing is summarized in this quote, attributed to Albert Einstein: 'If I had an hour to solve a problem, I'd spend 55 minutes thinking about the problem and 5 minutes thinking about the solution.'

Problem framing improves clarity around the what and why of a problem. It helps to check assumptions and reduce the risk of working on the wrong things:

- Exactly what is the problem?
- How well do you understand it?
- Why is it considered a problem? What is the impact on the business?
- Who is affected by the problem?
- How would you know if a solution is working?

Business problem statement

The formula below is a useful way to articulate a business problem. While it's focused on the outcome, it is not prescriptive about what the solution looks like:

> We have observed that [our website/app/component] isn't meeting [these goals], which is causing [this adverse effect/business issue] to our business.

> How could we improve [our website/app/component] so that our customers are more successful? We will know we have achieved this by measuring [these measurable criteria].

SOURCE Adapted from *Lean UX* (2016) by Josh Seiden and Jeff Gothelf.[15]

Identify research questions

Once the problem is clearly understood, break it down into questions that can be answered with data. Good questions meet the criteria set out below, making up the acronym FINER:

F – Feasible. You have the means, budget and technical expertise to answer the question. This includes access to a relevant data source, with a large enough sample.

I – Interesting/Important. The research covers a topic of strategic importance. Answers would be of interest to management and stakeholders.

N – Novel. Just like in the scientific community, your research should generate new knowledge. It should aim to confirm, refute or expand on previous findings.

E – Ethical. Research should be compliant with legal, regulatory, company policy and other relevant frameworks. For example, personally identifiable data have to be processed in accordance with GDPR or its equivalent in your region.

R – Relevant. Does the research really matter to your business? Is a particular question relevant to understanding that problem?

Research canvas

We developed the practical tool shown in Table 3.2, which you can use to translate the problem into research questions.

Table 3.2 A research canvas can be used to translate business problems into research questions

Business problem		
What is the problem? Why is it a problem? What is its impact? What are the untested assumptions?		
Research questions	**Data sources**	**Methodology**
Which questions can shed light on the problem?	Where can you find data relating to the question?	Which forms of research are most relevant?
What assumptions or theories do you have in relation to the problem?	Can you get information from more than one data source for a richer picture?	This depends on the questions and source of data.
Good questions explore who, what, why, how.	Approach the question from various angles (eg quantitative, qualitative, behavioural and attitudinal).	Different research methodologies are discussed in upcoming chapters.
Do questions meet the criteria set out in the FINER framework?		

Summary

E-commerce optimization starts with gathering data to show you where the problems and opportunities are, as well as how much they could be worth to you.

Data in their original state are meaningless. Give them meaning through analysis, which is simply making observations – what you see and hear in the data.

The purpose of research is to find actionable insights, not to produce reports with pretty graphs and charts. Insights spawn ideas about how online sales can be increased. Those ideas can then be tested and measured.

You'll use a number of different data sources to get a full picture of the world of your customers, their motivations to purchase as well as the barriers and frustrations they experience on your site.

Quantitative data tell you what is happening, whereas qualitative research can tell you why it is happening. Quantitative research and analysis can help you identify patterns, whereas qualitative research is a good way to discover new insights. Because what people say is not always the same as what they do, you should also aim for a mix of attitudinal and behavioural insights.

Notes

1 Kohavi, R *et al* (2009) Online experimentation at Microsoft, *Data Mining Case Studies*, 11, p 39
2 Hall, E, Zeldmaneditor, J and Fox, R (2014) *Just Enough Research*, A Book Apart, New York
3 Weick, K E (1995) *Sensemaking in Organizations*, vol 3, SAGE, London
4 Pirolli, P and Card, S (2005) The sensemaking process and leverage points for analyst technology as identified through cognitive task analysis, *Proceedings of the International Conference on Intelligence Analysis*, 2–6 May, pp 2–4, McLean, VA
5 Reinhardt, A (1998) Steve Jobs: There's sanity returning, *Business Week*, 25 May www.bloomberg.com/news/articles/1998-05-25/steve-jobs-theres-sanity-returning (archived at https://perma.cc/557F-5DKR)
6 Mulder, S (2006) *The User Is Always Right: A practical guide to creating and using personas for the web*, New Riders, Berkeley, CA
7 The Economist (1955) [Accessed 5 August 2020] Parkinson's law [Online] www.economist.com/news/1955/11/19/parkinsons-law1 (archived at https://perma.cc/7FBW-KLVJ)

8 Clarke, A (2005) *Situational Analysis: Grounded theory after the postmodern turn*, p 202, SAGE, Thousand Oaks, CA

9 Saldaña, J (2013) *The Coding Manual for Qualitative Researchers*, SAGE, Los Angeles, CA

10 Bernard, H R (2006) *Research Methods in Anthropology: Qualitative and quantitative approaches*, p 452, AltaMira Press, Lanham, MD

11 Hatch, J A (2002) *Doing Qualitative Research in Education Settings*, State University of New York Press, Albany, NY

12 Nelson, G S (2018) *The Analytics Lifecycle Toolkit: A practical guide for an effective analytics capability*, John Wiley & Sons, Hoboken, NJ

13 Denning, S (2004) Telling tales, *Harvard Business Review*, 82, pp 122–29, 152

14 Bhargava, R (2017) [Accessed 5 August 2020] Hands on Approaches to data storytelling, *SlideShare* [Online] www.slideshare.net/rahulbot/hands-on-approaches-to-data-storytelling-82401114 (archived at https://perma.cc/T4B5-PKVP)

15 Seiden, J and Gothelf, J (2016) *Lean UX*, O'Reilly Media, Sebastopol, CA

Behavioural research

04

It's time to start digging for insights.

In the previous chapter, we discussed the journey from data to insights by means of analysis. Over the next three chapters you will learn more about a number of research tools and methods, focused on generating actionable insights.

You'll find that it's not a linear approach of moving from one data source to the next in an orderly sequence. More likely you will loop back to a data set at times, prompted by an insight from another piece of data. It's okay; that is the process.

But where to begin? Analysis can be broken out into these key four areas,[1] says Brent Dykes, author of two highly recommended books about analytics:

Acquisition: What are the primary sources of traffic? How do they compare in terms of sales activity? If your business pays for traffic, how does this 'bought traffic' perform? If you can increase the conversion rates and average order values of paid traffic, it will have a big impact on ROI. E-mail is an area you have more control over than others, and in some organizations this presents a massive opportunity.

Site interactions: What is happening on your site? What are the dominant journeys? Which paths are more profitable, and which are most leaky? How easily are users able to carry out key tasks that lead up to the final conversion event?

Conversion process: Identify the roadblocks to conversion. Start by looking at the micro conversion events: activities higher up the funnel that build up to the transaction. Examples are finding and selecting products, adding to cart and navigating the site. Where in the journey do visitors become stuck? Where do they drop out of the funnel?

Visitor value: In Chapter 1 we introduced the concept of customer profitability. Not all your customers are equal in value. What are the different patterns between users who purchase and those who don't? Focus your efforts on customers that will give you the best long-term return.

In this chapter, we focus on data sources, tools and research methods to form a backdrop of behavioural insights. Where do they come from, what do they do, where do things go wrong?

Remember to diligently document every noteworthy observation, and capture any questions and ideas before they are gone.

Website analytics

You probably have Google Analytics (GA) installed on your site. In fact, you are probably already familiar with it and the types of reports it can generate.

At the time of writing, industry rumours have it that GA is about to be comprehensively upgraded. The principles shared here are timeless, even if you find the platform has evolved significantly by the time you're reading this.

GA is so vast that we could write an entire book on this topic alone. It also means that you can easily get stuck in analysis paralysis. Don't allow that to happen; look for answers to specific questions rather than aimlessly clicking about.

When you feel that the outline of a story is starting to take shape, move on. GA analysis is something you can come back to at any time. There will be ample opportunity to work your way into the granular detail. Each time you return with fresh knowledge, gained from other data sources, your analysis is more fruitful.

As you go along, make screenshots of any interesting reports. Export data sets from GA to Excel or Google Sheets for further analysis, maybe at a later point. This goes into the proverbial shoebox from Chapter 3, along with your notes and observations. There should be no pressure to walk away with any earth-shattering insights. Just record what you observe, take down relevant questions – and answers if you can find them.

Get an overview

If you are doing targeted research to explore a specific problem or opportunity, you will be guided by specific research questions as discussed in Chapter 3.

If this is part of your exploratory research, start by dipping in and out of the various native GA reports. Cover all four analysis zones identified in the introduction to this chapter. Use a relatively broad date range, preferably a year to counter seasonal effects.

Examples of questions of interest at this stage:

- Where are your visitors coming from (source/medium)?
- In which countries or regions are they? Are they what you would expect?
- What devices are they using?
- Mostly Android or iOS, or something else?
- What are the top three browsers?
- Where do visitors enter the site?
- Which are the most visited pages?
- Which pages have a high bounce rate?
- On which pages are they leaving the site?
- Where in the checkout funnel are visitors dropping out?

What are some questions that you want to know about the visitors to your website, and their behaviour? What assumptions do you hold that GA could help to validate or refute?

Conversion rate

It's one of the biggest obsessions in e-commerce, yet absent from the list above: 'What is your conversion rate?'

We unpack this in a later chapter, but for now, let's jump straight to the punchline: **in isolation, conversion rate is a meaningless data point**. Let's say your conversion rate is 2 per cent or 5 per cent or whatever. What does it really mean? What can do you do with that information? How can you act on it?

The first problem is that it is not a static number. Your Black Friday conversion rate is not the same as your post-Christmas conversion rate, which is not the same as your weekend conversion rate… you get the point. So, without doing anything to your site, it goes up and down. Depending on when you put the dipstick into GA, you'll get a different value.

Conversion rate is not a pointless metric *per se*; it is valuable if used wisely. For example, compare the conversion rate of different groups of users. Paid search converts worse than Organic? Ah, suddenly questions worth asking start popping out.

Return to the list of questions in the section above. This time, compare the conversion rate of the top three to five segments in each of those reports. See anything interesting? Make a note of it. Does it trigger a few questions? Put them in the shoebox.

Segment the data

Whatever GA reports you use, segmenting those data is the difference between wasting your time and using it productively. Analytics guru Avinash Kaushik doesn't mince his words: 'no segments, no insights, no job'.[2]

By default, GA reports are aggregates based on the activities of all your visitors. They hide important nuances in behaviour and how that affects performance. Segmentation reveals those individual groups, allowing you to compare the behaviour and commercial value of the various segments.

If you're not yet sure exactly how to do this thing called 'analysis' – this is a key part of it. **Segment and compare** is how you learn about behaviour, and it's a good way to make sense of almost any data – not just GA.

Figure 4.1 shows drop-off rates at various stages in the journey. Overall, 21 per cent of users are lost at the basket page. However, looking a bit deeper reveals a different picture. Most of that leakage comes from mobile users (30 per cent) and tablet users (34 per cent). On desktop, only 8 per cent are lost here.

GA gives you several options for creating segments, including:

- inline segments;
- advanced segments.

Inline segments

This is a quick 'on-the-fly' method. In Figure 4.2, we are getting more granular in the landing pages report by adding *Source/Medium* as a secondary dimension. Now, instead of seeing a list of pages where users entered the site, we'll see where they entered – depending on where they came from.

Advanced segments

An optimizer's best friend! Unlike inline segmentation, advanced segments are applied at a global level. You can really dig deep and use this feature to answer almost any question as long as the key attributes are available in GA.

Figure 4.1 Basic user journey map, constructed with GA user data. The rows show drop-off rate at each stage of the journey, segmented by device type.

Drop-off rate by device

	Visits	Category	Product	Add to basket	Basket	Login/ Sign In	Delivery	Payment	Order Confirm
All	0%	42%	91%	33%	21%	5%	3%	11%	
Desktop	0%	37%	91%	36%	8%	4%	4%	10%	
Tablet	0%	37%	91%	27%	34%	5%	1%	16%	
Mobile	0%	60%	93%	32%	30%	10%	2%	17%	

Figure 4.2 Segmenting data in GA by using inline segmentation

Set up advanced segments to compare the behaviour and performance of different groups of visitors. The list of potential segments is endless. You'd have to think about the ones that would be useful in your own business.

Here are some examples:

- Acquisition channel
- Device type
- Browser/browser version
- New vs returning visitors
- Customers vs non-customers
- High-value vs low-value purchasers
- Users who completed specific actions on the site
- Users who visited a certain page
- Users who completed a specific series of actions
- Users/device who add to cart but don't convert
- Users/sessions with transactions
- Users/sessions with more than one transaction
- Device with transactions
- Lots of page views but no add-to-basket
- Users who used site search
- Desktop/mobile users who bought more than x times
- Users who spent between x and y
- Users who came from Facebook and whose first session was on x date
- Customers who bought product x after seeing page y
- Paid search traffic who saw advertisement x and then added a product to cart

To start, click 'Add Segment' at the top of the page next to the default 'All Users'. This opens a window that looks similar to what you see in Figure 4.3. Here, we are creating a segment for users who purchased furniture, by specifying the relevant product categories. Build your own custom segments by mixing and matching various attributes. Pick from demographics, technology, behaviour and others on the left. Once you've created and named your new segment, you can apply it to almost any report in GA.

Figure 4.3 Create advanced segments in Google Analytics – a powerful way to build your own audiences based on various attributes

Funnel visualization

If funnels have already been created in GA, you will be able to get a useful funnel visualization like the example shown in Figure 4.4. At a glance, you can see how visitors are moving through the steps and where they are dropping out, to identify the major leaks. It also shows where visitors are entering the various steps, on the left, and where they go when they abandon.

If funnels haven't been configured, this isn't hard to do and you'll find easy-to-follow instructions in the GA help files on the official website. Set up funnels for your checkout and other key journeys, for example PLP (product listing page) and PDP (product detail page) progression to basket.

Assuming funnels have been set up, follow this path to generate a funnel visualization for your site:

Reports > Conversions > Goals > Funnel Visualization, and then pick the relevant funnel from the Goal dropdown box at top left.

In this particular example, the checkout funnel has a conversion rate of 19.7 per cent – out of all the visitors who start on the cart page, only 19.7 per cent of them eventually check out. The biggest drop-off is on the checkout page; almost 60 per cent abandoned the funnel at this point.

Another very insightful visualization can be found in the checkout funnel report *Checkout Behaviour.* You will have access to this if *Enhanced E-commerce* has been added to your GA installation. If it hasn't been done, ask your developers to do this as soon as possible.

Web analytics tools

There are other tools similar to GA. Some of these are positioned as alternatives, while others are useful additions. Large corporations often have GA running in parallel with enterprise products like Adobe Analytics or IBM Digital Analytics (formerly Coremetrics).

Others include:

- Kissmetrics
- Woopra
- Parse.ly.

Analytics for your mobile app:

- Google Firebase

Figure 4.4 Example of GA funnel visualization. This one shows the flow of visitors through three main stages in the checkout funnel of this e-commerce site

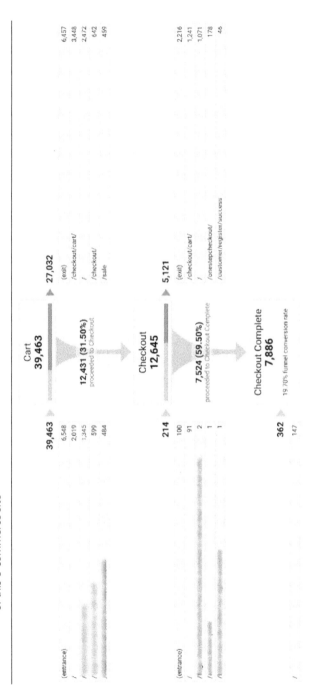

- Appsee
- Mixpanel
- Branch.io
- App Annie
- Kochava
- AppsFlyer
- Adjust
- Flurry
- Amplitude
- Countly.

User journey mapping

Built-in funnel visualization reports are insightful, but they're only accessible with some advanced configuration. Even then, the reports are only available from the day that they were created. This doesn't have to hold you back.

Your visitors leave behind trails of data in GA that you can use to manually plot their paths through the site. This forms a good backdrop to the rest of your research. In fact, many e-commerce marketers say that journey mapping is their single most valuable tool.[3]

A visualization of this data, as shown in Figure 4.1, gives you a great behavioural overview and can expose leaks on your site. This often highlights areas for further investigation, and might give you an early steer on potential opportunities.

A segmented view is always more meaningful than just looking at one block of aggregate data. Mapping out the differences between converting and non-converting segments can be very insightful. Think about what is most relevant for your particular context. The example in Figure 4.1 shows segmentation by device category. What jumps out at you? Certainly, the comparatively large drop-off on the basket page for mobile devices should prompt further examination.

PDPs often have a high drop-off rate. It's natural for people to look at products without buying, several times. Before they buy they're searching for solutions, evaluating alternatives, doing price comparisons, and they even come back to it after the purchase. There is more on purchase decision making in Chapter 13.

Create a journey map in GA

Identify the key pages that represent steps in your user journey. A typical e-commerce funnel looks something like this:

> All Users > Category Page > Product Listing Page > Product Detail Page > Add to Cart > Basket > Checkout > Transaction

Use GA to count the number of visitors to each step in the journey. There are many different ways in which to access these data. An easy approach is to create a new *dashboard* in GA, adding a widget for each step of the journey. Use regular expressions (regex; you'll find helpful tools online) to group pages together for each template. Once you've created a widget for each major step in the funnel, you can easily segment the journey by applying *advanced segments* and then export the result into Excel or Google Sheets for analysis.

Another approach is to use the advanced segments feature, shown in Figure 4.3. Go to *Sequences* on the left, then select 'Page' from the drop-down options and gradually add all the pages in the funnel. As you add another step, make a note of the visitor and session numbers to the right.

Use an extended time frame to account for seasonal differences. All that remains then is to calculate the drop-off rate between different steps and present it in an easy-to-understand visual.

Heatmaps

This is a more visual representation of user activity, compared to analytics. That also makes it effective in presentations and in discussions with stakeholders. It's easy to understand and helps to create talking points around user behaviour.

The reports are based on mouse movements (desktop) or finger movements (mobile), and show you how people interact with your pages. Examples are:

- heatmaps
- clickmaps
- scrollmaps
- mouse movement maps
- confetti maps
- overlay maps

- list views
- attention maps
- gaze plot maps

Clickmaps and heatmaps track where users click, scroll or tap on your website. Once you install the software, it runs on your site and monitors the mouse movements and click patterns of visitors. Reports are based on actual data (Table 4.1).

Table 4.1 A breakdown of the different types of visitor behaviour visualization tools

Type of heatmap	What it shows	Use the data to...
Scrollmap	How far down the page visitors are scrolling, where on the page they are spending more time	Identify whether the content you want visitors to see is being noticed or whether you need to reorganize the page to put the most important content in a more prominent location
Mouse movement map	Where your visitors are moving their mouse to and what elements they're hovering over	Infer where visitors are looking based on their mouse movements. Identify links with a low mouse movement-to-click ratio, which implies that users look at it, but choose not to interact.
Clickmap	Shows exactly where visitors are clicking on the page; GA can't give you this granular view	Discover where visitors click – and importantly, where they don't click. Are they clicking on elements that are not linked?
Overlay map	Click activity for each item on the page	Get exact numbers of clicks on each link, rather than comparing shades of colours
Confetti map	A segmented view of where your visitors are clicking	Analyse clicks by visitor type. For example, how does the behaviour of PPC, e-mail and organic traffic differ? Do visitors who convert behave any differently from those who don't convert?

(continued)

Table 4.1 (Continnued)

Type of heatmap	What it shows	Use the data to...
List view	Quantifies clicks on visible and non-visible areas of the page	Compare the user engagement with every element of your web page. Which items on the drop-down navigation are most popular? Which are the most popular products in your carousel? What percentage of clicks go to which elements?
Attention map	Algorithmic prediction of which areas on the page attract the most attention, before a visitor clicks	Discover whether content you want your visitors to see and read is visible enough. Are visitors likely to notice your value proposition? Are there distractions?
Gaze plot	Where your visitors are looking, in what order they look at on-page items and how long they look at them for	Understand how your visitors are viewing your web page – what is drawing their attention? How long are they looking at or reading your copy? Where do people look after they've looked at the product?

Unlike GA, **heatmaps** show exactly where people clicked on a page, regardless of whether it's a link or not. The more clicks, the brighter the spot. It shows which elements on a page generate the most interest. Is it in line with what you would expect, or are there surprises? Are people clicking where you want them to click? Are they being distracted, or going down less profitable paths? If so, is it because of design, or does it possibly tell you something about your visitors' goals, needs and intentions? What can you infer about user behaviour by looking at the distribution of clicks?

As with most analysis, the most interesting jewels of insight are usually hidden in segmentation. Don't ever miss this trick. In the clickmap of the login page in Figure 4.5, new visitors are represented by darker (red) dots

Figure 4.5 Segmented clickmap of a login page, where darker dots are new visitors and white dots are returning visitors

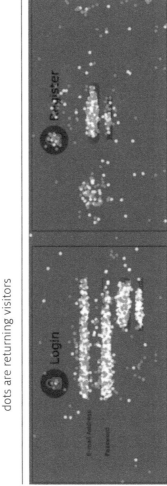

SOURCE Courtesy of Crazy Egg

and returning visitors by white dots. A large number of new visitors appear to be interacting with the login area. This prompts the question – why? Surely, if they were new to the site, they would not previously have registered an account to log into. This insight may lead to the hypothesis that the distinction is not clear enough and should be better messaged.

Scrollmaps

The idea behind **scrollmaps** is to show you how far down the page visitors scroll, and where on the page they are spending most of their time. It's always interesting to see how much of what happens 'below the fold' is noticed. The fold is a concept inherited from newspapers, which are of course literally folded in half on the newsstand. Passers-by can see only the top half of the page, which is meant to grab the attention. In a similar way, only the top section of your web page is visible when a user first looks at it. On a mobile device, an even smaller portion is in the initial view. Does it work hard enough in generating interest? What percentage of people see key content if it's further down the page? Are there any areas lower down that receive a lot of attention? Why would that be – what does it say about user needs that they seek it out? And should you elevate that content?

If you integrate the heat- and scrollmap tool with your experimentation platform, you'll be able to compare user behaviour with test variations against the control. This can be very helpful in figuring out how the variation changes behaviour. Some testing platforms, like VWO, have built-in heatmapping capabilities. Others, like Optimizely, integrate smoothly with Crazy Egg or some of the alternatives listed below.

A list of suppliers:

- Clicktale
- Crazy Egg
- Decibel Insight
- Hotjar
- Inspectlet
- Mouseflow
- MouseStats
- Sessioncam

- Sessionstack
- Truconversion
- Trymyui/stream
- UXCam (for mobile apps)
- VWO

Some of these offer much more than just heat- and scrollmaps. Hotjar is a popular tool that also includes funnel analysis, form analysis and on-site surveys. VWO is an experimentation platform with a range of discovery tools around it.

Enterprise tools, like Sessioncam and Clicktale, incorporate AI (artificial intelligence), which does much of the hard work for you in the background. Sessioncam, for example, has an algorithm that flags recordings (covered below) of sessions with poor user experience.

Session replay

You can learn a lot by watching actual people using your site. Session replay consists of video clips of mouse and finger movements, from when the user starts a session to where they leave the site. Most of the heatmap software listed above also offers session replay.

Captured by always-on software, recordings are made of every interaction by each visitor who meets your specified criteria. For example, the recording can start when a user arrives on a specific page, or when they click on a certain button on that page. Set criteria based on your insights from elsewhere and any research questions you may have. At a minimum, make sure you have activated session replay for the main device categories on key pages and templates – homepage, PLP, PDP, basket and so on.

Rather than static images, the videos show how the mouse/finger moves around the page, where they click or tap, where there's hesitation and backtracking. You see the exact sequence of these events, which heatmaps can't give you. More importantly, you can see how the site responds to that user interaction, which can surface usability issues, errors and unexpected behaviours.

Watching these clips can be revealing, but it can quickly become an unproductive time sink if not managed properly. To avoid aimlessly playing everything from beginning to end, have a plan.

First, decide which touchpoints in the journey you want to analyse and then filter videos by URL. Use insights from GA to guide the investigation, so you might target areas with a high drop-off rate or bounce rate. Then, apply the segment-and-compare strategy mentioned earlier.

Now you're ready to play the clips back to back at high speed. There's no need to watch every single clip. Soon, you'll start noticing behavioural patterns. Different segments of users behave differently. As always, make a note of every observation, linking it back to segment, device and area of the site.

CASE STUDY

One of our clients, a well-known retailer, redesigned their mobile site. In GA, we noticed a small increase in visitors abandoning PDPs of clothing products. All other categories were performing better, but fashion is one of the main revenue drivers, so this was a problem.

To understand why this was happening, we filtered session recordings for mobile visitors who abandoned the PDP without clicking the 'Add to Cart' button. It didn't take long to discover two separate problems.

The first was a general usability issue. Immediately below the product image is the quantity selector and 'Add to Cart' button. Almost a third of abandoning users were tapping the quantity selector repeatedly, but couldn't get the dropdown to work. They didn't realize they first had to pick colour and size – and to do that, they would simply have to scroll down. Out of sight, out of mind.

The second issue was a bug. The quantity button genuinely did not work if they used a certain phone model and browser combination. Even if the user had selected colour and size, the button did not respond. Because the session replay software gives you those details, we were able to pin it down and have the client's developers apply an urgent fix for that segment of users.

Usability testing

GA and heatmaps are excellent ways of finding out what is happening on your site, and to surface opportunities for optimization. It tells you what is happening, but not why. Without further information about the observed problem, it's hard to figure out how to solve it. Often, you can fill in the gaps with usability testing.

Imagine the knowledge you would gain if you could be a fly on the wall when a visitor is using your site, if you could somehow hear what they are thinking at the same time. That could give you a great insight into the road-blocks on the path to conversions.

This is exactly what usability testing is – observing users interacting with your site or app while verbalizing their thoughts. One thing to be absolutely firm on: it is never a test of the user! You are testing usability.

The official definition of usability, according to the International Organization for Standardization (ISO), is: '(the) extent to which a system… can be used by specified users to achieve specified goals with effectiveness, efficiency and satisfaction in a specified context of use'.[4] In plain English: can your users do what they want to do on your site, without suffering too much frustration?

Officially, usability testing is a way to assess 'effectiveness, efficiency and satisfaction' in relation to carrying out tasks on the site. In practice, it's simply this: see where users are getting stuck, why it's happening and get specific ideas to improve the journey.

Formative usability testing is used to find and fix issues, whereas **summative** usability testing is more descriptive, for example measuring and comparing usability.[5] E-commerce optimization tends to rely more on the formative type, but summative can come in useful if you want to explore specific problems in more detail. An interesting exercise is doing usability testing on competitor sites, and here summative will be better at facilitating a comparison.

Within these two broad divisions, there are several different approaches to conducting usability testing, as explained below.

Remote vs on-site

At one time, all usability testing was done in a laboratory. Research subjects would take time out of their day to visit the lab and conduct the test, while being observed from behind one-way glass. It was hugely expensive as well as being an artificial environment, which may cause users to behave differently from how they would at home.

Lab-based testing definitely still has its place, but it's not the only option or even the best one. The travel site Booking.com, known for their strong experimentation and optimization culture, use different approaches:

> Our product teams can order funnel tests in our lab, where they observe how people navigate through the website, what they think, and how they struggle. It's very powerful for teams to see this, especially when they think a new function is obvious but users don't understand it. Tests at users' homes show us how they

behave with our product in their own environment, spending their own money. We run tests on the street, in bars, and in cafés here in Amsterdam. We show mockups, so people can try a new user interface. (Gerben Langendijk, Booking.com[6])

Nowadays, it's easy to do this exercise remotely, without the need for a specialized lab environment. Quite literally, you can be on the other side of the world, talking to a customer, in their home, watching how they use your site.

Remote usability studies can be facilitated by a moderator, or be unmoderated. Let's look at the difference.

Unmoderated

Unmoderated testing is quick and inexpensive thanks to automated platforms like the ones listed here:

- usertesting.com
- Loop11
- Userzoom
- trymyui.com
- Validately

Typically lasting just a few minutes per session, participants log in from their own home at a time of their choosing and carry out specific tasks, speaking their thoughts out loud.

Their voice and all on-screen activities are recorded for you to watch later. All the platforms offer a feature where you can create short video clips of relevant observations to share with your team and management. This is a powerful tool that we encourage you to use.

Setting the tasks

At the start of the session, give the participant tasks to perform. These should be linked to the goals of your website. For example, in order to make a purchase on your site, users should be able to find a suitable product and add it to their cart. Marieke McCloskey offers the following guidelines for setting meaningful tasks:[7]

- Set the task in a scenario, rather than issuing a blunt instruction without any context. So rather than just 'Buy a bunch of flowers', say, 'Imagine that it's your mum's birthday tomorrow, and you want to have flowers delivered to her house. Visit my-flowers-site.com and choose something that you think your mum would like.'

- Keep it realistic for the user. The example above is not too prescriptive about either the item to be purchased or amount to be spent. This gives users the freedom to adapt the task to their circumstances and encourages natural behaviour. Asking someone to buy a particular bouquet in this case would be too specific. It may be that a user dislikes that type of flower and would never buy them in real life.

- Make it actionable. Don't ask users what they would do. Ask them to do it. Continuing the example from above, they have to click their way through the journey rather than explain what they would do next.

- Don't explain the process in too much detail or list the steps to be followed, as this could give them clues on what to do. Since they don't have that benefit in real life, usability problems may not come to light if you hold their hand. Instead of 'Add the item to your basket, then click on the green button at the bottom of the screen', simply state: 'Proceed to buy the item.'

Selecting your participants

Finding people to test is easy when you use automated platforms, because they offer ever-growing networks of testers ready and willing to take part.

Be warned, though, that this can be a double-edged sword: those testers are not necessarily representative of your visitors and customers. Many panellists are doing it semi-professionally, which can result in responses coming across as predictable and rehearsed. Some panels seem to attract individuals from a design or UX background who can't resist giving 'professional' advice, rather than reflecting on their own individual experience. Unfortunately, though well meant, that input is worthless.

The way around this problem is to screen your panel, which is a standard feature on these platforms. Don't rely only on basic demographic profiling alone; include custom questions to get as close as possible to your target customers. One of our clients sell products aimed at mothers of young children. We would ask a screening question like 'Do you have any children under the age of two?' You can also use these questions to filter out undesirable tester profiles; for example, 'Do you have a background in design or UX?'

Moderated

As the name suggests, moderated usability testing refers to the study being conducted in the presence of a facilitator. Instead of the user completing the tasks on their own, they do it while someone is watching. That someone is you, or a team member.

It can be done in person, at your office for example, or remotely using simple technology – nothing more than phone and screen-sharing tools like GoToMeeting, Zoom and Adobe Connect. We have even used Skype and Google Hangouts, although both require accounts and may be a barrier for some as these tools can represent personal space.

The advantage of moderated usability testing is that you can interact with the participant and ask follow-up questions, like 'what did you mean by that' or 'could you say a bit more about why you think that'. It allows you to explore unexpected paths, which can be extremely valuable.

This 'go with the flow' aspect has led to some of our greatest insights and discoveries. During one study, for a well-known bakery chain, the moderator observed that the user was struggling to carry out the task of ordering fresh cakes from the website. The moderator gently explored why this was, being careful not to give specific instructions like 'why don't you click there?'

Eventually the user remarked: 'What?! You mean I can actually order these cakes online and have them delivered to me?' At this point, it dawned on the moderator that despite lots of visual clues, such as a basket icon and banners about delivery, it had not even occurred to the user that it was possible to buy fresh cakes online. It seemed obvious to the client, but was clearly not obvious to all users.

This was an 'Aha!' moment that would not have surfaced in an unmoderated setting. It also required the researcher to recognize it as a valuable insight and not dismiss the user as an idiot. This casual remark was developed into the hypothesis that sales would go up if more visitors were made explicitly aware that they could buy from the site.

A simple experiment was developed in which everything was the same as before, apart from an additional headline on the homepage saying 'Shop online now – from our bakery to your door'. These nine words delivered an 18 per cent increase in revenue per visitor. It led to a series of tests, challenging a core assumption everyone had – that users actually knew they could order fresh cakes online.

Recruiting the panel

To recruit people for usability testing, we recommend that you intercept users on your site as they are actually using it. This allows you to observe a truly authentic experience. Known as live recruiting, two popular tools are Ethnio and Hotjar. They serve a pop-up to users like the one shown in Figure 4.6 and when someone responds, you can call them immediately and conduct the session right there and then.

Figure 4.6 Example of a pop-up served by Ethnio to recruit usability testing participants in real time

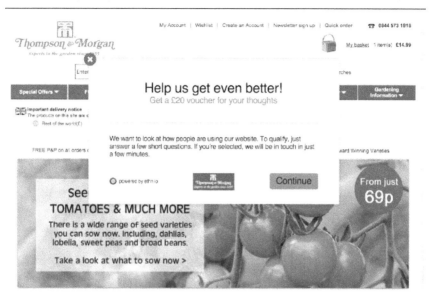

If live recruiting is not possible, you can reach out to your database by e-mail or telephone. Regardless of the method you use, it's a good idea to offer a small incentive, usually a gift voucher to spend on the site. It will increase your response rate, and it's also fair to thank people and compensate them for their time – which should be limited to no more than 15 minutes. Detractors of this inducement say that it can skew the results, but it's still better than not having any data.

How to conduct a session

Once you've found a participant via live recruiting, phone them up right away and direct them to the screen-sharing facility. Ask them to continue the session as though you weren't there.

A big difference between recruiting from your own customer base, as opposed to using panels, is that this is probably a new experience for them. They don't know anything about usability testing. Use the first few minutes to help them feel at ease and explain the rules of engagement carefully:

- This is a test of the website, not of the user. If they find something confusing or problematic, there are other people who will have the same experience.
- Reassure them that you can see only what they are sharing with you. If at any point they feel uncomfortable for whatever reason, they may stop the session immediately.

- It is very important that they share with you what is going through their mind, even if they feel it is irrelevant.

Your role then is to observe, listen and take notes. This is important: have them speak their thoughts out loud. Don't interrupt! And don't guide them.

When they go quiet, give them a gentle nudge, for example 'what are you looking at now?' or 'is this what you were expecting to see?' Apart from that, keep out of their way and let them get on with it. Resist the temptation to tell them how to do it, especially if they get stuck. Rather, let that one individual struggle, even if it means losing a sale, so that you can see what's going wrong and fix it for everyone else.

If they ask you a question, turn it back to them. For example, if someone wants to know how to proceed to checkout, you could ask: 'what do you think you should do next?' Giving them any directions kills your opportunity to learn.

Quantitative and qualitative insights

Usability testing really shines in its ability to generate qualitative insights, but quantification is still possible.

It is especially common with summative usability testing, given the nature of its being more descriptive. Two metrics that are often used in this type of analysis are task completion rate and time on task.

Task completion rate simply measures how many participants managed to complete the task. It is expressed as the percentage of successful attempts. To measure **time on task**, record how long it takes for each user to complete the task. This is mainly used for benchmarking and comparison.

To do quantitative analysis effectively requires slightly bigger sample sizes. For this reason, remote unmoderated usability testing lends itself well to quantitative analysis, as it's easier to increase panel size.

Documenting insights

It shouldn't be necessary to say this, but jot down every observation. One thing worse than not doing usability testing is wasting the opportunity by not keeping notes diligently. Include verbatim quotes to provide colour to your observations; it's an effective way to underscore an insight.

A simple system that works well for us is using a spreadsheet similar to Table 4.2. Each unique observation is captured on a separate row, while each column represents a participant in the study. You can see at a glance

Table 4.2 A basic log for capturing observations during usability testing

	User 1	User 2	User 3	User ...	TOTAL
Observation 1	1				1
Observation 2	1	1	1		3
Observation 3	1	1			1

which users experienced which issues. In the example in the table, User 1 encountered three issues compared to only one for User 3. Observation 2 was experienced by all users.

The last column adds up the total for each row. While this may be an indication of how widespread an issue is, be careful of reading too much into it. You'll mostly be working with small samples, and the purpose of this exercise is not to make statistically robust inferences.

Still, if you count the number of occurrences per observation, it can be used as a signal of importance. It is also good practice to assign a **severity rank** to each issue. Keep it simple, for example:

- **Major:** A show stopper. The user is unlikely to continue beyond this point, so the task cannot be successfully completed.

- **Moderate:** The task may still be successfully completed, but this issue causes user frustration and delays.

- **Minor:** Minor irritation, but the conversion is not jeopardized.

Severity, and to some extent occurrence rate, can help you to prioritize the issues you've observed.

How many users do you need?

When you are doing formative usability testing as part of a broad exploration, don't stress about sample size.

An often-quoted statistic comes from the seminal work of Jakob Nielsen and Tom Landauer.[8] They found that just five testers reveal 85 per cent of a site's usability issues, after which the law of diminishing returns sets in. They also make the point that one is better than none, which is a good way of saying that the focus should be on finding insights rather than chasing sample quotas.

There is a caveat to the five-user rule. When you have two or more distinct groups of users, it's good practice to include representatives from each group. If you have created personas, a topic for the next chapter, aim to test three or four users from the core persona groupings. If your study spans different device categories, our advice is to target mobile and desktop separately, with three to five users on each.

Try to do follow-up studies throughout the optimization lifecycle and as you make changes to the site. At the very least it may validate some of your interventions, but invariably fresh opportunities will emerge. It's better to do more frequent sessions of smaller batches.

Heuristic evaluation

The method was originally developed in 1990 by Dr Jakob Nielsen with Rolf Mollich as a formal process of evaluating a website against 10 general principles. It has subsequently been adapted for the purposes of UX and optimization.

Some optimizers start the ideation process with heuristic evaluation. Often it's nothing more than one person's subjective opinion about the site. In our view it's more effective to do this if you already have some data and insights to bring to the exercise.

A framework

Six principles commonly found in heuristic evaluation models are:

1 motivation

2 value proposition

3 relevance

4 incentive and urgency

5 distractions/attention

6 anxiety/friction

Motivation

People buy stuff because they have a need. They need to solve a problem, or to get something done. Harvard marketing professor Theodore Levitt famously said: 'People don't want to buy a quarter-inch drill. They want a quarter-inch hole!'[9]

The stronger that need, the more motivated they are to purchase. You can uncover the needs and motivations of your customers by using the research methodologies covered in Chapter 5.

Value proposition

Strong motivation to purchase is not enough to clinch the sale, partly because the consumer has alternatives. They could buy from a competitor, or choose to do nothing at all.

> Value proposition = Perceived benefit – Perceived cost

Note it's all about perception. What you and your team think about value is far less important than what your customer values. Through user research, you can determine what your customers find valuable. For the purpose of the heuristic evaluation, check the following:

- Does your copy pass the 'so what' test?
- Why should someone buy this product from your site? Are you giving visitors compelling reasons?
- Is the value proposition easy to understand?
- Is it communicated and articulated well?
- How does it stack up against the customer's expectations of value?
- Is it clear what difference the purchase will make in their lives?
- How does it compare against the value propositions of competitors?
- Is there a sense of uniqueness, of differentiation?

Relevance

All consumers are tuned into the same radio station – WII.FM (What's In It For Me?)

We often hear that people don't read on the web. That's not true. People read if it's relevant to them. Unfortunately, web copy is often badly written, hence it doesn't get read.

Are the key messages relevant to the visitor, in the context of their motivation and need? Are they aligned with expectations created upstream, for example in search advertising campaigns? Is it specific and unambiguous?

For example, if I clicked on an advert that promises a 50 per cent discount, is that promise carried forward to the page that I arrive on? Do I see a reinforcing message with links to the marked-down products? If not, there's a potential disruption of that initial thought pattern.

Incentive/urgency

Hotel booking sites use the urgency principle very effectively. By showing you how many other people are looking at the same hotel – and, by the way, only one room is left – you know that you have to act quickly.

Robert Cialdini points out that, on the whole, people want to maximize gain and minimize cost[10] (see Chapter 13). Is anything offered to sweeten the deal, or to make the user act now instead of delaying?

Often, these mechanisms already exist, but can be improved or amplified. For example, the incentive might be presented at the wrong time in the decision-making process. Or it might not be communicated compellingly enough.

Distractions/attention

Humans have a limited attention span. Treat it as a scarce resource! Every additional design element and call to action potentially adds to cognitive load. This hampers a user's decision-making process and may cause them to abandon altogether.

Which elements on the page could be diverting attention from the main objectives? For example, links in the main navigation, or other calls to action, can lead users down a side path further away from a sale. Heatmaps are useful tools when trying to identify distractions.

You can also use tools like Eye Quant and Feng-GUI. They use predictive algorithms to reflect on the ability of a design to distribute attention effectively (Figure 4.7). These tools will show you which parts are most likely to be seen within the first few seconds, and where users are most likely to look.

Anxiety/friction

These are negative forces that get in the way of conversions, even when a user is highly motivated. Reducing anxiety and friction is one of the most common ways of improving the conversion rate.

The difference between the two is that anxiety plays out in the user's mind, whereas friction comes from the web page. Wondering whether fragile goods will arrive undamaged may cause anxiety. Being confronted by a long, badly designed form is an example of friction, as it increases the effort required by the user.

If you have identified pages with a high drop-off rate or exit rate, chances are that users are experiencing one of these forces. Do you see anything on the page that can potentially cause FUD (Fear, Uncertainty, Doubt)? Is there any part of the process that can be simpler?

Figure 4.7 Using EyeQuant to compare the perception map of two design variations. The predictive algorithm, developed by analysing thousands of eye movements, shows where users are likely to look within the first few seconds

Variant

Control

Session replay analysis can expose areas of friction. Similarly, you can explore hypotheses about friction and anxiety with usability testing.

Setting up for heuristics evaluation

It's not uncommon for businesses to employ a consultant to tell them what's wrong with their site, or where the opportunities are. No matter how qualified and experienced that person may be, they can't give you that answer. Nobody can.

The importance of having a diverse number of inputs was amply illustrated by an experiment conducted by Jakob Nielsen. He asked 19 evaluators to work together, and they found 16 usability issues. No one picked up every issue, and some evaluators spotted as few as three. The results are shown in Figure 4.8, with black squares representing an issue that was spotted, and white those that were missed.

Looking at the top row, you'll see that the least successful evaluator found only 3 out of a possible 16 issues. On the far left of the chart, where the more hard-to-spot issues are plotted, there are only two black squares, indicating that they were picked up by only two evaluators. Overall, there are far more white squares than black, testament to just how difficult it can be. In fact, Nielsen also discovered that an evaluator typically finds only around a third of usability problems.

Figure 4.8 Jakob Nielsen's experiment. The black squares represent an opportunity spotted and white squares are those that were missed

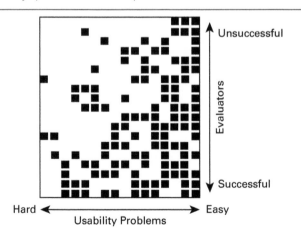

SOURCE Nielsen Norman Group[11]

To get the best results with heuristic evaluation, follow these guidelines:

- **Use two or more people**. Different issues will be picked up by different individuals. Nielsen suggests using three to five.

- **Work collaboratively**. One school of thought favours independent evaluations so that individuals aren't influenced by each other, but our experience is that a collaborative effort works well. Having evaluators together in one session avoids duplication and saves time. Issues can be discussed and prioritized in real time. You don't even have to have everyone in one room. With video conferencing or screen-sharing, a group heuristic evaluation is just as effective when done remotely, but always have one person keeping track of all the insights as they emerge.

- **Use a framework**. The point of the exercise is not for each person to list what they dislike about the site. Systematically work through recognized heuristic principles, which brings clarity and focus to the evaluation.

To conduct a group heuristic evaluation, start by issuing a brief containing the following:

- **URL of the site,** or of specific pages if you're limiting it to an area of the site. Presumably this is your own site, but nothing prevents you from making this exercise part of competitor analysis.

- **Framework** to be used. Have everyone use the same framework, or give them the same list of heuristics.

- **Personas**. Try to imagine yourself in the world of a customer. What are they trying to do on the site?

- **Tasks** that the evaluator has to perform. These can be based on the most dominant, or broken, journeys obtained from GA analysis.

- **Device**. Try to cover a range of devices.

Collect responses either individually or in a group. If done individually, give everyone a template where they can list all the issues and opportunities they notice under relevant headings. A good method is to use a screen capture tool to take and annotate screen grabs. If evaluators collaborate, then have one person aggregate everything in real time.

Customer immersion

When did you last buy something from your own site, or use your own product? One of the most revealing ways to find out what it's really like to buy from your site is to become a customer yourself. You may be astonished at what you discover.

This can be done as an extension of heuristic evaluation. Place an order, just as if you were a customer; the only difference is that you log each step and take notice of your actions, feelings and observations. Your aim is to inspect the entire purchase chain, including the checkout process as well as the post-purchase experience. Screenshot the process, and look at any e-mails or other communication as part of your transaction.

Often, the last mile is owned by a courier service. For a pure-play e-commerce business, that may be the only human interface with the customer. Many people won't make a distinction between your business and the carrier, so what impression is left? Try to return the item. How easy or cumbersome is that?

Compare the reality you experience to the messaging and promises on the site. Does it match up? Is there something in the experience you can improve? Are there positive elements around the fulfilment currently not reflected online? For example, one of our clients had a white-glove delivery service that we discovered by chance after placing an order. It was actually a pleasant delivery experience – but not a word of it in key places on the site!

The authors of *Rules to Break and Laws to Follow*[12] highlighted a number of questions that you should be able to answer about your customer experience. The list below is based on their recommendations:

- What is it like to be your customer?
- Exactly what is the customer experience that you deliver, in specific practical terms?
- What is it like to deal with the call centre or support system?
- What is the experience of receiving and opening the package?
- Do you need instructions, are they easy to find and follow?
- Was everything exactly as promised?

Site search

It's amazing how much you can tell about user intent and needs by analysing the phrases used to search your site. It also plays a role in merchandising analytics, covered in Chapter 6. Site searchers tend to be more prolific spenders, so this journey usually deserves attention.

Table 4.3 shows an actual example, comparing searchers against non-searchers. What's so revealing is that only a very small percentage of visitors use site search – about 14 per cent, but they're responsible for a massive 40 per cent of revenue.

To find optimization opportunities in the search experience, look at the following:

- most common search terms;
- terms with highest/lowest exit rates;
- terms with highest/lowest conversion rates;
- top search terms ranked by Revenue/Per Search Value;
- pages where most search events originate;
- failed search terms, resulting in no matches found.

Review your search results pages for the 20 most searched terms. Often, just improving the performance of the top 20 can have an impact. Are the most relevant products displayed first? There's some research that suggests that users pay disproportionately more attention to the first few items. Are there any distractions? Too much choice, perhaps?

Take a step back from the search pages and look at your site with a fresh eye in the light of what you know people are searching for. Are the products that people search for prominently signposted on relevant pages?

Table 4.3 Data obtained from GA that compares the behaviour of visitors who used site search versus those who didn't

Site search status	Sessions	Revenue contribution	Average order value	E-commerce conversion rate	Per-session value
Without site search	86%	60%	£17.87	4.40%	£0.79
With site search	14%	40%	£30.92	10.25%	£3.17

The GA metric % *Search Exits* tells you the percentage of people who left your site straight after doing a search. Sort by this column to see which search terms are causing most dropouts. Now run a search for those terms with high exit rates to see if you can figure out why they're causing visitors to give up. Are the search results relevant? Conduct a similar search on your main competitor's site. How do you compare? The purpose is to look at it in the same context as your visitor, never to copy what competitors are doing.

You can also see how demand is influenced by seasonality. To find out, export the top unique searches for each month over the last year from GA. Then stitch them together in 12 columns, one for each month. What patterns do you pick up?

With a little extra configuration, you can track failed searches in GA. This will show you which search queries return no results. Are products not showing because they're not in stock, or has something else gone wrong? If you don't carry the products that users are searching for, is that an opportunity? What has brought your visitors to your site under the impression that they can buy something from you that you don't stock?

Looking at the pages your users were on when they started their search will give you different insights. Are there any surprises when you look at this report? For example, what does it mean if a lot of people search for things from the product detail pages? Are they not finding what they were looking for? How do search patterns differ between page templates? For example, do people in the checkout funnel search for delivery information?

Form analysis

How much do you like filling in forms? Nobody does, and yet forms are central in many online journeys. It's easy to see how they can get in the way of conversions. To illustrate this, an analysis of data from 650,000 form users revealed that the conversion rate for Order/Payment forms averaged only 9 per cent![13]

Assess the performance of pages containing forms in GA. First, review top-level indicators for those pages, such as bounce rate, exit rate and drop-off rate. This will give you some context and direction in terms of which forms to analyse and prioritize. As for the forms, check the following:

- How many people saw the form?
- How many started filling it out?

- How many completed the form?
- Which fields caused users to abandon?

The good news is that all of these data can be made available to you by setting up event tracking in GA, which involves just a tiny bit of technical work for your developer.

Another approach may be to use a tool designed for this purpose. These tools can show you things like which fields cause the most hesitation, where errors occur and identify the fields that lead to abandonment. If forms are an important part of your visitor journey, it may be worth investing in bespoke form analysis software like Formisimo. It's also included in some other tools like Hotjar and Clicktale.

Session replays, discussed in detail earlier, can also come in handy. Filter recordings of people interacting with the form. You should spot the issues as you review the clips: where people pause, errors that come up, and where they abandon.

Finally, build forms into your heuristic evaluation. Here are some principles, which you could use as a basis for the evaluation:

- **Form length**. The more fields, the more daunting the task will appear. Every field has to justify its existence. Ask of each one, why do you need it? Is it to the benefit of the business or the user?

- **Layout**. Would a single-column form with the field name above be better than two columns with the field name to the side?

- **Nomenclature**. What you call a part of the form can make a difference as to how people react. For example, 'verification required' may be off-putting, whereas 'activate now' sounds perhaps more inviting.

- **Phone number**. People generally resist sharing their phone number. If you need it, could you tell the user why it's in their interest to provide it? For example, 'We may call you to schedule delivery.'

- **CAPTCHA**. Do you really need it? What is the risk in dropping it? If you can't do without it, make it as easy as possible. A simple puzzle like '3+1=' means they only have to type in one digit, not a string that you struggle to read. Even better, just a tick-box to indicate they're not a bot.

- **Error messages**. Is the error message specific to the error? Does it leave the user with clear instructions on how to recover? Does the message make it sound as though the user is at fault? Is it worded in a helpful way so that the user understands what to do? Is it in close proximity to where the error occurred?

Summary

Ideas are born out of insights, which start by gathering and analysing data. There are many different data sources that will each give you a different piece of the puzzle.

Start by understanding what is happening on your web and mobile site. How are visitors interacting with it? Where do they come from, where do they land, what do they do – and what do they not do?

Analytics data are a rich source of insights. Use funnel visualization and journey maps to find out where visitors are leaking out of your funnel. There are many other signals in analytics data to point out potential opportunities, such as bounce rate, exit rate, page value and conversion rate. Use conversion rate to compare different segments. In isolation, it's a meaningless metric that causes managers to obsess over the wrong thing.

You can learn a lot by seeing how visitors interact with your site. Heat- and scrollmaps show you exactly where on a page users click and pay more attention, which is not visible in analytics data. Session replay tools make video recordings of all user interactions, including mouse and finger movements, clicks and taps. Watching these video clips can reveal behavioural patterns, usability issues and even bugs.

Usability testing is the process of observing users interacting with your site or app. It is arguably the best method for uncovering usability issues and roadblocks in the path to conversion. The easiest approach is to use an online service. Filter their vast panel, give panellists a script to tell them what to do on your site and come back later to watch the video recordings.

Try to combine that with moderated usability testing, where you are physically present during the session. This can even be done with people recruited live from your site. The advantage is that you watch an actual user doing what they normally would do, rather than following a script. This is a good way to discover issues that you're not aware of yet.

The tools and methodologies covered in this chapter will give you a good insight into behavioural patterns. The next chapter will help you understand what's driving that behaviour. Armed with that knowledge, you can shape this behaviour.

Notes

1 Dykes, B (2012) *Web Analytics Action Hero: Using analysis to gain insight and optimize your business*, Adobe Press, Berkeley, CA

2 Kaushik, A (2010) *Web Analytics 2.0: The art of online accountability and science of customer centricity*, John Wiley & Sons, Hoboken, NJ

3 Econsultancy (2015) [Accessed 5 August 2020] Conversion rate optimization report 2015, *Econsultancy* [Online] https://econsultancy.com/reports/conversion-rate-optimization-report/ (archived at https://perma.cc/R8N7-4EER)

4 International Organization for Standardization (ISO) (nd) [Accessed 5 August 2020] Ergonomics of human–system interaction – Part 11: Usability: Definitions and concepts, *ISO* [Online] www.iso.org/obp/ui/#iso:std:iso:9241:-11: ed-2:v1:en (archived at https://perma.cc/DX76-LQQE)

5 Sauro, J (2010) *A Practical Guide to Measuring Usability: 72 answers to the most common questions about quantifying the usability of websites and software*, Measuring Usability LLC, Denver, CO

6 Thomke, S and Beyersdorfer, D (2018) Booking.com, Harvard Business School Case 619-015, October

7 McCloskey, M (2014) [Accessed 5 August 2020] Turn user goals into task scenarios for usability testing, *Nielsen Norman Group* [Online] www.nngroup.com/articles/task-scenarios-usability-testing/ (archived at https://perma.cc/K4AE-ZEC4)

8 Nielsen, J and Landauer, T (1993) A mathematical model of the finding of usability problems, *Proceedings of ACM INTERCHI'93 Conference*, pp 206–13, Amsterdam, Netherlands, 24–29 April

9 Christensen, C M, Cook, S and Hall, T (2006) [Accessed 5 August 2020] What customers want from your products, *Harvard Business School Newsletter: Working Knowledge* [Online] https://hbswk.hbs.edu/item/what-customers-want-from-your-products (archived at https://perma.cc/QN53-RVF8)

10 Cialdini, R (2007) *Influence: The psychology of persuasion*, HarperCollins, New York

11 Nielsen, J (1995) [Accessed 5 August 2020] How to conduct a heuristic evaluation, *Nielsen Norman Group* [Online] www.nngroup.com/articles/how-to-conduct-a-heuristic-evaluation/ (archived at https://perma.cc/WQ6A-5DLP)

12 Peppers, D and Rogers, M (2008) *Rules to Break and Laws to Follow,* John Wiley & Sons, New York

13 Formstack (2015) [Accessed 5 August 2020] The 2015 form conversion report, *Formstack* [Online] www.formstack.com/infographics/form-conversion-report-2015 (archived at https://perma.cc/6KAW-FFGZ)

Voice of customer

05

Having dug the foundations with behavioural research, the stage is set for the most valuable insight of them all – voice of customer (VoC). Listening to the stories behind data will help you understand quantitative and behavioural data better.

'Numbers alone won't convince others', Nick Morgan wrote in *Harvard Business Review*.[1] He continued: 'Good stories… are what attach emotions to your argument, prompt people into unconscious decision making, and ultimately move them to action.'

VoC is not just shorthand for customer feedback. It has the following attributes:[2]

- detailed set of customer wants and needs, in their own words;
- organized into a hierarchical structure, from the customer's perspective;
- prioritized in terms of importance and satisfaction with current alternatives.

Interviewing customers is by far the best method for obtaining VoC insights. In this chapter, we look at this and other mainly qualitative research methods.

Interviews

Arguably one of the most underrated research methods, an interview is a unique opportunity to learn about customer motivation, **needs and wants**.

The practical importance of this is stressed by the world's greatest car salesperson, Joe Girard, to whom we return in Chapter 13: 'The more you understand about their needs and wants, the better equipped you'll be to provide them with the right solution.'[3]

Interviewing is different from moderated usability testing, covered in Chapter 4, where you also have one-on-one interactions with users. In that context it's not about having a conversation with the user. On the contrary, we emphasized that the moderator must stay quiet and give the user space to get on with the task.

Dialogue gives you the ability to explore, clarify and follow up. Interviews will take you down unexpected paths, and often that's exactly where you'll find the best insights.

'There are no facts inside the building so get the heck outside,' Steve Blank from Stanford University famously said.[4] Interviewing someone in person in their own environment is ideal, but it's not always practical. It can be time consuming and expensive, and is not necessary in most cases. Telephone interviews have advantages of scale, efficiency and geographic reach.

Customer interviews

'A deep dive into the lives of customers.'[5] That's how Steve Portigal, author of *Interviewing Users: How to uncover compelling insights*, describes it.

Only by talking to customers can you truly begin to understand their context, needs, motivations and pain points. No other research method can let you get into the hearts and minds of your customers to the same extent.

Customer research is not about profiling customers; rather it is done to discover what drives behaviour. It's not demographics that makes someone buy. As Clayton Christensen explains: 'We live our lives in circumstances. During the course of the day, problems arise and we look around to hire products to solve these problems.'[6]

This fresh way of thinking is the essence of the Jobs To Be Done (JTBD) framework. In their daily lives, people are trying to get stuff done. In doing so, the overall experience is an important consideration. And their circumstances dictate the purchase decision more than customer traits or product attributes.[7]

Use interviews to uncover the core motivation behind the purchase decision, by understanding what 'job' they are trying to get done. It's not always **functional**. Your customer might buy an expensive piece of furniture to make a statement in their home (**emotional** driver). Or buy fashionable sneakers to fit in with the crowd (**social** driver).

'What should I ask?' 'That's the wrong question,' an academic tells her students whenever they want to know what questions to ask. 'You have to have a question that you are really interested in. Not make it up, but find out what you are really interested in.'[8]

In *The PDMA Handbook*, VoC is said to be best explored with indirect questions, grounded in reality.[9] Let's explore what is meant by that.

Ground it in reality. Let them talk about past experiences, rather than asking about hypothetical scenarios.

Customers are not good at telling us what they want. Henry Ford is quoted as saying: 'If I had asked people what they wanted, they would have said a faster horse.' There is no evidence that he actually said it,[10] but it underscores the point that people can't tell you what they want. So don't ask them that. They are much better at telling you about their needs, the problems they are trying to solve and their frustrations in doing so. It's your job to figure out a solution once you have all the relevant information about what causes the problem in the first place.

The best questions begin something like this: 'Tell me about the last time you….' This line of questioning will take you down a path of discovery where you can learn about relevant circumstances, needs, wants, motivational forces and frustrations. The response is based on an actual experience, not predictions relating to some hypothetical scenario.

Ask indirect questions. Avoid starting off with direct questions like 'what do you want?' Ask about current behavioural patterns, solutions and frustrations.

When we worked with a large gardening and plant retailer, some of the questions we asked target customers were:

- When you last purchased plants, where did you buy them?

- What alternatives did you consider?

- Why did you buy from that particular outlet on that occasion?

- How did you decide which plants to purchase?

- Tell us about the last time you bought plants online.

It's best to go into interviews with a handful of seed questions, rather than a complete list to work through. This method, called a **semi-structured** interview, will allow the conversation to unfold naturally.

What may not be clear at this point is that the insights come from the open response, including side paths and tangents. In fact, it's a good idea to leave a few moments of silence before following up, in case the interviewee wants to fill that space. The real nuggets are often hidden in tangents and extended responses. Without asking directly what their frustrations are, these will soon come out in the detail around decisions made and real experiences.

Even a broad and seemingly vague opening question like 'what do you like about gardening?' invites the customer to share underlying needs. In this case, the drivers were more social and emotional than functional. For many, gardening is an escape as well as a way to connect with others. This leads to a particular way of buying flowers and plants. If you understand that journey, you can optimize it.

Customer service representatives

The operators in the inbound call centre, if you have one, have the thankless task of listening to people moan at them every day. What a gold mine! If you don't have a call centre, speak to colleagues who deal with those customer calls.

Ask them to identify the three to five top queries and complaints. What goes wrong before an order is placed? What information do they want? What do online customers ask about? Why have they contacted the call centre, rather than look at the online help section?

And here is the secret sauce: also ask these colleagues how they respond, and what reaction they get. What do they say that melts away the anxieties and sales objections? Which themes do customers respond well to, and less so?

Tapping into that knowledge can inform a lot of test ideas. One of our clients makes a habit of spending a day in their call centre from time to time. She emerges full of ideas, entirely focused on the customer's agenda.

Store managers and salespeople

If you operate in an omnichannel environment, do yourself a favour and go hang out in your bricks and mortar stores. Shop assistants are at the sharp end of dealing with customers. They get real-time feedback and adjust their sales messages accordingly. They are in the incredibly privileged position of seeing how the purchase decision unfolds, hearing the burning questions and sales objections, and learning which responses push undecided shoppers over the purchase line.

I visited a client's store to look at a high-ticket item that was a big seller, but suffered a high abandonment rate on their site. Seeing how the assistant 'sold' me was an eye-opener, not only for me, but also for the client's online team when I later presented this to them. The pitch was completely different from the online approach. That salesperson knew from talking to hundreds of customers how to pinpoint my needs, and which buttons to push to help my make up my mind.

Most omnichannel stores will have Click and Collect counters. This is where your online customers interface with the business in the real world. What can the staff behind that counter share with you? What are their observations of your customers?

E-mail surveys

An e-mail survey is easy to launch and can generate a large number of responses. That makes it one of the most effective methods for gathering customer feedback and data across a broad spectrum.

This low barrier also has a downside. It's easy to get carried away with a long list of questions dumped into SurveyMonkey. We see too much of this survey spam. Before writing your first survey question, have a plan.

What do you need to find out? What is the main purpose of your survey? That will inform what questions to ask. Here are some of the topics you can explore via e-mail surveys:

- Sentiment – what do people say and feel?
- Who are your customers? Are they who you think they are?
- How are loyal customers different from one-time buyers?
- What has caused lapsed customers to stop buying from you?
- Who are your key competitors? Are they who you think they are?
- What do your customers like about your competitors?
- What do your customers value about your business/product?
- What is their motivation to buy your products, regardless of where they buy them?
- How do they make the purchase decision?
- Post-purchase satisfaction (overall, product, service etc).
- Long-term satisfaction.

Don't ask it just because you can! Every question has to have a reason for being there. For each question, you should be able to state in advance how you will act on the data. If you can't do anything with that feedback, don't ask the question.

Target the right audience. Who to send the survey to depends on the research objectives. Are you targeting customers, non-customers or both?

First-time buyers, one-time buyers or loyal customers? Customers who made a purchase recently or lapsed? Customers who bought particular product categories?

Keep it short. Limit both the number and length of questions. Before you send it out, test how long it takes someone to complete it. Try to keep it around 5–10 minutes. Long surveys tend to have lower response rates. The quality of your responses might also suffer as survey fatigue sets it. Give the option to skip questions unless you have a good reason to make it mandatory, such as 'conditional branching questions' where you need a response in order to channel the respondent down the appropriate path.

Ask clear questions. Avoid using technical, marketing and business jargon. Customer-friendly language, not corporate gobbledygook. Don't assume that users will understand your terminology. Avoid using stilted and formal phrasing. Just ask the question how you would ask a friend. Let customer interviews inspire your survey language. Use the same terms and descriptions that you heard from interviewees. Before launching the survey, ask a few colleagues if they understand the questions.

Incentivize responses. Offering a small incentive increases the likelihood that people will take part. This could be important if you have a small database, or if your network is known to be unresponsive. A gift voucher is always popular, but entry into a prize draw can also be used. Although purists say this affects the results, it is certainly preferable to having too little or no data to work on. It's also fair to offer people something for their time and input.

Open questions

There is no doubt that open questions and open-text responses are more valuable, though they also take more time to process. These are questions where a more considered response is required, and can't be answered with one word like 'yes' or 'no'.

You will benefit from seeing the respondent's own words. Sometimes the way in which something is expressed, or the specific words chosen, is as important as what is being said. This is lost when respondents are given answers to choose from.

These responses can also help you later on with creative work, because the actual quotes can be valuable to inform copy, and may even end up being used semi-verbatim in copy or headlines. Column D in Table 5.1 is used for the purpose of creating an 'ordinary person' vocabulary, as opposed to marketing speak. This may later be used in sales copy on the website.

Nothing beats reading through user feedback, line by line. That's the point of it, and it's another good reason to limit the number of questions. As

Table 5.1 Codifying open-text responses to identify themes and patterns. Column D in this example highlights actual words used by respondents to build up an 'ordinary person' vocabulary. This may later be used in sales copy on the website and elsewhere.

	A	B	C	D
1	Response	Theme	Sub-theme	Words used
2	I was looking for the thinnest sole	Comfort	Sole	
3	It was what i was looking for. Min	Protection		Minimalist
4	This was one of the only sandals	Comfort	Unique design	Toe thong
5	Probably because it was about th	Price		
6	I wanted a pair of sandals that co	Versatility		
7	A combination of both customer	Hiking	Sole	Thin-soled, hikin
8	ability to tie it my own way to my	Comfort		Tie it my own wa
9	I chose the sturdier looking sanda	Durability	Running	Challenging terra
10	I thought this would be the most	Performance	Performance	Most fun

the UX researcher Chrissie Brodigan said: 'No amount of machine learning or text analysis can surface the insights reading open text does.'[11]

Export responses to a spreadsheet and highlight the ones that stand out. Use a colour coding system such as red for high severity, yellow for interesting or noteworthy and green for positive.

Although primarily a qualitative research technique, it's necessary to apply some quantification to open question analysis, as explained later. Categorize each response according to its high-level theme, then count the number of instances per theme. This makes it easier to observe patterns.

Closed questions

Closed questions give respondents answers to choose from. Make sure that you cover the entire range of possible answers. The best way to do this is by including options for 'other, please specify' and even 'don't know' or 'not sure'.

These questions are easier to process quantitatively, but you don't get the real VoC benefit. Where relevant, follow up with an open question. If someone responds to that first closed question, they are generally more likely to provide a follow-up response too.

A big advantage of closed questions is **conditional branching**. This is where the direction of the survey changes, depending on the response. This way you can have respondents self-select their segment, and then tailor the rest of the survey to them. Each segment will see different questions. Examples of segments that we use regularly include:

- one-time buyers
- multi-buyers
- non-buyers
- lapsed buyers
- big spenders.

Sample questions

It's impossible to offer a universal list. The following, along with those presented elsewhere in this chapter, are just meant as inspiration. Think about your unique situation, and what you need to know about your customers and their needs.

Closed questions:

- Demographics: age, education etc
- How many times have you bought from our online shop?
  - o Never
  - o In the last 30 days
  - o 1–3 months ago
  - o More than 3 months ago
- How often do you visit our site to look at an item, but go into one of our stores to buy it?
  - o Not usually
  - o Sometimes
  - o Routinely

- How would you describe yourself?
  - ○ Professional photographer
  - ○ Serious amateur
  - ○ Novice
- Do you
  - ○ own your house?
  - ○ rent your house?
- What products have you purchased from our site?
- How frequently do you purchase X product?
- When did you last purchase from us?

Open or closed, depending on your objectives and existing intelligence. If closed, always offer an 'Other, please specify' option:

- What alternative products/technologies did you consider before buying this item?
- At which shops or online stores have you shopped for the product you most recently purchased from our site?
- What factors did you consider when buying the product you most recently purchased from our site?
- Which website do you like buying from?
- What is it about your favourite shopping site that you like?

Open-text answers, where the purpose is to get attitudinal insight:

- How would you describe our site/product/brand to a friend?
- What influenced your decision to purchase online as opposed to in-store?
- Why did you buy from us and not another website or shop?
- What do you like about Competitor X?
- What do you like about us compared to Competitor X?
- What has been the best/worst thing about your experience as our customer?
- What concerns and fears did you have when shopping on our site?
- What one thing could we change to persuade you to shop with us more?
- Please describe your entire decision-making process behind your most recent purchase. For example: I was looking for blinds, but didn't want

to pay too much, and a friend recommended your brand. I had a look online and was impressed with the prices. I visited one of your stores to look at the blinds, then went home to order online.

- How are you using product X?
- Why exactly did you need the product that you came to the site for?
- It can be said that we buy things to improve aspects of our lives. What difference in your life did you *expect* this product to make?
- How would your life be different if you weren't able to use X product?

Pitfalls to avoid

Avoid **leading questions**. This is where the question is framed in a way that could influence the response. Not 'We take great pride in our award-winning customer service. What do you think about our service?' but 'The last time you bought from us, how would you rate the service?' Not 'How important is free delivery?' but 'Which factors did you consider when you bought from our competitor?'

Don't ask people to **recall from memory**. 'What almost stopped you buying from us?' is a great question, and one of the staples in our agency. However, it's more appropriate to ask immediately following a transaction, when the experience is still fresh in the memory.

Be careful when **reporting quantified results**. Unless you have performed statistical analysis against a large enough sample, concrete conclusions are impossible. Caveat it by using statements like 'indications are…' and 'it appears that…'. The purpose is to gain qualitative insights; use quantification as an analysis tool but don't get side-tracked.

E-mail survey platforms

- SurveyMonkey
- Google Surveys
- Google Forms
- Typeform
- QuestionPro
- Client Heartbeat
- SurveyGizmo
- Crowdsignal

Feedback and transcript analysis

If you have one of the following, these are gold mines:

- customer support e-mail account;
- live chat;
- social media;
- customer reviews.

Analyse e-mails to the customer support address and live chat transcripts for common themes and patterns. Don't try to trawl through everything. Randomly select around 200 responses from each channel, going back two to three months. Categorize the responses into headline topics so that you're able to identify the most important issues. Live chat software will show you on which pages queries originated, so you can trace it back for further investigation.

Social media and customer reviews are visible to the world, and undoubtedly influence purchase decisions. But they are also a source of insight for you. How are customers talking about value? What do they find appealing, what do they rave about? What are the positive points that you could possibly amplify? What are the negatives that you should maybe counter in the sales process? Are there product or other questions that can be incorporated into the copy on the site? What can you learn about the customers from their language?

On-site polls

The best time to get qualitative insights from your users about the online experience is when they are still in that experience. On-site polls and surveys allow your visitors to give real-time feedback, directly from a page. It's especially useful in situations where you want to examine observed on-site behaviour (Figure 5.1).

For example, a particular handbag product detail page on a client's site was able to draw in the crowds, but battled to turn it into sales. Targeting only those visitors who looked like they were leaving the site from this page, we asked bluntly: 'Why did you not purchase this handbag?' A few comments suggested that they were not sure what to match the handbag with. It was an insight that we could act on, and not even close to what we had anticipated.

Figure 5.1 An example of an on-site poll box, using Qualaroo

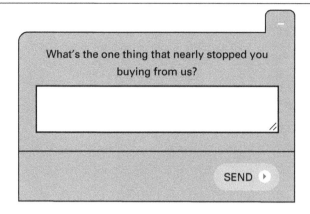

Lock onto the problem by targeting your questions as precisely as possible. Is a particular product category performing below average? Ask users on those pages what's missing or why they won't buy. High basket abandonment rate? Ask abandoners why they're leaving. Mobile site not converting? Target mobile visitors to understand their context better. If you have identified sources of anxiety or friction through heuristic evaluation or another method, this is a good way to validate and explore it.

In our experience, most users respond favourably to one or two well-placed polls as it gives them an opportunity to raise any feedback they may have. But it can be annoying if done too aggressively. Use it sparingly to fill specific gaps in your knowledge of customers and their behaviour. Limit the number of surveys and questions that a user will see.

As always, the questions you should ask depend on what you are hoping to find out. Identify the gaps in your knowledge before popping the question. Here are some starters:

- Landing pages and intent:
  - What is the purpose of your visit today?
  - What were you expecting to find on this page?
  - What persuaded you to visit our site rather than that of a competitor?
- Abandonment/hesitation:
  - If you didn't make a purchase, please tell us why not.
  - What could have persuaded you to check out?
  - What is holding you back from making a purchase?

- Post-purchase exit:
  - What was the one thing that almost stopped you buying from us?
  - How did you justify the investment in x?
  - What was your biggest fear or concern about buying from us?
  - Which other options did you consider before choosing this product?
  - What persuaded you to buy x product instead of y?
- Tools that offer on-site polling and surveys include:
  - ForeSee
  - GetFeedback
  - Informizely
  - iPerceptions
  - Qeryz
  - Qualaroo
  - Survicate
  - Usabilla
  - Hotjar

NPS survey

Net Promoter Score (NPS) has been endorsed by *Harvard Business Review*, calling it the best predictor of loyalty and growth.[12] In the context of optimization, NPS offers limited value. It fails to give you anything specific to act on that is measurable in the short term. A simple tweak fixes that.

NPS poses this question:

How likely are you to recommend our company to a friend or colleague?

Users are asked to choose a response on a scale from 0 to 10. To calculate your NPS, subtract the number of detractors (0–6) from promoters (9 and 10). Tools like Qualaroo handle this automatically.

To make it more actionable, ask a follow-up question:

What is the reason for your response?

Using pivot tables in Excel or Google Sheets, you can easily map these reasons to the numerical rating the respondent provided. Look carefully at the issues raised by detractors. They are shouting: 'Fix me or your business will die.'

Some will be outside your sphere of influence – escalate them to the relevant managers. Take note of the ones that can become hypotheses to be tested.

It can be probed by e-mail or via an on-site poll. If done online, you can decide to target customers by only posting it on the purchase confirmation page, or cast the net wider by having it earlier in the funnel.

Value proposition

One of the primary objectives with VoC analysis is understanding your value proposition. It may surprise you to hear that this is not brainstormed in a boardroom, but co-created with customers.

An enormous body of research points to a link between a well-developed value proposition and business success.[13] Without a compelling value proposition, the visitor may not convert even if they came to your site with a strong motivation to buy. MECLABS deems it to be 'a major key to conversions';[14] Widerfunnel goes further: 'Your value proposition determines your potential conversion rate.'[15]

Unfortunately, the true ethos of the concept has been diluted over the years. It's often confused with the USP (unique selling proposition), but it's not the same thing.[16] Neither is it those boxes dotted around the site, shouting 'Free delivery' and 'Money back guarantee'. Michael Lanning, a former McKinsey consultant who first coined the term, laments: 'Often, the term "value proposition" has been misinterpreted as the simplistic marketing notion of positioning, the meagre content of which is largely antithetical to the term's true meaning.'[17]

What is the value proposition?

Let's start with a definition of value:

Value = Perceived benefits – Perceived cost

Note that we are dealing with perception. Value is what your customer thinks and believes. If you can shape that perception, you can alter that constructed reality and tip this value equation in your favour. The more you increase perceived benefits and decrease perceived cost, the more likely a sufficiently motivated visitor is to purchase. This is what you can do:

- Amplify perceived benefits in your messaging.
- Make sure these benefits resonate with your customers, by checking directly with them what matters.

- Reduce perceived cost, which is not the same as lowering price.

The value proposition is your promise to customers of how you intend to deliver this value to them. Essentially, it is the answer to this question: 'Why should I buy from you as opposed to your competitor?' If you can write down an answer to that question, you're in a good place. But not so fast; your answer has to pass these filters:

- **WIIFM** (What's In It For Me)? It must matter to your customer, which is not the same as what matters to you. To be sure, you have to validate any core assumptions about this – you'll see how in later chapters.

- **Say what?** Many supposed value proposition statements are nothing but marketing waffle. If the customer doesn't understand your message, how can they be expected to take action?

- **So what?** Consumers have strong BS-filters. Their default stance is to distrust any sales talk. You have to convince them that you're the real deal. There is more on this later in this section.

Total net experience

Benefits relate mainly to products, so it's easy to go into product-centric tunnel vision mode. However, the value proposition encompasses the *total experience* of the customer. Lanning refers to the value proposition as 'the entire set of resulting experiences' that your customer has by buying from you.

To illustrate: A retailer delivered a box of very expensive wine to a loyal customer. A slightly annoyed lady pondered loudly why her husband kept buying 'all this wine', when there was nowhere to put any more boxes.

In terms of the value equation, perceived cost for the customer (the wine-buying husband) includes:

- the price of the item itself, an expensive premium wine;
- storage challenges;
- justifying the purchase to his wife.

There's a lot of cost in this transaction (not just monetary), yet overall there must have been sufficient perceived benefit, as that scale tipped in the retailer's favour.

When this customer was interviewed later, it became evident that it was not the *wine* he was buying. He was buying the net resulting *experience*, to borrow Lanning's phrase. Despite the price tag, storage problems and nagging wife, he was still one up. How?

Only a few cases of this rare wine were available, so first there was the badge of owning something quite exclusive. After reading Chapter 13, it will be clear to you why. What really sealed the deal, though, was the prospect of sharing it with his dinner guests. Who wouldn't feel special? Who wouldn't be impressed with our customer's taste for the finer things in life? So who are the lucky dinner guests, the interviewer asked. Astoundingly, there was no confirmed dinner date. Such is the power of a compelling value proposition that an imagined event sold an expensive case of wine, which ended up being squeezed into a cupboard by an unimpressed spouse.

Discover your value proposition

Discover is a deliberate choice of words. Business often talks about *determining* the value proposition, but it's the wrong mindset. Your value promise does not matter to customers unless it matches *their* perception of value. Management is unfortunately often out of sync with the reality of their customers. In a study of 326 firms by management consultants Bain & Co, 80 per cent believed they were providing a superior customer experience. However, only 8 per cent of their customers thought that was the case![18]

Ask your customers what matters to them. Here are a few sample questions, again related to actual experiences instead of hypothetical scenarios:

- What made you buy from us as opposed to a competitor?
- What made you buy from a competitor instead of us?
- What persuaded you to make this purchase?
- How would you justify the expense to X?
- How did you think product X would make your life better?
- How would things be different if you stopped using product X?
- How would your life change if you no longer had access to product X?

Here's an exercise you can do today to get a sense of what matters to your customers. Compare the click-through rates (CTR) of paid search campaigns, including ones that have been paused. Divide the headlines and ad content into broad themes. You may end up with categories like price match, free delivery, range, guarantee and so on. Are there any patterns when you compare the CTR performance across these broad categories? Users may consistently respond more favourably to one theme over another.

Also test candidate value propositions using the same method. You have the benefit of far more traffic in search results than you have on your site, and it's a relatively inexpensive way of validating your value proposition.

Create different text advertisements, each containing a distinct value theme. Then, compare the results over a period of time in the same way, using CTR as a proxy for customer appeal.

Crafting a value proposition

When expressing your value proposition, use insights from VoC sources covered in this chapter, such as e-mail surveys, on-site polls, customer interviews:

- What are the things that customers tell you matter most to them when they consider buying from you?
- What is the total net experience that they are buying? Think beyond the functional benefit. What are the social and emotional drivers?
- Which negative experiences are they trying to avoid by considering your offer?
- What promises do your competitors make to your customers? How do they match the desires of your customers? What gaps are left for you to own?

How to express your value proposition

Lanning offers three characteristics of a well-communicated value proposition.[19]

Clarity

If the customer doesn't understand your message, how can they ever be expected to act on it? This is not the time for clever word play. Be specific about the benefit they will get, why it matters to them and why they should believe you.

Make it easy for the customer to visualize the post-purchase benefit. Images and sensory language can help us to feel and taste something. When someone is imagining themselves experiencing the benefit of the product, the sale is more likely to happen.

Differentiation

What is unique about your offer, or what aspect of it is unique? What makes it stand out from the alternatives? How is it better than alternative solutions? Do a competitor analysis (see next section) to identify gaps in the marketing noise that you can exploit.

Remember, for your customer doing nothing is also an option.[20] Create the perception of a net resulting experience that overcomes both competitors and consumer inertia.

Credibility

People are sceptical about marketing messages and 'sales talk'. Your statement needs to have 'verisimilitude' – the appearance of truth. Below are mechanisms to improve the credibility of your claims. You'll see some of it put into practice in the value proposition case study:

- Offer objective support, such as ratings, testimonials and endorsements.

- Be specific. For example, '2,378 products in stock' sounds more credible than 'we have the largest range'.

- Use language that resonates with your customers. To achieve this, many copywriters draw inspiration from qualitative customer surveys and interviews. They may even quote specific phrases used by customers.

- Connect with a persona. Know your customers; create your value messages for one person that represents a dominant segment. This is covered in detail at the end of this chapter.

CASE STUDY   Value proposition

This case study shows a compelling value proposition, forcefully communicated on an e-commerce site, for the UK's largest retailer of specialist toys and food for exotic birds.

Heather is a widow in her late 60s, living in the north of England. Her parrot is more than a pet – he's a companion, a child ('perpetual toddler' in her words). She is the persona around whom this page was developed.

You'll never hear Heather refer to 'my parrot' – only by his name, Buddy. She loves buying nice things for him, but is always concerned about his safety, as toys that come apart from rough parrot play can cause injury. She heard about Northern Parrots from another parrot owner, who had been recommended by her vet.

From surveys and interviews, we knew what customers valued. We changed the homepage, Heather's entry point, replacing the hero image at the top of the page with messaging that reflected those insights:

- Trusted shop, recommended by veterinarians – so your parrot is safe.

- Widest range of things for your parrot – so your parrot can have fun, playing with something new.

- Next day delivery – so your parrot doesn't have to wait.

Figure 5.2 This value-infused homepage delivered a sizable uplift in revenue per visitor as it matched the desires of key personas. It also used mechanisms proposed by Michael Lanning to improve messaging

Everything your Parrot needs - delivered next day

Choose from the UK's widest range of Parrot supplies

With over 1,500 toys, foods, cages and accessories for Parrots and cockatiels, budgies, lovebirds and more, we're the UK's favourite Parrot supplies store.

You won't find a bigger range anywhere else. In fact, we have so many high quality products that many pet shops and online stores buy from us and vets regularly recommend us.

Plus, you're guaranteed a fantastic service with 97.1% of UK orders delivered in 2 days or less. We've delivered abroad to 123 countries, and since we started in 1995 have made more than 250,000 birds very happy.

"I regularly refer my clients to Northern Parrots as I know they can get whatever they need for their Parrot quickly and reliably"

Richard Jones (BVSc MSc MRCVS)
Avian Veterinarian
Northwich, Cheshire

Find something for your Parrot

African Grey (843)

What are you looking for?

- Food (181)
- Toys (456)
- Cages (26)
- Accessories (145)
- Supplements (46)

Click to find

This homepage also included a subtle rewrite of the client's previous headline, from 'Everything you need for your parrot' to 'Everything your parrot needs' (Figure 5.2). This may be only a few words of difference, but the former is a promise to Heather while the latter is a promise to the parrot, and it is the parrot's needs that are really important to Heather.

Competitor analysis

Don't confuse this with copying competitors, which is unfortunately all too common. That's not wise, because as growth marketing expert Peep Laja said, 'they don't know what they're doing either'.[21]

The purpose is to see your offer, as your customers do, in the context of alternatives. Though not strictly speaking VoC analysis, it falls under the same umbrella because you are trying to understand the totality of your customer's perceptions.

How to do it:

- Do a Google search for your offer, using the phrases that your customers use (you can check in Google Analytics, or draw on direct user feedback).
- Which competing offers come up in the results?
- Visit the competitor sites and their social media accounts, and take note of their key messages and value claims.
- What is their core message? What value claims do they make, both in organic and paid search results? How do they differentiate themselves?

Categorize and compare your competitors' core messages, stated benefits and differentiation claims in a table similar to Table 5.2. At a glance, you can see all the messages that your users are exposed to.

The missing perspective here is what actually matters to your customers. That insight will come from other data sources, such as surveys. When you have that information, you can use the two data sets to fine-tune your sales conversation and value proposition. Is there anything your users rated that is drowned in white noise? Is there any space in the landscape of messages that you can own? The biggest opportunity is a theme your customers care about a lot, but doesn't feature highly in competitor messaging.

Finally, it can be interesting to do usability testing on your competition. See Chapter 4 for details. This will let you see their offer and journey through the eyes of your customers. As we've said, just don't fall into the trap of wanting to copy them.

Table 5.2 Summary table comparing your competitors' core messages

Themes	Competitors									Total
	1	2	3	4	5	6	7	8	9	
Price guarantee	✓							✓		2
Free shipping		✓	✓	✓	✓	✓	✓		✓	7
Locally made	✓									1

Put it all together in personas

Meetings at Amazon always have an extra seat, empty and reserved for The Customer.[22] It's a reminder to everyone that the customer's voice should be present.

It's easy to lose sight of the fact that behind all the data you have collected are real people – your site visitors and customers. Yet, anything that appears on a web page is ultimately there to try to get human beings to take a certain action. In this chapter we have looked at ways to understand who those people are. What are their interests, needs and pain points? What motivates them to buy?

Personas can help you to package all of these data meaningfully. A persona is a character who represents an archetypal user. Though fictional, they are firmly based on data and grounded in reality. Personas remind you that you are not optimizing for yourself, but for a user. You are not your user. Your boss is not your user. The UX consultant is not your user.

Personas also serve as a reminder that not all your customers are the same. There is a small risk in optimizing your site for the *average user*, but such a thing doesn't exist. As the *Wizard of Ads* author, Roy H Williams, said: 'Your business has only 3 or 4 customers living at thousands of different addresses.'[23]

Some practitioners write personas off as a bit woolly, and Jason Fried of 37signals may have spoken on behalf of many others when he dismissed personas as 'artificial, abstract, and fictitious'.[24] Indeed, if your personas are formulated in a brainstorming session, without much user data, they're pointless. However, if you base them on actual people, if they are informed by research, they are actually immensely useful. One study claimed that the use of personas led to superior user experience in design.[25]

A strong argument in favour of personas came from an interaction designer, who used to view the practice with 'disdain'. Later, he became an advocate. Explaining this twist in *Smashing Magazine*, he writes: 'My process became more efficient and fun, while the fruits of my labor became more impactful and useful to others. Never before had I seen such a boost in clarity, productivity and success in my own work.'[26] When you create a wireframe with one person in mind, or when you rewrite a product description to talk directly to that person, it brings clarity and focus.

One of our clients has three personas – expectant parents, parents and gifters. We called one Julia, based on real interviews conducted with mothers of young babies. In the early hours of the morning, in a quiet part of the house away from the rest of the family, she is feeding her baby. Julia is inspired by several customers who described to us how they would start browsing our client's mobile site, making mental notes of things to come back to later. Do you think that a wireframe designed with her in mind looks different from one without this vision of Julia? Absolutely.

What does a persona look like?

The essence of persona creation is described by Alan Cooper, a pioneer of the method: 'Develop a precise description of your user and what they wish to accomplish.'[27] Fundamentally, that boils down to two things: a biography of sorts plus a goal statement.

Cooper emphasized that **goals** and personas are two sides of the same coin. It's easy to fall into the trap of focusing too much on the person and not enough on goals. Make it your number one priority to understand what each persona wants to achieve, what their needs are, what problem they are trying to solve. That becomes the distinguishing attribute that sets one persona apart from another.

Some find it useful to adopt the mindset of JTBD, the framework mentioned earlier in this chapter. What is the 'job' that your customer wants to get done – functional, social and/or emotional? How does 'hiring' your product help them get this job done?[28] The aim is to think about your user's core goal, which might be something like:

- Impress guests with exclusive, expensive wine.
- Encourage young child to read by buying story books.
- Let my wife know I'm thinking of her by sending her some flowers.

Another component of personas is scenarios: stories that outline the sequence of activities carried out by the user to achieve this goal.

The biographical content varies depending on your context. Unless demographics are central to your business model, it doesn't take centre stage in your personas. As we said earlier, it's not demographics that drive behaviour. Don't neglect it though, as it serves to complete the narrative and make the persona real and memorable. For the same reason, your persona should be polished with a name and, preferably, even a face (Figure 5.3).

How to create personas

Whatever you do, don't brainstorm them from your own assumptions about users. Useful personas are not fabricated, but discovered through analysis. A strong research bedrock is what makes them credible. Brainstorming can be a starting point, what is known as a proto-persona, but these personas must be validated with actual data and adjusted as necessary.

Figure 5.3 Personas should be goal driven and focused on motivations

Harry

Job Software Engineer
Location London
Age 28

Goals and Motivations:

- Works long hours and wants to have better work-life balanc
- Likes the idea of being barefoot in nature, but not the thorns

Scenario:

- Reads about the concept of barefoot shoes in a blo
- Conducts a Google search for 'barefoot shoes'
- Looks at three different competitor websites
- Compares features and prices of shoes
- Reads several customer reviews
- Opts for a running sandal that suits his style

A great first step in building personas is to run a dedicated e-mail survey. Collect demographic details, but focus on core motivations. What do they want to achieve by visiting your site or buying your product? What alternatives do they explore? How, in specific terms, is your offer better for them than the alternatives? When you have enough responses, look for patterns of difference and similarity. That will be the start of the various persona groupings.

Nothing beats semi-structured interviews for learning about your users' needs, goals and motivations. Visiting users at their home or office provides a richer experience, but telephone interviews may be easier and more cost-effective. Allow the conversation to unfold naturally and let the interviewee do most of the talking. Stick to open-ended and indirect questions, asking only one question at a time. Below is a list of sample questions:

- Context:
  o Tell us a bit about yourself.
  o How did you first become aware of the site/product? Describe the circumstances.
  o What was your first interaction with the brand? Store, computer, mobile device, call centre, app, catalogue etc?
  o Where were you when you first/last visited the site?
  o How often do you buy online?
  o What is your favourite shopping site?
  o What is your favourite non-shopping site?
- Needs:
  o What exactly was it that prompted you to visit the site the first time?
  o Tell me about the first time you bought from the site/used product X.
  o What has made you come back to the site?
  o What did you do before you discovered product X?
  o At the time of buying the product, what difference did you think it would make in your life?
- Goals:
  o When you first visited the site/the last time you visited the site, what was it that you wanted to do?
  o What alternatives did you consider?

- o When you last visited the site of a competitor, what was it that you wanted to do?
- o Did you manage to achieve that goal? If not, why not?
- o Tell me about the last time you considered buying something on our site/that of a competitor, but didn't.
- o How would your life be different without this product?
- o How are you using the product?
- o Are you using feature X of product Y?
- Motivations:
  - o Before you made the purchase, did you imagine what owning this product would be like?
  - o Tell me about the last time you made a purchase on the site, or that of a competitor.
  - o Tell me about a time you were going to buy X (or from Y), but then decided against it.
  - o What other solutions did you try? Why?
  - o What was it that persuaded you to buy from us the first time/last time?
  - o What was it that persuaded you to buy from a competitor instead?
- Attitudes:
  - o Did you have any doubts or fears about buying on the site?
  - o What were your first impressions of the brand/site?
  - o How has that view changed over time?
  - o How would you describe this brand/site to a friend?
  - o What do you like about competitors and their sites?
  - o How does this site compare to the competitors'?
  - o If this site disappeared today, how would it affect you? What would you use instead?
- Behaviours:
  - o How did you go about looking for solutions to X?
  - o Before you made the purchase, did you discuss it with anyone?
  - o How do you normally interact with the brand? Store, computer, mobile device, call centre, app etc
  - o How often do you visit this site?

- o How often do you visit the site of a competitor?

- o When last did you visit this site, or that of a competitor?

- o Think back to your last visit to the site. What can you tell me about that experience?

How many personas do you need?

Each persona represents a different customer segment. Segment by goals and behaviour, not demographics.

At first, you won't know what those segments should be. Don't let it distract you. As you speak to customers it will become clear, and you'll see personas taking shape naturally. If you kick-start the process with an internal brainstorm, don't let fictional pen portraits created out of uninformed beliefs stop you putting together well-researched personas. Treat them as hypotheses to be validated with research.

Some experts recommend creating a persona for each segment across the entire spectrum, including ones you don't cater for. That is boiling the ocean in our view. One primary persona, and around three to four secondary personas, should suffice in most cases. The exact number is not important, as long as you have covered the key ones for your situation.

Aim for at least five interviews per persona. In our experience, this is enough to provide depth and colour alongside your quantitative data. As you're gathering the data, start breaking them into themes. Look out for patterns and commonalities that you can base the different personas on.

Summary

As important as it is to have the backdrop of behavioural insights, voice-of-customer data is where you'll strike gold. It will give you a new perspective on quantitative and behavioural data.

Steve Blank famously said: 'There are no facts inside the building so get the heck outside!'[29]

Yet, too often boardrooms are filled with managers who think they can read the minds of their customers, talk on their behalf, make decisions on their behalf.

You are not your customer. Your boss is not your customer. Your marketing agency is not your customer.

If you want to serve more customers, and you want to sell more goods to them more frequently, you have to understand their world. What are the driving forces that have them come to you, or go to a competitor?

One of the best ways to find out is to speak to them directly. A customer interview is a rare opportunity to immerse yourself in the world of the customer. Don't ask them for solutions, or try to predict how they would behave under hypothetical conditions. Ask them to talk about actual direct experiences they've had. Let them talk while you listen actively. From that, you can learn about their needs, motivations and frustrations.

Surveys have the advantage of ease and scale. You can do surveys via e-mail as well as on the website, asking context-sensitive questions in situ. It's a good way to discover what is behind quantitative observations like drop-off rate and cart abandonment. Feedback channels, such as live chat and customer support e-mails, will add more layers of insight.

Your value proposition can be summarized as the answer to this question: 'Why should I buy from you as opposed to your competitors?' This should go beyond features and benefits to encompass the entire experience. Your message should deliver a clear promise of value, balancing perceived benefits and perceived cost.

The value proposition will have to compete with claims made by competitors, so conduct a competitive analysis to be aware of that context. Audit core themes that your users are exposed to, and make a judgement on how you fit in with that.

Personas are controversial because too often they are not real, but based on guesses and intuition. Think of it as a way to package all your insights about customers. Personas are valuable if they are grounded in research and analysis.

Wireframes, A/B test variations and sales copy are more likely to resonate with customers if they were created with them in mind. Properly formed personas give them a voice in the optimization process.

Notes

1 Morgan, N (2018) Decisions don't start with data, *HBR Guide to Data Analytics Basics for Managers*, Harvard Business Review Press, Boston, MA

2 Gaskin, S *et al* (2010) Voice of the customer, *Wiley International Encyclopedia of Marketing*, ed J N Sheth and N Malhotra, John Wiley & Sons, Hoboken, NJ

3 Girard, J (2013) *Joe Girard's 13 Essential Rules of Selling: How to be a top achiever and lead a great life*, McGraw-Hill, New York

4 Blank, S (2009) Get out of my building, *Steve Blank* [Online] https://steveblank.com/2009/10/08/get-out-of-my-building/ (archived at https://perma.cc/A9C6-779Z)

5 Portigal, S (2013) *Interviewing Users: How to uncover compelling insights*, Rosenfeld Media, New York

6 Christensen, C, Anthony, S and Roth, E (2004) *Seeing What's Next: Using the theories of innovation to predict industry change*, p 101, Harvard Business School Press, Boston, MA

7 Christensen, C *et al* (2016) Know your customers' jobs to be done, *Harvard Business Review*, 94 (9), pp 54–62

8 Kiegelmann, M (2009) 'Making oneself vulnerable to discovery', Carol Gilligan in conversation with Mechthild Kiegelmann, *Forum Qualitative Sozialforschung*, 10 (2), Art 3

9 Kahn, K (2005) *The PDMA Handbook of New Product Development*, John Wiley & Sons, Hoboken, NJ

10 Vlaskovits, P (2011) Henry Ford, innovation, and that 'faster horse' quote, *Harvard Business Review* [Online] https://hbr.org/2011/08/henry-ford-never-said-the-fast (archived at https://perma.cc/YD2R-NA6M)

11 Brodigen, C (2016) UX research at Github: Measuring hard-to-measure things, *O'Reilly Case Studies* [Online] https://learning.oreilly.com/case-studies/user-research/ux-research-at-github-measuri/9781491991336-video308629/ (archived at https://perma.cc/J8NA-84ZT)

12 Reichheld, F (2003) The one number you need to grow, *Harvard Business Review* [Online] https://hbr.org/2003/12/the-one-number-you-need-to-grow (archived at https://perma.cc/P47N-8MJB)

13 Parnell, J A (2006) Generic strategies after two decades: A reconceptualization of competitive strategy, *Management Decision*, 44 (8), pp 1139–54; Lusch, R, Vargo, S and Tanniru, M (2010) Service, value networks and learning, *Journal of the Academy of Marketing Science*, 38, pp 19–31

14 Jacobson, A (2008) Powerful value propositions, *Marketing Experiments* [Online] www.marketingexperiments.com/improving-website-conversion/powerful-value-propositions.html (archived at https://perma.cc/68FR-PSNP)

15 Goward, C (2013) Use these 3 points to create an awesome value proposition, *Widerfunnel* [Online] www.widerfunnel.com/blog/how-to-create-an-awesome-value-proposition/ (archived at https://perma.cc/ZG9B-549Q)

16 Lanning, M J (2015) MJL MECLs Intrv Total, *YouTube* [Online] www.youtube.com/watch?v=-Bzqlxnh9uw&feature=youtu.be (archived at https://perma.cc/ZCM9-HEF3)

17   Lanning, M (2000) *Delivering Profitable Value: A revolutionary framework to accelerate growth, generate wealth, and rediscover the heart of business*, p 61, Perseus Books, New York

18   Allen, J *et al* (2005) Closing the delivery gap, *Bain & Company* [Online] www.bain.com/bainweb/pdfs/cms/hotTopics/closingdeliverygap.pdf (archived at https://perma.cc/QY6V-TXZC)

19   Helmut, M and Lanning, M (2016) Communicating the value proposition: How to turn a brilliant product idea into a marketing success, *DPV Group* [Online] www.dpvgroup.com/articleswhite-papersbook/articles-white-papers/communicating-the-value-proposition/ (archived at https://perma.cc/C3NM-GBJJ)

20   Anderson, J and Narus, J (1998) Business marketing: Understand what customers value, *Harvard Business Review*, **76** (6), pp 53–65

21   Laja, P (2013) Stop copying your competitors: They don't know what they're doing either, *CXL Institute* [Online] http://conversionxl.com/stop-copying-your-competitors-they-dont-know-what-theyre-doing-either/ (archived at https://perma.cc/B4PA-JQ6P)

22   Koetsier, J (2108) Why every Amazon meeting has at least 1 empty chair, *Inc.* [Online] www.inc.com/john-koetsier/why-every-amazon-meeting-has-at-least-one-empty-chair.html (archived at https://perma.cc/7397-8AP7)

23   Williams, R H (2008) 3 marketing lessons, *sclohoreally* [Online] https://sclohoreally.wordpress.com/2008/08/05/3-marketing-lessons/ (archived at https://perma.cc/8D7A-MN2E)

24   Fried, J (2007) Ask 37signals: Personas?, *Signal v. Noise*, 6 November [Online] https://signalvnoise.com/posts/690-ask-37signals-personas (archived at https://perma.cc/5MUU-EYZV)

25   Long, F (2009) Real or imaginary: The effectiveness of using personas in product design, *Irish Ergonomics Review*, Proceedings of the IES Conference 2009, Dublin, *Frontend.com* [Online] https://www.frontend.com/thinking/using-personas-in-product-design/ (archived at https://perma.cc/CB2V-NXWW)

26   Goltz, S (2014) A closer look at personas: What they are and how they work | 1, *Smashing Magazine* [Online] www.smashingmagazine.com/2014/08/a-closer-look-at-personas-part-1/ (archived at https://perma.cc/9R5N-9JUY)

27   Cooper, A (2004) *The Inmates Are Running the Asylum: Why high tech products drive us crazy*, Sams Publishing, Indianapolis, IN

28   Bettencourt, L and Ulwick, A (2008) The customer-centered innovation map, *Harvard Business Review* [Online] https://hbr.org/2008/05/the-customer-centered-innovation-map/ar/1 (archived at https://perma.cc/6RR3-KT43)

29   Blank, S (2009) Get out of my building, *Steve Blank* [Online] https:// steveblank.com/2009/10/08/get-out-of-my-building (archived at https://perma. cc/KPA5-JYLX)

Merchandising analytics   06

'A website converts because customers want to buy the merchandise presented to them,' said Kevin Hillstrom,[1] one of the world's foremost experts in merchandising data mining.

So, to optimize your e-commerce website and sell more, show your visitors things they want to buy. How do you know what those are?

The answer lies in a specialist form of research and analysis known as merchandising analytics. It involves looking in detail at the interaction between your customers and the product ranges, including categories and pricing.

There are several different merchandising analytics techniques you can use to find out where within your existing product range you can squeeze more sales. Two methods recommended by Hillstrom stand out:

- **new product analysis**: the rate at which new products are introduced, and their productivity (ie contribution of each new product to total sales);
- **bestseller analysis**: the rate of decay of best-selling items.

Specific techniques include:

- product category analysis;
- look-to-book analysis;
- price-point analysis;
- price testing.

New product analysis

Hillstrom[2] advocates that businesses should constantly introduce new products, and cultivate them to bestseller status, in order to grow sales. Merchandising analytics can give you the insights to help you achieve this. Here's how you do it.

Introducing new products

The first step is to analyse what you're doing now. Total up the quantity of new items introduced over the previous three years and the revenue they have generated. If a product was introduced in Year 1 then you will need to capture the revenue it took in its first year and Years 2 and 3.

If a product was introduced in Year 2 or 3, you will need to pro-rata them to calculate their likely sales over this three-year period. For example, if you had first-year sales of £100,000, multiply this by three to get the total sales over a three-year period. It's a little rough and ready but will suffice for your analysis.

You will end up with a table that looks something like Table 6.1.

This simple exercise can be quite an eye-opener. For example, in the scenario in Table 6.1, we can see that over the last three years:

- The rate at which new products have been introduced has fallen by 25 per cent, from 393 per year to 291 per year.

- Sales from new products have plummeted by 41 per cent, from £3.5 million to just over £2 million.

- Productivity – the total sales that each new product contributes – has also gone down by 22 per cent, from around £9,000 to around £7,000.

This fictional example paints a gloomy picture. New products are the life-blood of many e-commerce websites, and here it's ebbing away. 'Businesses that develop new merchandise today will experience marketing success tomorrow,' according to Hillstrom,[3] so the declining sales and productivity from new products could have a detrimental effect on their ability to attract new customers and retain existing ones.

Table 6.1 Example showing total new product revenue and average revenue per new product over the last three years

Year	Number of new products introduced	Revenue from new products	Productivity of new products
1	383	£3,546,011	£9,258
2	320	£2,889,318	£9,029
3	291	£2,111,065	£7,254

How to identify potential new products

Continuing with the above example, this picture may lead the company to launch more new products. So, what products should they introduce? Simply putting out a bigger range of a number of new products does not guarantee high sales. Not all new products are a success, so revenue from the shiny new items may not make up for all that has been lost.

How can you improve the chances of introducing high-performing new products rather than duds? If you're looking for rich sources of inspiration for successful new product development, try the following:

1 Look at your failed on-site search data, where visitors typed in something they were looking for, but it came up with no matches. This is a golden insight into what people really want to buy from you.

2 Rank your products by sales, then look at the bestsellers to identify common themes.

3 Use search data to analyse trends and search terms that correspond to your current categories and products. For example, if you sell mirrors, look at the volume of searches for 'oval mirrors', 'round mirrors' and so on.

4 Identify categories that are growing in sales and items that are doing better than expected. Develop subcategories to increase your authority in this product category and analyse the performance of new products brought into these subcategories.

5 Survey your customers and what problems your current merchandise solves. Their answers could surprise you, and give you valuable ideas on new products to address those problems.

At the same time, it's also worth analysing which products to cull to make room for more profitable lines, by:

1 identifying those paid search terms on exact match, eg 'oval mirrors', that convert poorly;

2 examining products that have high rates of returns and refunds;

3 ranking your products by sales and then looking at the least popular items at the bottom of the list to identify common themes.

You can also gain clues from analysing your competitors' bestsellers, and those in their clearance section. These relatively simple exercises put you in a position to put together a successful new product development programme.

Bestseller analysis – how to analyse bestsellers and their rate of decay

There is a circularity around bestsellers. They get to the top of the list precisely because they are innately desirable and large numbers of people want to buy them. That's important, because these are the products that bring people to your site and trigger them to put the first product in their basket.

What is a bestseller? Your criteria will depend on your particular business models, but Hillstrom[4] suggests making the cut at the top 5 per cent ranked by revenue and volume, and also the top 5 per cent ranked by revenue alone:

1 **Revenue and volume:** These items bring in considerable revenue and also sell in large quantities.

2 **Revenue alone:** These items have a higher ticket price, so they generate considerable revenue but do not sell in such large quantities.

You'll often find that these few products make up over half of total sales, so they are critical to the success of the business.

When you've split out your top sellers, simply count the actual number of bestsellers you've had in each of the last three years. It may look something like Table 6.2.

In the example in Table 6.2, there has been a 36 per cent reduction in the number of bestsellers, down from 28 to 18. This decline represents a lost opportunity to promote desirable items to new and existing customers. Behind the scenes, the decline could also lead to reduced purchasing power with suppliers and erode margins.

With fewer product introductions and weaker performance of bestsellers, this business needs to:

1 ramp up the rate of new product introduction;

2 work on promoting existing items to bestseller status by marketing them better.

Table 6.2 Count of bestsellers by year

Year	Number of items in 'bestsellers' categories
Year 1	28
Year 2	21
Year 3	18

Product category analysis

The way in which you organize and promote your product categories can have a significant impact on how well the products within those categories perform.

Some simple analysis will immediately tell you which categories generate the most product views, add-to-baskets, orders and revenue. Once you know this, you can see which categories perform well in terms of converting visitors into viewing them, adding to basket and finally paying for them. You can also perform this analysis to reposition categories in your navigation to increase sales.

To analyse the category performance, capture the following data:

1 **Category name** (eg sofas, lighting, kitchenware etc).

2 **Category views:** Number of visits to the site that included a visit to the particular category.

3 **Product views:** The number of times that any product page was viewed within the same visit as the particular category page was viewed.

4 **Baskets:** Number of times that any product was added to the basket within the same visit as the category was viewed.

5 **Transactions:** Number of transactions that took place in the same visit as the category was viewed.

6 **Revenue:** Amount of revenue from orders placed in the same visit as the category was viewed.

Your analytics platform can probably produce this report for you, but if not, then simply fill in the data on a table similar to Table 6.3. If your business has clear seasons, separate this data into peak and non-peak time periods, otherwise the data captured should cover a calendar 12 months.

Table 6.3 Example of raw data required for product category analysis

Category name	Category views	Product page views	Baskets	Transactions	Revenue
Category A	12,784	4,333	1,233	412	£22,933
Category B	15,898	3,736	1,112	598	£21,121
Category C	9,764	4,119	1,089	512	£18,083

New product analysis

Ratio analysis

Next, use the raw data shown in Table 6.3 to convert into ratios. These represent the performance of particular categories in terms of converting visitors into a product view, creating a basket and placing an order (Table 6.4).

You now can sort the columns to produce the following views:

- Sort the **£ per category view** column with the highest £ at the top to identify those categories that generate the most revenue.
- Sort the **category: Transaction** column with the greatest number of orders at the top to identify those categories where propensity to buy is highest and lowest.
- Sort the **category: Basket** column with the highest at the top to identify those categories where propensity to add to basket is higher, and lowest.

While you get a clear overview of sales by category, you can study the visitors' journey through a category onto a product page, into the basket and then through the checkout at a more granular level. For a particular category, it may be that while overall 'sales per category view' are higher than for other categories, the ratio of baskets to order is relatively lower.

This discovery means you have an opportunity to improve this part of the customer journey for a particular category. For example, if you were to compare categories containing higher-priced items (such as sofas) with lower-priced items (such as lighting), you might discover that while both categories had similar Category: Basket ratios, the sofa category had a much lower Baskets: Order ratio.

In other words, there is a barrier in the checkout part of the journey for sofa category visitors. This insight could prompt you to collect more data and take action to address the weaker performance in the checkout. For example, through using exit surveys, you might discover that delivery of

Table 6.4 Ratios within product category data

Category: Name	Category: Product	Category: Basket	Category: Order	Baskets: Order	£ per category view
Category A	33.9%	9.6%	3.2%	33.4%	£1.79
Category B	23.5%	7.0%	3.8%	53.8%	£1.33
Category C	42.2%	11.2%	5.2%	47.0%	£1.85

large items like sofas is a key consideration for potential purchasers. You can then hypothesize that providing reassurance about the quality of your delivery service to these visitors at this point in their journey would increase their Basket: Order ratio, and ultimately boost sales. A split test would give you the answer, and if you're right, you'll soon be selling more sofas.

Navigation analysis

You can also use these data to optimize the way you display categories in your navigation. In the example above, Category C has a much higher conversion rate to basket and order, and has the highest £ per category view.

Armed with this knowledge, you may want to consider putting Category C in a more prominent position in the navigation, promoting it through banners, and moving products into Category C from other categories, provided they are a sensible fit.

Then just run a simple split test to determine whether moving the high-performing category to a different place in the navigation gains additional sales.

Look-to-book analysis

Look-to-book is a nifty bit of analysis that helps you to identify a strategy for all your products based on the number of product page views and their add-to-basket ratio.

Proposed by Bryan Eisenberg,[5] one of the earliest exponents of website optimization, this analysis is simple to do and yields great insights on your products based on how your website visitors behave. First decide whether you are going to do seasonal analysis, such as peak and non-peak, or over a 12-month period.

To perform look-to-book analysis, you need the following information:

A Total number of all unique product views (by unique visitor).

B Total number of products (don't worry about individual SKUs, just the product lines).

C Total number of unique views of the basket page (irrespective of whether the products end up being purchased or not).

D Number of unique product views by product.

E Number of unique views of the basket page, by product.

This data will help you produce two vital numbers:

- Your average number of product page views
- Your average add-to-basket ratio.

Let's say you have 450 products, and each page is viewed 350,000 times. Your average unique view per page is 777.

Your data say that your basket page gets 33,500 unique views. Dividing this by the total number of unique product page views (ie 350,000) gives an average add-to-basket ratio of 9.5 per cent.

You now have two numbers:

- Average product page views – 777
- Average add-to-basket ratio – 9.5%.

Use them to benchmark every one of your products.

To calculate the add-to-basket ratio for each product, simply divide views of the basket when that product is in the basket by its number of page views.

Let's say that Product A has 1,100 unique page views and an add-to-basket ratio of 8.1 per cent.

- In terms of being viewed by your web visitors, it is above average (1,100 vs. 777).
- In terms of it being added to basket, it is below average (8.1 per cent vs 9.5 per cent).

When you have done this for all of your products, the next step is to segment them into one of four segments as shown in Table 6.5. HIGH means above average and LOW means below average.

This knowledge gives you a platform to decide which products to push (Segment A), which ones to get rid of (Segment D), and which ones need some attention (Segments B and C). So what sort of attention should you give them?

For low-converting products that fall into segment B (high page views but low add-to-basket ratio), use online survey tools such as Qualaroo to understand why visitors are not adding items to their basket. Useful questions to ask include 'Is there any information missing on this product'? or, more directly, 'Why didn't you add this item to your basket?' The answers to this question will give you insight as how you can better merchandise these products.

For high-converting products that fall into segment C (low product page views but high add-to-basket ratio), there is an opportunity to bundle products together with other bestsellers from segment A. This helps get them noticed and can encourage visitors to place larger orders, which will increase your average order value.

Table 6.5 Segmenting each of your products by PDP views and intent to purchase

	Product page views	Add to basket ratio	What this means
A	HIGH (Above average)	HIGH (Above average)	These are your stars
B	HIGH (Above average)	LOW (Below average)	Visitors like the look of these products but don't buy. Why?
C	LOW (Below average	HIGH Above average)	These have hidden potential
D	LOW (Below average)	LOW (Below average)	These are the underperformers

In summary, use look-to-book analysis to develop a clear merchandising strategy for each one of your products based on the way your website visitors interact with them, as summarized in Table 6.6.

If you have a seasonal business with clear peak and non-peak periods, repeat this analysis for these two time frames, as the products in each segment will change, and so will your strategy for each segment.

Price-point analysis

This useful form of analysis was born out of a pre-internet offline technique called SQUINCH or 'square inch analysis', used by catalogue marketers. They would quite literally measure exactly how much space was given to each product in the catalogue and divide it by the revenue generated to assess which ones were paying their way, and which were taking up too much valuable room.

To perform modern-day price-point analysis, first set out the total number of products at each price point. Ignore SKUs (eg colour and size variations) for the purposes of this analysis. The bands you use will depend on the spread of your product prices.

Table 6.6 Product strategies after performing look-to-book analysis

	#	LOW add-to-basket ratio	#	HIGH add-to-basket ratio
HIGH product page views	B	Research and improve merchandising	A	Maintain or promote
LOW product page views	D	Remove or replace	C	Bundle with other products

If you find you have a lot of products all bunched into one or two price bands, use smaller bands. In the example in Table 6.7, most of the price points are set at £10 intervals, but at £30, the bands are only £5 (£30–£34.99 and £35.00–£39.99). This was done to avoid bunching, because nearly a third of products fall into the £30–£39.99 band. Splitting this highly populated band into two gives a more even spread.

Then capture the total number of orders for all the items included in each price band. You can then work out the percentage for items offered and items ordered, and the variance between the two. Your table will probably look something like Table 6.7.

Price-point analysis is designed to show you the price bands that your most popular products fall into. It is a message from your customers that gives a strong signal that you can offer them more items that cost that sort of price.

In Table 6.7, we can see that items in the price band of £50–£59.99 make up just 2.5 per cent of total items offered, but comprise 6.3 per cent of total sales. This is a firm indication that you can increase the number of items offered at this price point.

Conversely, the £10–£19.99 bracket accounts for 13.9 per cent of all sales but 18.8 per cent of all items. This is where you could look to reduce the number of items you sell.

However, do look at the bigger picture before delisting. Before making the final cut, check to see whether any of these items regularly appear in the first order a customer places with you. Removing popular items for first-time orders could have a detrimental effect on your ability to convert new visitors into first-time buyers.

Table 6.7 An example of price-point analysis

Price point	Number of items offered	% of total items	No of orders containing items at this price point	% of total orders containing items at this price point	Variance
£0–£9.99	43	9.4%	6,230	9.0%	−0.3%
£10–£19.99	86	18.8%	9,561	13.9%	−4.9%
£20–£29.99	111	24.2%	17,665	25.6%	1.4%
£30–£34.99	80	17.5%	11,001	16.0%	−1.5%
£35–£39.99	65	14.2%	9,873	14.3%	0.1%
£40–£49.99	56	12.2%	7,892	11.5%	−0.8%
£50–£59.99	11	2.4%	4,332	6.3%	3.9%
>£60	6	1.3%	2,343	3.4%	2.1%
Total	458		68,897		

Price testing

As a rule of thumb, as the price increases, demand falls. However, people will almost always pay more for something if it's presented in the right way. The problem is that you never really know how much more unless you engage in some form of price testing.

It's unreliable to simply ask people what they would be prepared to pay; consumers are notorious for saying one thing but doing another.

As the pioneering ad agency founder David Ogilvy asserted: 'Customers don't know what they feel, don't say what they know, and don't do what they say. Market research is three steps removed from real behaviour.'[6]

Therefore, in order to understand how much you can charge for your products – or their demand elasticity – without losing sales, quantitative testing is more reliable.

There are a number of ways you can do this, including increasing your prices and analysing the sales before and after the price increase. However, with this method it is difficult to trust the results because there could be several other factors at play.

There is a way to use a scientific approach to price testing and discover the maximum price you can charge for selected products without harming overall demand. The last few years have seen the launch of a number of price-testing tools, including WisePricer and Tatvic. It's also something you can do with server-side experimentation platforms.

Tatvic, for example, offers a service called LiftSuggest, which allows you to test one or more different prices to a proportion of your website visitors. You can then compare sales on both the higher- and lower-priced groups and see whether the higher price makes a difference. Although it's not actually illegal to offer the same product at two or more different prices at once, it's generally considered immoral, and consumers are outraged if they discover it.

To avoid negatives of this kind, LiftSuggest reduces the price for the customer at the last minute. It does this by showing the higher price on the category and product pages only. Once the visitor has added the product to the basket, they are shown a message that tells them how to reduce the cost to get the lower price, such as 'Your price has been reduced by £x. Please click OK to continue' (Figure 6.1).

The LiftSuggest reporting dashboard lets you see whether the add-to-basket ratio of the product offered at the higher price is different from the product offered at the base price. You may find that pricing a product 10 per cent higher does not lower the add-to-basket ratio, but when you price it

Figure 6.1 Example of price reduction after higher-priced item has been added to basket

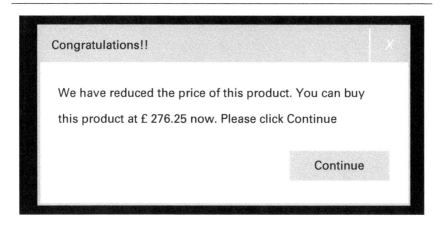

Congratulations!!
x

We have reduced the price of this product. You can buy

this product at £ 276.25 now. Please click Continue

Continue

15 per cent higher, there is a reduction. This will give you the confidence that increasing your product's price by 10 per cent will not harm sales. Price testing in this way can also be used to evaluate the impact of cutting prices to see whether a lower price results in higher levels of gross margin.

Price testing helps avoid under-pricing (where you give away too much margin) and overpricing (where you lose sales because the price puts too many people off). Either way, when you price test in an objective and scientific way, you'll optimize your revenue – a key part of website optimization.

Summary

Merchandising analytics is a range of valuable research techniques to use as part of your website optimization programme. It gives you useful insights into the interaction between your visitors, the merchandise you offer and the actions your visitors take.

Using merchandising analytics allows you to determine the impact on sales of a declining rate of new product introduction, and how a fall in revenue from bestsellers over time could damage your business.

Category analysis identifies poorly performing categories as well as the chance to understand underlying reasons. You can optimize your navigation for higher sales by examining which categories result in higher and lower levels of conversion and revenue.

Look-to-book analysis is a simple and easy way to develop a strategy for each of your products based on the number of views they receive and how likely it is that they are added to the customer's basket.

Using price-point analysis enables you to scientifically pinpoint where you have authority to sell more products in this price band, and the products that could be culled without damaging sales. Price testing gives you the opportunity to determine the maximum selling price without reducing order volume.

For e-commerce businesses selling products, merchandising analytics can reveal insights that are often missing from optimization programmes. It's worth repeating on a regular (eg six-monthly or seasonal) basis.

Notes

1 Hillstrom, K (2013) *Hillstrom's Merchandise Forensics: A case study in understanding why merchandising issues impact marketing productivity and business health*, CreateSpace Independent Publishing Platform, Scotts Valley, CA

2 Hillstrom, K (2013) *Hillstrom's Merchandise Forensics: A case study in understanding why merchandising issues impact marketing productivity and business health*, CreateSpace Independent Publishing Platform, Scotts Valley, CA

3 Hillstrom, K (2013) *Hillstrom's Merchandise Forensics: A case study in understanding why merchandising issues impact marketing productivity and business health*, CreateSpace Independent Publishing Platform, Scotts Valley, CA

4 Hillstrom, K (2013) *Hillstrom's Merchandise Forensics: A case study in understanding why merchandising issues impact marketing productivity and business health*, CreateSpace Independent Publishing Platform, Scotts Valley, CA

5 Eisenberg, B and Eisenberg, J (2005) *Call to Action*, Wizard Academy Press, Austin, TX

6 Ogilvy, D (1985) *Ogilvy on Advertising*, Vintage, New York

Create an experimentation roadmap

In the early days of Amazon, experimentation was democratized throughout the organization. Almost anyone could test almost anything. Feel like changing a button colour today? If you had access to the platform, you could make it happen. There was a flood of dumb experiments.

An ex-Amazon senior staffer recalls: '(The tests) had no chance of yielding any value. There wasn't any point to them. We were just kind of curious. We were just running a lot of experiments, which have a cost by the way, and taking up experimental slots...'[1]

They were throwing mud against the wall, seeing if any of it would stick. In the industry this is jokingly referred to as RATs – Random Acts of Testing. It is surprisingly common, even today. In case there is any doubt at this point, it's a waste of time and resources. RATs will devour your budget with nothing to show but lots of testing activity, meaning negative ROI.

High-ROI teams use logic to determine what gets tested when.

How to prioritize test ideas

Coming up with ideas to test is easy. The trickier part is deciding which ones to start with, and which ones to relegate to the bottom of the list. That is prioritization.

If it sounds like a purely operational endeavour, it's not. Fundamentally prioritization is about ROI. To quote Bill Gates: 'Prioritization is effectiveness.'[2]

On optimization programmes, prioritization generally happens on two levels. First, there is **top-down prioritization,** which aligns the programme with strategic focus areas. This does not mean that management get to decide the final order of tests, or whether something gets tested. It's guiding the team to work on things that matter from a business perspective.

As an example, one of our agency clients asked us to focus on two product categories. It formed part of a broader initiative designed at corporate level to improve gross margins and profitability. For another client we honed in on mobile customer journeys, in line with their strategic agenda for that year.

Bottom-up prioritization is performed by the team on a day-to-day basis to separate the wheat from the chaff. It relies on set rules and data points to score ideas relative to one another. Opinion, emotion and intuition are more or less stripped away.

At the start of an experimentation programme, an unrestricted bottom-up view can be useful. It will help you to identify areas with the biggest promise in terms of ROI, which could shape any top-down view.

Value/Effort

The most basic approximation for ROI is value divided by effort. Plotted as a matrix as shown in Figure 7.1, ideas with the highest ROI can be easily identified.

Value

It should come as no surprise that two perspectives are important when thinking about value:

- value to your users;
- value to the business.

Figure 7.1 A basic Value/Effort prioritization matrix. Ideas with the highest ROI sit in the top left quadrant. In optimization, these are experiments that cost less to execute yet return strong increases in online sales

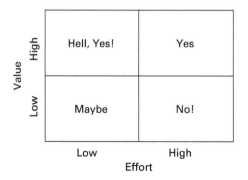

The observations and insights in your evidence file (see Chapter 3) should by now be packed with ideas about how to improve the experience for users and customers. When you test these ideas, you'd want to monitor changes in user behaviour.

The test should also be set up to validate business value, by measuring the impact on KPIs (key performance indicators). The outcome of the experiment is usually judged against an appropriate metric. There is more on this in Chapter 9.

Impact

Your tests should directly impact business KPIs in a measurable way. For example, it's unlikely that a test on the About Us page would impact revenue directly. One of the factors in determining value is therefore the extent to which a test is likely to directly impact KPIs such as revenue.

To measure the business value of an experiment, core e-commerce metrics are tracked. These are generally average order value (AOV) and sales conversion rate, which together make up revenue per visitor (RPV). In Chapter 9, we'll discuss this in more detail.

Detecting a confident win tracking conversion rate is easier than using a revenue-based metric, such as AOV or RPV. This is because conversion rate is binary – there are only two possibilities (either a user converted, or not), whereas revenue can vary greatly. The implication is that it may not be feasible to directly measure the impact of a test on revenue. You would then default to sales conversion rate.

Even that could prove tough under certain conditions. The further a test is located from the final conversion point, the less feasible it is to use conversion rate as a metric. Then you have to rely on a *proxy metric*, ideally a user-based metric that is positively correlated with a core business metric. For example, clicks on the 'Add to Cart' button could be a valid proxy metric for conversion rate. It shows purchase intent, even if the user didn't buy after adding the item to their basket.

An approach often used on low-traffic sites is to track visits to the next page in the funnel. For example, a test on the PLP might track visits to the PDP as a measure of how effective the test is. The idea is that the sales funnel is more effective in driving users towards the final conversion point.

Tests containing changes that impact sales directly should score higher than those that don't. Tests that allow you to track core metrics should score higher than those where you would have to rely on proxy metrics.

A retailer we work with has a blog that receives enormous volumes of organic search traffic. It's a great customer acquisition tool. That said, only a small portion of blog readers ever become paying customers. When it happens, it's usually a nurturing process spanning weeks or months.

While it certainly has a positive effect on conversion rate and revenue, the link is so tenuous that it can't be directly measured in experiments. Instead of e-commerce metrics, on those tests we track engagement and lead generation. Did more blog readers visit the online shop? Was there an increase in the number of e-mail addresses captured?

Naturally, those experiments that track user-based proxy metrics, instead of core e-commerce metrics, are assigned lower priority.

Value by testing slot

Your tests are like spaces in a car park. If you have a test running on one area, that is one of your car park spaces occupied. You won't be able to run another test on this area until the first one has been declared.

A testing slot is an area where experiments can be run. There is a finite number of testing slots, which makes it a scarce resource. The easiest way to think of testing slots on an e-commerce site is to split it up into different parts of the funnel. Typically, this is how it breaks down:

- homepage;
- category pages;
- product listings pages;
- product details pages;
- basket page;
- checkout;
- about us;
- main menu;
- site search;
- header;
- footer;
- content/blog pages.

Before even considering the merits of individual test ideas, the relative value of each testing slot can be determined by comparing the testable population and the revenue multipliers.

Population

In Chapter 9, we discuss the importance of sample size when calculating the outcome of a test. For now, accept that the higher the number of visitors (sample) in our test, the easier it is to be confident about the outcome. So the more visitors a page receives, the faster an experiment can be concluded. It follows that the most frequently visited pages present a more solid testing ground as a rule.

Clustering pages together for experimentation purposes can ramp up sample size dramatically. It's common practice to test at template level rather than targeting individual pages. For example, by grouping together all the product detail pages (PDPs), the sample size is the sum of all the individual PDP visitors. On a site that sells cameras and lenses, you might have a separate grouping for each product category. The more granular, the smaller the sample size.

The area of the page where the change is introduced can also play a role. Say you want to treat an element in the lower half of a page. Google Analytics counts 100,000 visitors on that page, but not everyone scrolls down far enough to see this change. If only 20 per cent of those visitors scroll down to the area where the change is located, the available population for this experiment is sliced from 100,000 to 20,000 visitors. Scrollmaps, as discussed in Chapter 4, can give you this perspective.

Site-wide elements, like the header and main navigation, offer a comparatively large test population. Nearly all visitors see the global header, only some will see a category page, and even fewer will make it to the PDP. However, there is a trade-off with 'Impact', as you'll see later in this section.

Revenue multiplier

In scenario B below, a 10 per cent increase in sales is worth double that of scenario A. All things being equal, it makes sense to give priority to the opportunity with the bigger upside.

1 A: Baseline $100,000. 10 per cent increase = $10,000

2 B: Baseline $200,000. 10 per cent increase = $20,000

The closer to the checkout, the higher the monetary value of each percentage point lift, as more revenue passes through that part of the funnel. To be clear, this does not mean that the checkout should be higher priority than other pages by default. For one, the checkout has a lot less visitor traffic than higher up the funnel.

Use Google Analytics to calculate and compare the revenue multiplier for each testing slot. To do this, create an advanced segment as explained in Chapter 4 and compare this segment against *All Sessions* in the *E-commerce Overview* report.

This should give you a view like the one in Figure 7.2. In this example, homepage viewers contribute roughly 32 per cent to total site revenue, so that is the multiplier for this page. A 10 per cent increase in sales on the homepage is actually worth only 3.2 per cent (10 per cent increase × 32 per cent revenue contribution = 3.2 per cent site-wide impact). In contrast, PDP viewers contribute roughly 80 per cent to overall revenue, so a 10 per cent uplift on PDP would translate into 8 per cent site-wide.

Effort

Some experiments require more effort to bring to life than others. Effort increases cost, which drives down ROI. Effort can be technical or political in nature.

Changing a line of copy is reasonably straightforward; someone with a very rudimentary knowledge of coding should be able to build this test. Other tests may require advanced front-end coding skills, visual design and specialist testing platform knowledge.

More specialist skills + More time = Increased cost = Lower ROI

It's also worth considering the complexity and cost of deploying a winning test to the code base of the website or app.

Figure 7.2 Using GA advanced segments to compare revenue for homepage views to all sessions reveals a multiplier of 32 per cent That's the revenue contribution of homepage viewers to site-wide revenue (£173,287 / £547,524 = 31.6 per cent), rounded up to 32 per cent.

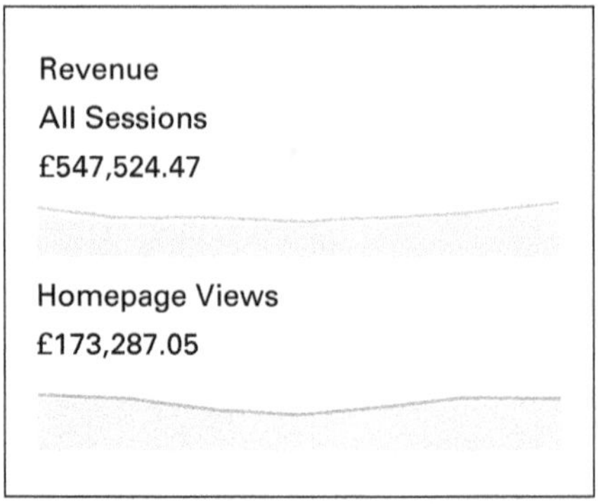

Revenue
All Sessions
£547,524.47

Homepage Views
£173,287.05

Political complexities are often harder to crack than technical ones. We know of a giant international brand that would occasionally exclude their company's internal IP address range from experiments to limit the chances of colleagues seeing the changes!

Expect some pushback on certain ideas. Over time, as the programme builds credibility, resistance will ease. Even then, pick your battles wisely.

The homepage is often especially sensitive. Different silos in the business all want their interest to be represented there. In some organizations it's sacrosanct. We worked with an optimization team at a well-known fashion retailer that believed their homepage was rich in potential. However, they were at odds with their colleagues in the marketing department who were concerned that testing would result in 'hard sell' messages on the homepage diluting the brand.

Some of our clients operate in a highly regulated environment. Whereas small copy changes are usually relatively stress free, in those organizations almost every phrase has to be checked by the legal department. This can introduce long delays and several iterations to get the copy legal-proof, by which time it may have lost its punch. Needless to say, these ideas score low on the grounds of effort.

Cost of delay

In product development circles, *cost of delay (CoD)* is often used as a factor in prioritization. 'Being wrong may be less costly than you think,' explains Jeff Bezos, 'whereas being slow is going to be expensive for sure.'[3] CoD is a measure of revenue loss or deferment as a result of delays.

This practice is less common in optimization. One of the biggest risks for delay in optimization is around test duration. Sample sizes can be enlarged by extending the run of an experiment, thereby exposing it to a bigger population.

A larger sample size is required to be able to detect smaller differences with confidence. So, a 3 per cent lift will take longer to detect than a 5 per cent lift, which in turn will take longer to detect than a 10 per cent lift. Bear in mind that most wins are modest.

Increasing test duration for the sake of detecting that smaller effect is not always a good trade-off. There's an opportunity cost in extending the life of an experiment, as it occupies a testing slot. It could be making way for another experiment with a better chance of producing a more compelling win.

The *minimum detectable effect* (MDE), which is the smallest lift that can be confidently detected in an experiment, can be calculated in advance.[4] You can find MDE calculators online if your testing platform doesn't offer one. This will give you the *minimum required sample size* (MRSS). Then it's a simple matter of calculating how long a test would need to run based on visitor numbers for that testing slot.

Here's a real example using Optimizely's MDE calculator: Detecting a 10 per cent increase on a given page requires 31,000 visitors per variation. That's a combined sample of 62,000 for the control and our variation. So if this page draws 62,000 visitors per month, it would take a month to detect a 10 per cent lift on that page. Reducing MDE from 10 per cent to 5 per cent blows sample size requirements out of the water. MRSS shoots up by more than 300 per cent to 140,000 per variation! It will take 4.5 months for this experiment to reach statistical significance, compared to only 1 month if we settle on 10 per cent MDE.

It's not necessary to calculate MDE for each test you plan to run. If you know the MDE for a testing slot, consider the likelihood of a particular experiment meeting different MDE levels.

Prioritization frameworks

There are a number of established prioritization frameworks that have become widely adopted in the industry. It's beyond the scope of this book to discuss each of them.

What's more important than choice of framework is having a framework, and of course, using it. Below are two examples.

Value/Effort*Confidence

Grounded in the Value/Effort principle discussed above, the framework shown in Table 7.1 is easy to understand and implement. It's been endorsed by the highly regarded UX thought leader and prolific author Jared Spool[5] (look him up on Twitter).

For each idea, assign a value out of 3 for Value, Effort and Confidence. Set it up in a spreadsheet and format the cells so that you can select the appropriate value from a dropdown list. The formula for Score is V/E*C.[6]

Table 7.1 Example of a prioritization framework, which can be set up in a spreadsheet with dropdowns for ease of use. The formula for Score is V/E*C.

Test Idea	Value	Effort	Confidence	Score
Test 1	3	3	2	2
Test 2	3	2	2	3
Test 3	2	2	1	1

To make it more scientific and remove as much debate as possible, set rules to assign individual values. Here is an example of a basic rule set to quantify Effort:

1 Requires JavaScript coding; design resource needed

2 Some HTML and/or CSS required

3 No special coding or design needed.

Effort can be quantified by asking engineers to assign a value for technical complexity, or by estimating total person hours.

Here is an example of a more complex rubric, in this case to quantify Value (Table 7.2). Remember that one size doesn't fit all; adjust for your own situation.

Table 7.2 A sample rubric to quantify Value. Limit complexity in your framework as far as possible, but this is a good approach if you need more granularity. Remember to adapt this to your needs.

	1 Low value	2 Medium value	3 High value
Impact	Test will have to rely on proxy metrics	RPV not feasible, but another core metric can be used	RPV (revenue per visitor) can be used as primary metric
MDE 5%	Test will run more than a month to detect 5% uplift	Estimated test duration 1 month	Confident result likely in 14 days
Revenue multiplier	Testing slot revenue multiplier of <30%	Testing slot revenue multiplier >30% but <80%	Most revenue passes through testing slot; multiplier >80%

Confidence

How confident are you that the experiment will have the desired outcome? Unless something really obvious is wrong on a page, it is impossible to know in advance.

In fact, it goes somewhat against the spirit of prioritization, which is to remove personal intuition from the process. As Ronny Kohavi from Microsoft said: 'It is humbling to see how bad experts are at estimating the value of features....'[7]

One of the highest-earning experiments in the history of Bing, Microsoft's search engine, was deemed a low priority for months. An engineer made the call to launch it after realizing it would require relatively low effort to build. This experiment, which had been relegated to low-priority status for so long, added more than $100 million per annum in revenue in the United States alone.[8] The result was so surprising that a team was assigned to do a sense check. Nobody could have predicted it.

The famous PIE (Potential, Importance and Ease) framework has a similar dimension to Confidence. Potential refers to how much improvement you think can be made on a page. Chris Goward, who developed PIE, cautions that a 'certain amount of personal judgment and experience... comes into play at this stage'.[9]

Goward suggests looking at signals like bounce rate, exit rate and usability issues during analysis to inform this assessment. Say, for example, that GA data reveal a massive drop-off rate on a page. During usability testing you discover that visitors on that page get stuck because a key piece of information about the product is missing. This would indicate high potential around the hypothesis that inserting the missing information on this page would increase sales.

In our experience, another valuable data point for doing this is the outcome of previous A/B tests. Over time, you can get a sense of the inherent potential of each testing slot, as well as the types of intervention your users respond to.

Here is a basic recipe that can be used to quantify Confidence:

1 We have no evidence to back this idea.

2 There is some evidence from at least one source.

3 Strong evidence from more than one data source.

If you would like a more granular view, a sample rubric to quantify Confidence can be seen in Table 7.3.

Table 7.3 A sample rubric to quantify Confidence. Use this approach if you feel that you need more granularity in your decision-making

	1 Low confidence	2 Medium confidence	3 High confidence
Evidence	We have no evidence to back this idea	There is some evidence from at least one source	Strong evidence from more than one data source supports idea
Page statistics	Bounce rate and/or exit rate on this page is above average	Bounce rate and/or exit rate on this page is about average	Page or template has a high bounce rate and/or exit rate
Usability	Minor usability issue, or one with low occurrence rate	Moderate usability issue or medium occurrence rate	Severe usability issue, or one with high occurrence rate
A/B test history	Testing slot has not produced any confident wins	Testing slot has produced only modest wins	Testing slot has produced at least one strong, confident win

The binary model

Another approach is shown in Table 7.4. In this model, add 1 point if an idea satisfies the condition on the left, 0 points if it doesn't.[10]

Adapt this to your own needs and use your own labels. Don't be too zealous, though, as it can become a daunting exercise having to run through a long list of considerations. On the other hand, if you have too few points of reference in the table, you may end up with several ideas that have the same score.

The experimentation roadmap

The **experimentation roadmap** forms your action plan, showing test hypotheses in order of priority. How to formulate the hypothesis is covered in Chapter 8.

Simply pick the next one off the list when it's time to get a new test ready. The list is constantly updated and evaluated so that the highest ROI ideas are always at the top.

As shown in Table 7.5, a roadmap should at least include the hypothesis, prioritization and current status, which is discussed in the next section. It's a good idea to include a column for testing slot, which in this example has been incorporated into the test ID coding.

Table 7.4 The binary model is an alternative method of prioritizing ideas. First, agree a list of considerations to put in the first column. Add 1 if it satisfies the condition, 0 if it doesn't.

Consideration	Add +1 point if...	Give 0 points if...
Primary metric = RPV	It is feasible to track RPV as a primary metric	RPV can't be supported as a primary metric
Attrition rate	Targets an area of the site that has a high drop-off rate	Targets an area of the site that doesn't have high attrition
Bounce rate / Exit rate	The target page or template has a high bounce rate and/or exit rate	Bounce rate and/or exit rate is average or below average
Page value	The target page or template has a relatively high page value	Page value is average or below average
Usability issue frequency	The issue was seen frequently in usability testing	The issue was observed once only, or not at all
Usability issue severity	The issue has the potential to get in the way of conversions	Causes frustration, but does not block or hurt sales
Test duration	Test can be concluded in 14 days	Test duration is likely to be more than 14 days
Visibility	Targets an area of the page which is visible to all visitors	Scroll maps show the target area is not visible to everyone
Effort	The test is relatively easy to build and/or implement	The test requires advanced coding skills and/or design
Evidence	Hypothesis is supported by at least two credible sources of evidence	The idea is not backed by any credible evidence; it is based on intuition or opinion

Table 7.5 A basic roadmap, including hypothesis, prioritization (columns marked V, E and C represent value, effort, confidence) and current status

Test Id	Hypothesis	Prioritization				
		V	E	C	Score	Status
HP001						
PDP002						
PLP003						

The roadmap should never be set in stone. Be flexible if new insights warrant a change to the original plan. New insights may come from a range of sources:

- Insights from concluded experiments
- New data not previously available
- Previous research re-examined
- Changes in strategic priority
- fresh ideas from people in the organization.

Another good practice is to aim for a balance of low-, medium- and high-complexity tests. This way you avoid the risk of missing good opportunities in the high value, high effort quadrant (see Figure 7.1) by focusing only on low-effort experiments.

Keeping track of everything

The more experiments you run, the more difficult it becomes to maintain visibility on all the moving parts. This increases the risk of expensive delays, communication failures and unmatched expectations.

As Effective Experiments founder Manuel da Costa explains: 'Running an optimization programme is time consuming work with analysing data and running tests. We found that teams were becoming inefficient and unable to keep track of everything that was going on.' An experienced optimizer himself, he created a system designed with experimentation workflows in mind.

Just as with prioritization, which system is not as important as having a system. You may already have project management software. We've used Jira, Basecamp, Monday.com, Asana and Smartsheet very effectively. Alternatively, you can do it all for free with spreadsheets and Trello.

Scheduling

On high-velocity programmes especially, it's useful to have a plan that shows launch dates and even completion dates for each experiment. This helps to manage the pipeline of tests and make sure there's always something in the queue. A version of this can be seen in Table 7.6.

Don't plan too far into the future though. A good rule of thumb is a quarterly planning window, combined with a monthly review to ensure you're still working on the right stuff.

Table 7.6 Example of a slot-based schedule. Test 1 runs on the homepage for four weeks, and is replaced by Test 6 in the second month. The PDP has enough traffic to warrant a faster turnaround, so tests are replaced every 14 days.

Timeframe	Homepage	PLP	PDP	Basket	Sitewide
Wk 1–Wk 2	Test 1	Test 2	Test 3	Test 4	Test 5
Wk 3–Wk 4	Test 1	Test 7	Test 8	Test 4	Test 11
Wk 1–Wk 2	Test 6	Test 7	Test 9	Test 10	Test 12

Manage work-in-progress

It's important to keep track of tests as they pass through the various stages from idea to conclusion.

Harvard Business Review contrasted work-in-progress inventory in traditional factory environments with our world. In our environment 'inventory largely consists of information, such as design documentation, test procedures and results, and instructions for building prototypes'.[11] The recommendation is that these invisible inventory items should be given visibility.

You can do this by using a Kanban board such as Trello, or simply marking the status column in Table 7.5. Here are examples from our own programmes:

JDI (Just Do It). Some things are so obviously plain wrong, they just need to be fixed. These should be channelled to the relevant product team or go straight to the developers. Examples include browser and/or device compatibility issues and bugs.

Analysis. Further analysis is needed to complete the hypothesis or inform a solution. Go back to the relevant data sources with specific research questions. See Chapter 4.

Creative. A catch-all for wireframing, copywriting and visual assets. The first step in getting an idea ready for testing.

Dev. A test spec has been submitted to the developers for coding.

QA. Coding has been completed and the test has been set up in the experimentation platform. Quality assessment is now being performed to ensure it's free of bugs and behaving as expected.

Queue. A test is ready to be launched, pending approval or the conclusion of another test. To avoid losing any momentum, aim to have a test lined up for each slot.

Live. The experiment is running.

Concluded. The final bucket to indicate that a test has been completed.

Summary

The experimentation roadmap is a prioritized list of all your test ideas. Randomly moving from one test to another produces inferior results.

Use a prioritization framework to decide which ideas to progress, and how to order them on the roadmap. Fundamentally, prioritization is about managing resources.

The most basic framework is an impact–effort matrix, but it's important to also consider the location of a test. Robust experimentation requires minimum sample sizes to be observed. Therefore, it makes sense to give priority to pages that see more traffic. You can increase the test population by clustering pages together and testing at a template level, rather than on individual pages.

Some tests have direct line of sight to business KPIs like revenue and conversion rate. All things being equal, those tests should rank higher than ones where the link to KPIs may be more tenuous. This depends partly on the distance of your test to the final conversion point.

Cost of delay is often overlooked in many prioritization frameworks. Since there is a finite number of testing slots on your site, there is an opportunity cost associated with each test. The longer a test occupies a testing slot, the higher that cost.

To keep track of everything, use status labels to give visibility to work-in-progress items. There are bespoke tools that have been developed specifically for this purpose, but standard project management software works as well. Smaller programmes can be managed effectively using spreadsheets and Trello.

Always allow for some flexibility with your roadmap. The list should be updated every time new insights come to light. It should also be reviewed regularly as priorities may have changed on the back of new information. Limit advance planning to a quarterly window, reviewed on a monthly basis to ensure that you're still working on the biggest opportunities.

Notes

1   Diamandis, P (2016) [Accessed 6 August 2020] Culture & experimentation – with Uber's Chief Product Officer, *Medium* [Online] https://medium.com/ abundance-insights/culture-experimentation-with-uber-s-chief-product-officer-520dc22cfcb4 (archived at https://perma.cc/N652-G3PE)

2   BBC (2016) [Accessed 6 August 2020] Bill Gates, Desert Island Discs, *BBC Radio 4* [Online] www.bbc.co.uk/programmes/b06z1zdt (archived at https:// perma.cc/PS2F-C3Z5)

3   Bezos, J (2016) [Accessed 6 August 2020] 2016 letter to shareholders, *About Amazon* [Online] https://blog.aboutamazon.com/company-news/2016-letter-to-shareholders (archived at https://perma.cc/XS8L-YZD3)

4   Bloom, H S (2008) The core analytics of randomized experiments for social research, in *The Sage Handbook of Social Research Methods*, ed P Alasuutari, L Bickman and J Brannen, pp 115–33, SAGE, London

5   Spool, J (2019) [Accessed 6 August 2020] (Value ÷ Effort) × Confidence = Priority, *Medium* [Online] https://medium.com/@jmspool/value-effort-x-confidence-priority-46dfad80f936 (archived at https://perma.cc/GQ9Z-2WFE)

6   Moreira, M E (2017) *The Agile Enterprise: Building and running agile organizations*, Apress, New York

7   Kohavi, R *et al* (2009) Online experimentation at Microsoft, *Data Mining Case Studies*, 11, p 39

8   Kohavi, R and Thomke, S H (2017) The surprising power of online experiments, *Harvard Business Review*, September–October, pp 74–82

9   Goward, C (2013) *You Should Test That! Conversion optimization for more leads, sales and revenue or the art and science of optimized marketing*, John Wiley & Sons, Hoboken, NJ

10 Rusonis, S (2015) [Accessed 6 August 2020] A method for prioritizing A/B test ideas that won't hurt feelings, *Optimizely* [Online] https://blog.optimizely. com/2015/05/05/how-to-prioritize-ab-testing-ideas/ (archived at https://perma. cc/ZAN7-GLQW)

11 Thomke, S and Reinersten, D (2012) Six myths of product development, *Harvard Business Review*, **90** (5), pp 84–94

From hypothesis 08
to experiment

Spotify have developed their own framework, called DIBB. It stands for Data–Insight–Belief–Bet.[1] It's similar to the one in this book, but with a deliberately different vocabulary. This subtle departure aims to foster a mindset and environment conducive to experimentation.

The first two steps – *Data* and *Insights* – should be familiar to you. In Chapter 3, we discussed how data breed insights through analysis and sensemaking. Some years back, Spotify noticed a trend that mobile usage was rising sharply, while desktop usage was declining. The insight, that mobile would soon dominate, prompted suggestions of radical change throughout the organization.[2]

Belief, the third step in DIBB, refers to our interpretation of the data and insights, how we make sense of data and the meaning we attach to them. Belief is personal. According to the dictionary, it is 'the feeling of being certain that something exists or is true'.[3]

Bet suggests there are two possible outcomes. That's the beauty of this phrasing; everyone understands what it means: it could go your way, but there's an equal chance it could swing the other way.

In a more traditional or scientific framework, the bet would be similar to an experiment. Like a bet, there is always a chance that the test doesn't win.

The equivalent of a belief would be a hypothesis. While it is something you believe to be true, you are not emotionally invested in it.

What is a hypothesis?

A hypothesis is a statement about cause and effect, based on what you believe to be true. If you change x, you believe y will happen. In e-commerce optimization, it is a prediction that making a change to the website will result in a positive outcome.

A well-formulated hypothesis:

- Links to data. State the observations which inform what you believe to be true about the current situation.
- Shows cause and effect. What will you change, and what will be the effect of that change?
- Can be measured. How will the effect be measured, what metric(s) can be used to track and report the impact of the change(s)?
- Is testable. You must be able to run an experiment that can disprove your prediction.

Optimization specialist Craig Sullivan proposed the following framework, which has been widely adopted:

1 Because we saw [qual & quant data].

2 We expect that [change] for [population] will cause [impact(s)].

3 We expect to see [data metric(s) change] over a period of [x business cycles].[4]

Apart from satisfying all the conditions mentioned earlier, using this format means you are truly focused on the users and their needs. It helps you to test things that are meaningful to both your customers and the business.

Below is an example of a hypothesis using this format. It was for a home-wares retailer, where merchandise can be bought on credit:

1 Because we observed a large drop-off between the product and basket page (quant), and users were confused about which items were included in a bedding set (qual).

2 We expect that making the most popular bedding set the default option, and offering a pop-up to 'View Bedding Set' with a complete list of items (change) for users on bedding set PDPs (population), would lead to an increase in sales of bedding products (impact).

3 We expect to see the sales conversion rate increase for bedding products (metric change) over a period of four weeks (two business cycles).

The detail around population and number of business cycles can be dropped to simplify the formula, as below:

1 Because we saw [qual & quant data].

2 We expect that [change]... will cause [impact(s)].

3 We expect to see [data metric(s) change].[5]

In the example below, this simplified formula is used. The context is the same as the first example above, but a different qualitative observation prompted a different treatment:

1 Because we observed a large drop-off between the product and basket page (quant), and users had concerns about whether they could afford the repayments, wondering if there was some kind of 'deal' (qual).

2 We expect that giving more prominence to the finance calculator (change) would increase revenue per visitor (impact).

3 We expect to see more clicks on the calculator and an increase in average order value (metric changes).

Why you need hypotheses

A hypothesis sets you up to learn something from the experiment. It provides the basis on which causation (x leads to y) is established.

Part 3 of the above formula defines how that causal link is established. If the metric goes up, it bolsters confidence in our theory. If it does not go up, the hypothesis is disproved. But you can learn from that. It means you have to rethink a belief or assumption.

Either way, a good hypothesis is the first step in gaining insight from the test. It defines what you will learn, in advance. A failed experiment is not one where your variation 'lost' to the control. You only fail if you don't learn anything from a test.

Some insights are so unique that they can only be obtained from a negative test result. If an insight obtained in that way gives rise to a win down the line, the initial 'failed' test must surely take the credit for subsequent success. The shoe retailer case study at the end of this section (see Figures 8.1–8.3) shows how a negative experiment led us to a win.

Dr Flint McLaughlin of research group MECLABS is emphatic about this: 'The goal of a test is not to get a lift, but rather to get a learning.'[6]

If the metric goes down, you can look back at the hypothesis to enhance your understanding. That negative result tells you that the variable being tested caused visitors to behave in a different way from what you expected. The question then is, why?

Fortunately, an experiment creates a pool of data that you can review to arrive at an answer to that question. Because this new insight is specific to the problem being treated, it can bring you a step closer to a winning solution. Revise the hypothesis accordingly and run a follow-on test.

If there really is an opportunity, a different treatment (part 2 in the hypothesis formula) should produce a different result next time.

CASE STUDY

A negative test result does not signal the end of the road. It simply means that the hypothesis is not valid and you should learn from it. If you've used the formula suggested in this chapter, you will be able to draw valuable insights from a 'loss'. This brings you a step closer to a winning solution, as this case study illustrates.

When working with shoe retailers, we often find size and fit concerns among users. This anxiety is so strong that many people don't buy the shoes, even if they really like them.

We worked with a large international shoe brand where this effect was pronounced. Figure 8.1 shows the original product detail page template. On heatmaps, we could see that a large percentage of users were clicking on the 'Size Information' tab. User feedback from on-site surveys suggested that the information in that tab was not helpful.

Figure 8.1   The PDP template of a major global shoe brand, where concerns about size and fit were a source of purchase anxiety. In our first treatment, we made use of the open white space above the size selector

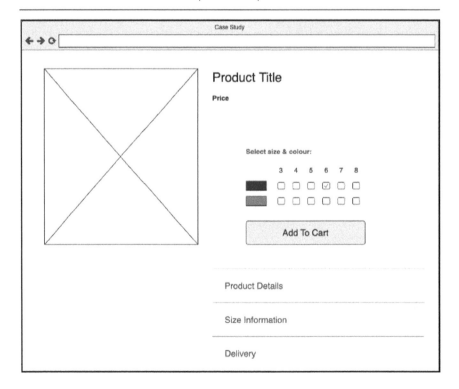

Figure 8.2 The first iteration of the experiment, showing the social proof element placed very prominently in the eye path. Revenue per visitor decreased by 12 per cent and there was a significant reduction in clicks on 'Size Information'

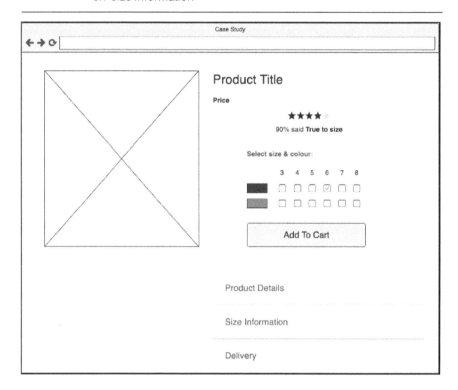

One solution invoked the principle of social proof, discussed in Chapter 13. A survey was sent out to all recent customers, asking them to rate how well the shoes they had purchased fitted them. They rated it on a scale from 1 to 3, where 1 = too small and 3 = too large.

We hypothesized that this form of social proof would reduce anxiety about how the shoes would fit. The first iteration of the experiment, shown in Figure 8.2, used the white space above the size selector. It placed the treatment very prominently in the eye path, so all users would see it.

That first test was negative. RPV was down 12 per cent and secondary metrics, tracked as part of the test, revealed a marked reduction in clicks on the 'Size Information' tab.

We hypothesized that the social proof element had been given too much prominence. It now had the opposite effect, and was raising anxiety levels. Our hypothesis was that it would be more effective if folded into the 'Size Information' tab, as there it would be seen in the right context. This formed the basis for the second iteration (Figure 8.3), which delivered in increase of 7.9 per cent in RPV.

Figure 8.3 The second iteration of the experiment folded the social proof element into the 'Size Information' tab. This time, it resulted in a 7.9 per cent increase in revenue per visitor

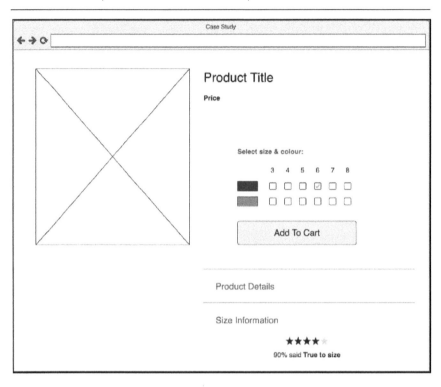

From hypothesis to test

Before the developers can start building the experiment, there are a few final steps:

1 Create wireframe and copy.

2 Review wireframe and copy.

3 Create the artwork if relevant.

4 Hand over to development team.

5 Do QA and UAT (user acceptance testing).

Step 1: Create wireframe and copy

Wireframe

A wireframe is a visual representation of the change(s) being proposed. It's primarily a communications tool to visualize the treatment as defined by your hypothesis statement. It sketches out the bare bones of the test variation.

Typically it goes through a few iterations, increasing in fidelity along the way. It may start as a simple low-fidelity (lo-fi) line drawing showing just the rough outlines of the proposed structure and layout (Figure 8.4). This is a useful first step if the treatment represents a significant departure from the current design, but if changes are subtle you can skip this and jump straight into the detail.

Figure 8.4 Early-stage lo-fi wireframe, created with Whimsical. It shows just the outlines of a mobile screen redesign

Eventually, the wireframe should sketch out what the proposed treatment will look like. There is a fine balance between showing the vital elements while, at the same time, cluttering it with unnecessary detail. Though there are no rules on this, here are some tips from our experience:

- Produce separate wireframes for different device types such as desktop and mobile.

- Focus on the hypothesis and user behaviour you want to influence and remember that the wireframe is not meant to be a final design.

- When it is compared against the existing page, it should be clear which new elements are being introduced (eg new sections, lightboxes and pop-ups) as well as which elements have been removed.

- Use actual copy, not *lorem ipsum* (filler text), to show how the words are contributing to the change in visitor behaviour you want to test. There is more on this in the next section.

The case study at the end of this chapter shows an example of a wireframe (Figure 8.5) and how it was translated into a final design (Figure 8.6). The lack of polish helps to keep the focus on the core functionality and the variables that are intended to alter user behaviour. What matters is that it clearly shows key changes and helps the team to visualize the proposed test.

Three reasons why it is important that a wireframe is lo-fi and looks somewhat unfinished:

1 The 'work-in-progress' nature of the wireframe allows everyone to focus on the core experience and functionality of the web page rather than getting distracted by pretty pictures.

2 The wireframe is a device to gather feedback. People are naturally polite, and when they are shown something very highly polished they are reluctant to criticize. A line drawing is clearly only work in progress, so reviewers are much more likely to say what they really think.

3 You can expect a lot of changes between your first and your final version of your wireframe. It will be seen by customers and peers, and their feedback will be incorporated into the final version. It is much quicker and more cost-effective to simply create a new wireframe rather than amend polished artwork time and again.

Specialist wireframing tools are available to make it quick and easy to create a wireframe. They usually come with grids and pre-set shapes and buttons to insert. Here are a few options to consider:

- Balsamiq: One of our all-time favourites, perfect for lo-fi wireframing (see Figure 8.5 for example).

- Whimsical: Another favourite, easy to use, sexy interface and well priced (see Figure 8.4 for example).

- Justinmind: Basic wireframing is free; paid version offers more advanced capabilities and interactive prototyping.

- OmniGraffle: Only for Mac and iOS. Expect a learning curve, in exchange for which you get a powerful tool including automation with JavaScript or AppleScript.

- Axure: Long established, capable of handling dynamic content, conditional logic and adaptive views for different screen sizes.

- Moqups: Boasts an extensive range of stencils for popular use cases, as well as big collections of icons and fonts. (The wireframes in Figures 8.1–8.3 were done in Moqups.)

- InVision: Very popular for high-fidelity wireframing and interactive prototyping; we are especially fond of the collaboration features.

- Figma: From lo-fi wireframes through prototyping to final design, Figma is the preferred tool of UX Designers on many teams, including ours.

Copy

Copy is an essential part of the wireframe, and the exact wording can make a big difference to the impact of a test variation. At Booking.com, some of the biggest wins come from small copy changes.[7] This can be extremely subtle, like a short phrase or even just one word – also called microcopy.

The reason why copy changes are so powerful is because they form the sales conversation. The site acts as a salesperson. A prospect has questions about the product and delivery, as well as anxieties and sales objections. The role of copy is to move them through the purchase cycle.

Often the first step is to work out exactly what the requirements of the message are at that particular point, rather than trying to write compelling copy straight off the bat. Is the purpose to educate the visitor? Help them find their way around? Clarify a complex point? Persuade them to take an action?

Use the early-stage lo-fi wireframe to work out where to put headlines and subheads to make the text scannable. Later on in the process, show actual words on the wireframe, in the right hierarchy, with more prominence given to important messages. Messages should be carefully placed to guide the viewer to the intended action.

Once you are clear about what the copy needs to convey, you can then rewrite it using copywriting techniques to give it the best chance of achieving its objectives. Here are some of the most valuable techniques:

- Start with an active word such as 'Discover' or 'Enjoy' rather than passive words like 'this' or 'A' or 'That'.

- Cut out unnecessary words.

- Use embedded commands such as 'You want that drink to be cold and refreshing'.

- Write in the present continuous tense: 'a luminous teapot adds fun and colour to your kitchen' rather than future tense 'a luminous teapot will add fun and colour to your kitchen'. Banish the word 'will'. This technique works because it communicates directly with the subconscious brain. Phrased as if something is actually happening right now, the reader imagines themselves using the product or pictures it in their home.

- Speak directly to the reader, by using words like 'you' and 'your', rather than writing passively in the third person, with phrases like 'we've worked hard'.

- Change company-centric messages ('Our biggest-ever range') into customer-benefit statements ('Your biggest-ever choice').

- Assume the sale. Write as if it's tacitly agreed that they are going to buy the product, and talk about 'when you have luminous teapots in your home' rather than 'if you buy the luminous teapots'.

Table 8.1 lists some examples of where a few tiny changes to the message resulted in much more powerful copy – even if at first glance they seem almost identical.

Table 8.1 Examples of very subtle, yet powerful, copy changes.

Original message	New copy	Rationale
7 Days Freshness Guaranteed	Guaranteed freshness for seven days or more	The word 'guaranteed' hooks the reader, and seven days is support for it. Leading with 'seven' has no meaning until the context is established.
Choose your special offers	You qualify for these special offers:	At this point in the journey, the customer was not aware they would be given an upsell. Copy had to introduce the concept. Starting with the word 'You' helps to hook the eye – everyone is interested in themselves!
Return within two days from delivery date for a full refund	Returns are easy – immediate no-quibble guarantee	At the point of order, people are anxious. Reassuring them that their decision can be reversed reduces risk, so increases propensity to go through with the purchase. A surprisingly high number of delivery and returns copy is written in a legalistic sounding style that can really deter customers from ordering.

Step 2: Review the wireframe and copy

It is in the nature of creative work that there could be more than one viable creative solution. We find it useful to get feedback before launching the test, especially from team members who understand the problem being solved.

Some practitioners also invite open feedback from the users who took part in earlier usability testing. Bear in mind that people can't predict their own behaviour, so don't ask them if this works better than the original. Limit it to questions related to user interaction; for example, 'where would you click', 'what would you expect to happen if...' and so on.

The reviewers can add to your thinking, spot gaps and generally act as a checkweight to make sure that the solution you are proposing in the wireframe genuinely solves the problem. They may also come up with other creative solutions, adding valuable dimensions to your idea.

Coordinate all the feedback from colleagues and users to determine whether this version of the wireframe and copy can be improved, before it proceeds to artwork. Many of the wireframing tools listed earlier incorporate a collaborative element. There are tools designed around collecting and coordinating comments, such as Red Pen, Notism, Cage and Miro.

Upload an image of the wireframe together with a description of the changes you have made. The aim is to give your reviewers enough background to be able to make informed comments. Include key information and some background to the wireframe, such as:

- What is the problem you're solving, for which audience?
- If the test is an iteration, what are the learnings so far?
- Relevant page statistics eg bounce rate, exit rate, drop-off rate.
- Observations from clickmaps, heatmaps and scrollmaps.
- Segmented view of behaviour on this page (eg new vs returning visitors).
- Observations and anecdotes from usability testing.
- Snippets from survey responses.
- Quotes from interviews with customer-facing staff such as live chat or customer service.
- Test metrics.

Commentators can click on an area of the wireframe to add notes and questions. Everyone sees the other comments and can reply, so you can see the dialogue developing. It is a great way to spark discussion, avoid duplication and have transparency. This also allows you to keep an audit trail of how your first version was influenced by your collaborators' comments.

When you have a well-oiled process in place, your collaborators will know what is expected. If you are doing this for the first time, send out some instructions with your invitation, so that they know what you want from them. It can also help to manage expectations, as it may not be possible to use everybody's ideas in the final wireframe. Below you can find a sample template:

Dear <collaborator's name>

We [conducted this research] and [made these observations]. To [solve x problem] for [y users], we've created this wireframe.

Please could you give me your feedback and ideas. Just log on to <noticeboard application> to view it and add your comments.

Feel free to be critical – it will help me enormously. Here are some things to bear in mind when you give your feedback:

- Be specific in your feedback.
- Offer suggestions, not only criticisms.
- Explain the reasons behind your suggestions.
- Think about situations where the proposed approach might not work eg out-of-stock item.
- Spot missing information.
- Let me know if you have any relevant data that can add a new perspective.
- Ask for clarification if anything is not clear.
- Reply to requests for clarification if your comments have not been clearly understood.

You can also add drawings and links if that helps. Thanks for your time and suggestions.

Of course, you do not have to take on board every suggestion. Incorporate comments that can move you forward into the final version and ignore the rest.

Some software can also be used to evaluate wireframes. Predictive attention mapping tools, such as EyeQuant and Feng-Gui, use an algorithm powered by thousands of previous eye-tracking studies. They predict what the human eye will notice and what is likely to fall outside of the eye path. Use them to ensure that visitors' eyes will be drawn to the most relevant part of the proposed wireframe.

Use the comments you receive on the wireframe, as well as the analysis you gather from tools like EyeQuant, to inform and inspire your current thinking and generate further ideas.

Step 3: Hand over to development team

Now it's time to ask your developers to implement the test on the experimentation platform.

Some testing platforms offer a drag-and-drop-style visual editor that allows anyone to make changes. Avoid using this as far as possible, limiting it to making small tweaks to static elements.

When a new element is to be created, or if the test involves a partial or complete redesign, a visual designer would have to first create design assets. For simple experiments, visual design should not be required. The development team can use existing cascading style sheets (CSS) to make the variations fit seamlessly into the existing website.

Hand over the wireframe, copy and any design assets along with a link to the live target page or pages. Also give them the following information:

- A description of the changes that are to be made, with reference to the wireframe(s).
- An outline of the hypothesis (ie why the changes are being made).
- Any corporate design guidelines, such as fonts, grids or colours.
- The page(s) where changes are to be made, with the URL(s).
- Goals, metrics to be tracked.
- Type of device targeted (eg mobile).
- Segment targeted (eg new visitors only).
- Traffic allocation (eg a 50:50 split).
- Any known browser issues that are likely to impact on correct rendering of the variation.
- An explanation (or use-case) of new functionality (eg pop-ups, change in data logic, scraping data from other parts of the site).
- How exceptions will be handled (eg what happens if the product is out of stock).

Step 4: QA and UAT

Ask the developers to perform thorough QA, including browser testing, before sending you a preview link to the test. This allows a limited audience – only those with the unique preview link – to do UAT.

UAT is one of your most important tasks, because it's the final filter before a test goes live. Take some time to check that the variation looks and behaves exactly as it should. If the experiment is intended to run across device types, open the preview link on a desktop machine as well as on your phone. Ask colleagues to check it on their different devices and browsers. Try to walk through a few typical use cases, making sure that nothing goes wrong when you click around the site.

If you find anything that looks out of place, or functionality that doesn't operate as expected, take a screenshot of the issue and send it back to the developers with as much information as possible. Explain exactly what the issue is and how they could replicate it as well as details about your desktop/phone and browser.

CASE STUDY   Xero Shoes

Xero Shoes are unique lightweight and low-profile running sandals. Wearing them is almost like being barefoot. From our research, we knew that customers loved the barefoot feeling, together with having just enough protection against dirt and thorns. The main pre-purchase concern was how comfortable these shoes were, though many reviews raved about comfort.

When we started working with Xero Shoes, they had no product links on the homepage. The top half of the page was dominated by inspirational images that appealed to their target market. Our research showed us that it was difficult for visitors to form an overall view of the various shoes on offer, and the differences between them. Visitors would sometimes return to the homepage to orientate themselves, but the only way to find the relevant information was to visit each product page separately.

Our hypothesis was that showing products on the homepage would send more traffic to the product detail pages, which would lead to an increase in sales. We wanted to infuse the page with value statements that we knew would appeal to prospective customers, like Harry, the persona you met in Chapter 5 (Figure 5.3). The resultant wireframe is shown in Figure 8.5, with the finished design, which yielded a 6.45 per cent increase in RPV, in Figure 8.6.

Figure 8.5 Lo-fi wireframe for the homepage of Xero Shoes. It shows the position of images, video and copy. Figure 8.6 shows how this was translated into the final design

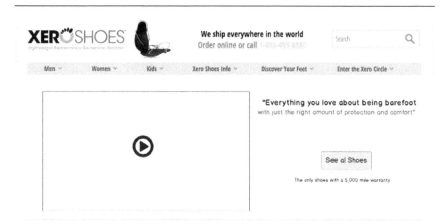

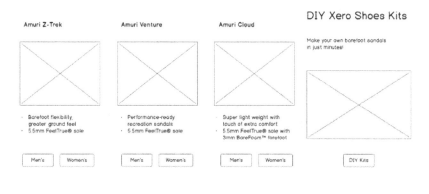

Figure 8.6 The final design of the wireframe shown in Figure 8.5 that resulted in a 6.45 per cent increase in RPV

Summary

A hypothesis is a prediction about cause and effect, a prediction that making certain changes will result in a positive outcome. Those changes should be informed by evidence obtained from data, as discussed in Chapter 3.

It must be testable. You should be able to validate or refute it through a controlled online experiment, usually an A/B test.

The purpose of an experiment is to learn something new about your customers, their behaviour and their interaction with your site. The idea is never to 'prove' your point of view or settle arguments. A well-formulated hypothesis helps to set up this mindset.

If the new experience performs better than the existing one, the hypothesis is validated. When the opposite happens, and the test is negative, it is an opportunity to learn by analysing the unexpected behaviour. You can use that new-found insight to develop alternative hypotheses and iterate on the test to get the desired behavioural change.

The changes proposed in the hypothesis are mapped out in a wireframe. It is used to spur discussion and get input from the team, and occasionally, customer feedback.

If necessary, a visual designer creates design assets for new images, icons or redesign. The final wireframe, copy and design assets are given to developers to implement in the testing platform.

Before the experiment can be made live, it is important to do thorough QA and UAT. This will ensure that the test is free of code errors or bugs, and that it behaves as expected.

Notes

1 Kniberg, H (2016) How we create focus, Presentation delivered at Agila Sverige, *YouTube* [Online] www.youtube.com/watch?v=AqW18DmuGcs (archived at https://perma.cc/L7KJ-JHJD)

2 Kniberg, H (2016) How we create focus, Presentation delivered at Agila Sverige, *YouTube* [Online] www.youtube.com/watch?v=AqW18DmuGcs (archived at https://perma.cc/U9CL-TX45)

3 Cambridge Dictionary (nd) Belief, *Cambridge Dictionary* [Online] https://dictionary.cambridge.org/dictionary/english/belief (archived at https://perma.cc/G7HD-H39R)

4 Sullivan, C (2015) Hypothesis kit 3, *Medium* [Online] https://medium.com/@optimiseordie/hypothesis-kit-2-eff0446e09fc (archived at https://perma.cc/JS8T-ZCYH)

5 Sullivan, C (2015) Hypothesis kit 3, *Medium* [Online] https://medium.com/@optimiseordie/hypothesis-kit-2-eff0446e09fc (archived at https://perma.cc/Z6DY-62GY)

6 Burstein, D (2012) Customer theory: How we learned from a previous test to drive a 40% increase in CTR, *Marketing Experiments* [Online] https://marketingexperiments.com/a-b-testing/customer-theory-increases-ppc-ct (archived at https://perma.cc/UT2T-FECL)

7 Dreyer, I and Scerbikova, M (2017) *99 Failed Experiments in 30 days?!* [Talk] 27 September, ProductTank, Cape Town, South Africa

Testing your hypothesis

There was a time when scurvy was thought to be caused by laziness. One of the first visible symptoms is intense, debilitating fatigue.[1] Soon, the gums start to swell, to the point of bulging over whatever remains of the teeth. One surgeon, having contracted the disease himself, took a knife to his own gums to release the black blood. And that's just the beginning – the signature of scurvy is the 'disintegration of the body'.[2]

A breakthrough in the fight against scurvy came in 1747, when a naval doctor did an experiment aboard HMS *Salisbury*. A group of 12 sailors, all suffering from scurvy, was split into six pairs of two. The pairs were kept in similar conditions and fed the same diet. But each pair was given a different dietary supplement. Only two sailors eventually made a recovery. Both were in the same group – the ones who received a daily dose of citrus fruit.

And so, James Lind conducted the first recorded clinical trial. By changing just one variable – dietary supplement – he was able to monitor its effect on another variable, the medical condition of those sailors. He wrote: '(The) most sudden and visible good effects were perceived from the use of the oranges and lemons; one of those who had taken them, being at the end of six days fit for duty... The other was the best recovered of any in his condition; and being now deemed pretty well, was appointed nurse to the rest of the sick.'[3]

Online experimentation

In this book, we use the terms *experimentation* and *A/B testing* interchangeably. An A/B test is one type of experiment.

By now, you are already familiar with the concept of A/B testing. It's showing one variation to half of your audience, and another variation to the other half, to see which one performs better. You'll find a more comprehensive explanation later in this chapter. It's also called an *online controlled experiment* (OCE), split testing, bucket testing and a few other names.

Experimentation can be defined as **the manipulation of one or more variables such that its effect on other variable(s) can be measured.**[4] In the opening story, James Lind manipulated the dietary supplement of sailors to measure its effect on their health.

From the previous chapter, you know that a hypothesis is a statement of cause and effect. If we do x, we expect to see y. You test and validate that with an experiment. So it's a mechanism by which to **establish causality,** that is, one thing caused another thing to happen.

Suppose, for example, that a business observes a sharp rise in revenue following the launch of a website redesign. They pat themselves on the back and reward the designers handsomely. The pattern is clear: immediately after the new website went live, revenue went up. This is illustrated in the graph on the left in Figure 9.1.

However, the relaunch wasn't the only thing that changed in this period. On the day that the site switched over, a key competitor shut down operations. Those customers now had to go to another supplier, to the benefit of our imaginary business. Had they kept a control group of visitors on their 'old' website, they would have seen the graph on the right. The new website is actually underperforming, and revenue would have been even higher with the old design.

An experiment has the following elements:

• Control group
• Treatment group

Figure 9.1 Revenue trend of an imaginary business, showing the impact of launching a website redesign. From the graph on the left, it looks as if the new site is performing well. However, it turns out that this performance is linked to external variables in the competitive environment. The dotted line in the graph on the right represents the old design. It shows that the old design would have produced an even better result

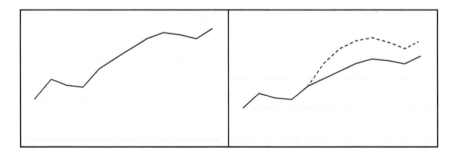

- something that changes (independent variable);
- something believed to be affected by that change (dependent variable);
- a way to measure this effect (metric).

Let's look at each of these in a bit more detail.

Control and treatment groups

How can you know that an observed uplift in an experiment is not the result of some external factor, such as a marketing campaign that coincided with the test?

This is a question we often hear. It reflects an enormous misunderstanding of even the basics of experimentation.

With an A/B test, the population (ie the visitors on your site) is split into two groups. This happens through a process of **randomization**, which means that visitors don't have control over whether they will see Variation A or B. They don't even know that they have been assigned to a specific variation.

The **control group** will see the original experience, without any changes applied to it. This is called the *control*, and typically it would be Variation A. The **treatment group** will see Variation B, the version where changes have been applied, also called the *treatment* or challenger.

Colin McFarland, who's led experimentation at Booking.com, Skyscanner and Netflix, sees an experiment as 'a means of gathering data to compare a theory against reality'.[5] Control (Variation A) is a view of the current reality. Variation B is a view of how you think that reality may be improved, as outlined in your hypothesis.

Because nothing changes for the control group, it provides a benchmark against which to compare Variation B. Both groups are equally exposed to any and all external factors – marketing campaigns, competitive forces, good or bad company news and so on. If the behaviour of the treatment group is significantly different, it can only be as a result of the change(s) in the treatment.

Independent variable and dependent variable

The **independent variable** is the thing(s) you change in the treatment. It is what makes your variation different from the control.

The independent variable is expected to have an effect on the **dependent variable**. You have little or no control over the dependent variable, but it is at the centre of your attention. You are very interested to see what happens to it.

If you have only one independent variable in an experiment, you can pinpoint precisely what caused any observed effect. As you introduce more independent variables, this becomes increasingly difficult to do. We return to this later in the chapter.

Metrics

Metrics are the measuring sticks for your experiment. They enable you to determine whether the change in the treatment had any effect on the dependent variable. They can also show you how the variation has changed user behaviour.

Metrics can measure either macro conversions or micro conversions. A *macro conversion* refers to the final conversion event – placing an order. *Micro conversions* are actions that users take higher up the funnel that may lead to a macro conversion.

Examples of micro conversions are:

- Visits to PDP
- Scroll to certain area of page
- Interact with Size/Colour selector
- Click on 'Add to Cart' button
- Visits to Basket Page.

Though the terms KPI and metric are often used interchangeably, there are subtle differences. *KPIs* are 'quantifiable metrics which reflect the performance of an organization in achieving its goals and objectives',[6] whereas *metrics* are, simply, what you measure.[7] All KPIs are metrics, but not all metrics are KPIs.

In experimentation then, KPIs are top-level metrics which align the testing programme with the strategic goals of the business.[8] In the context of e-commerce, typical KPIs are RPV (revenue per visitor), AOV (average order value) and conversion rate. Figure 9.2 shows how they are related (see the box 'E-commerce optimization KPIs').

One of these three KPIs will usually serve as the primary test metric is used to decide the outcome of an experiment: if it goes down, the hypothesis is rejected – even if another metric in the same test went up.

Causality is also established by monitoring the primary metric. If the change in your treatment is the only difference between Variation A and

Variation B, any statistically significant swing in the primary metric must be caused by that change.[9]

As important as the primary metric is, it provides a one-dimensional view. It tells only a small part of the story, whether a test is positive or negative. The bigger, often more interesting story is how the test changed user behaviour such to induce the observed outcome. To build this more comprehensive narrative, you will track a range of **secondary metrics**. Those tend to be more localized to the area where the change has been introduced. They may also include **guardrail metrics**,[10] ones which you don't want to see negatively affected.

Consider the example of an experiment on the PDP of a shoe retailer, as shown in Figures 8.1– 8.3 in the previous chapter. The primary metric in this case was RPV. Secondary metrics included AOV and conversion rate, to provide context around changes in RPV. Did more users buy products, or did the same number of customers spend more money, or both? Other secondary metrics would aim to explain user behaviour, such as clicks on the 'Add to Cart' button as well as clicks on the various tabs further down the page.

A guardrail metric used in that case study was 'product returns', relying on external data. The retailer had noticed a pattern of customers buying two pairs of shoes at a time to try on at home, and then returning one pair. It was important to monitor this, as the 'free returns' policy could cause profit margin to be degraded as a consequence of the test.

E-commerce optimization KPIs

KPIs are top-level metrics which align your testing programme with the strategic goals of the business.[11]

In e-commerce optimization, important KPIs are RPV, AOV and conversion rate (Figure 9.2). One of these often serves as a primary test metric.

Revenue per visitor, or sometimes *average revenue per user* (ARPU) measures the average amount of money earned per visitor to your site, including those who didn't purchase. It's a composite metric that rolls up two other KPIs – conversion rate and AOV.

RPV = Conversion rate $\times$ Average order value

Average order value measures the average amount of money your customers spend per transaction. Earning more from the same number of transactions is a good way to increase overall revenue and profitability.

Figure 9.2 E-commerce KPIs used as primary metrics in experimentation. RPV is a composite metric, a product of AOV × Conversion rate. It is a measure of how much revenue is earned per visitor on the site, including visitors who didn't make a purchase. When choosing a primary metric, always get as close as possible to revenue

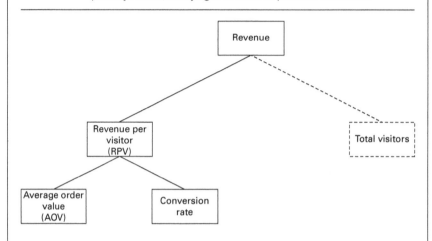

AOV = Revenue / Number of transactions

Conversion rate measures the percentage of all visitors who made a purchase on your site. If using revenue-base metrics is not feasible (more on this later), conversion rate is next in line to be used as primary metric.

Conversion rate = Number of transactions / Number of visitors

A note about conversion rate

Conversion rate is one of the most misunderstood metrics in e-commerce. There are times when a high conversion rate gives you less money. Take a look at these two (deliberately simplified) scenarios:

1 Scenario A: Four visitors come to your site. One of them places an order for £50 – that's a 25 per cent conversion rate.

2 Scenario B: Again you have four visitors, but this time two place an order – that's a 50 per cent conversion rate, a whopping 100 per cent increase. However, in this case each customer spends only £10. That's £20 in total revenue, less than half you earned in Scenario A.

Which would you rather have – the scenario with 25 per cent conversion rate or the one with 50 per cent conversion rate? If you're unsure, ask the accountant. You can't pay the bills with conversion rate.

Mechanisms like upselling and cross-selling can have an effect on AOV, but not on conversion rate. Measuring only conversion rate might lead you to the wrong conclusion if you tested the introduction of an upselling widget.

As you can see, conversion rate can be misleading.

Test revenue is not site-wide revenue

Any revenue uplift reported by the testing platform relates to the page on which the test was run. That is not the same as overall site-wide impact. To get the complete picture, you may have to decrement the reported value by the page revenue multiplier, as explained in Chapter 7.

For example, a test on your homepage reports a 10 per cent RPV increase. However, this uplift cannot be applied to everyone on the site, only the segment of visitors who pass through that page. If homepage revenue makes up 2 per cent of the total site-wide amount (revisit Figure 7.2), the site-wide effect of this test is 2 per cent and not 10 per cent [ie 10% × 2%].

Types of online experiments

There are mainly three different types of online experiments:

- A/B testing or A/B/n testing;
- multivariate testing (MVT);
- multi-arm bandit (MAB)

A/B and A/B/n testing

This is the staple of the industry, and most of your tests will fall into this category. It's simply comparing one variation against another, where 50 per cent of the audience see the control (the original, usually Version A) and the rest see the treatment or challenger (Variation B).

If there is more than one variation, it is known as an A/B/*n* test. If you have enough traffic to split up into more than two audiences, this approach has some advantages. First, you can move faster by fitting more than one idea into the same testing slot. Second, by directly comparing different treatments against each other, the opportunity for insight generation is much bigger.

Over time, you measure the relative performance of each variation against the primary metric. This gives you the data to decide which one should be kept.

There's a lot that you can A/B test, for example:

- UI elements such as images, forms, buttons and layout;
- copy elements such as headlines, sales copy, micro messaging;
- algorithms and product recommendation systems;
- a radical redesign of one page;
- redesign of a sequence of steps;
- product prices.

Multivariate testing

A number of variables are tested at the same time with MVT, dynamically mixed together in different combinations. Say you want to find the best headline and hero image combination. Load two alternative headlines and two alternative images into the testing tool, and it will present all possible combinations on the fly.

The major drawback of MVT is that it demands exponentially bigger sample sizes. Frankly, this puts it out of reach of most websites.

The number of variations in MVT is determined by this formula:

$$[\text{Nr of variations for element A}] \times [\text{Nr of variations for element B}]... = [\text{Total nr of variations}]^{12}$$

In the above example we have three headline variations and three image variations, counting the original. Total number of variations in this test is therefore $3 \times 3 = 9$. So your population will be split into nine buckets as opposed to two buckets like an A/B test. If the experiment added a third element, say the 'Add To Cart' button, it would bring the total to $3 \times 3 \times 3 = 27$ variations!

If you do have enough traffic to warrant MVT – and you probably don't – the number one benefit is accelerated learning. It's a way of pointing out the most profitable levers on a page. Use MVT to identify those elements, then target these with standard A/B tests.

Multi-arm bandit

This relies on machine learning algorithms to adjust the amount of exposure to test variations, depending on performance. More visitors will automatically be bucketed into winning variations, while losing variations would gradually start seeing less traffic.

Effectively outsourcing your decision to a machine removes the risk of prolonged exposure to a losing variation. However, that decision is often more nuanced and may require different layers of information and insight.

Jeremy Gu, Data Science Manager at Uber, explains that multi-armed bandit (MAB) and A/B testing serve different purposes. A/B testing is better in terms of decision making. At Uber, MAB is used to quickly find the best treatment among a large group of alternatives. 'However, MAB is undesirable to accurately estimate treatment effects for groups with small datasets', he cautions.[13]

On an e-commerce site, a visitor may arrive today for the first time, come back tomorrow to do more research and finally make the purchase next week. An A/B test would 'catch' this conversion, whereas the MAB may make a decision before the conversion event.

To a degree, MAB also assumes that conversion propensity holds constant over time, which is often not the case. For example, weekdays and weekends usually see different patterns, and time of day also plays a role.

When the experimentation time frame is not well suited to A/B testing, MAB may be a better option – a campaign related to Black Friday, for example, where the outcome of an A/B test would come too late to be fully exploited.

Big or small changes?

Should you be testing big, bold radical changes or small alterations?

The driving philosophy behind small-change testing is incremental improvement, and the buzz phrase *marginal gains*. These tests require less effort so presumably you can do more of them, continuously banking small uplifts all the way. All those 'almost nothings' eventually add up to something.

However, small changes often lack the muscle to deliver any noticeable effect, yielding inconclusive test results. This wastes weeks of testing time, and inconclusive results make it harder to draw meaningful insights. Even if you do get some small wins this way, some say it's an 'illusion of progress' if you're getting there one tiny step at a time.[14]

Radical changes, such as the complete redesign of a page, are more likely to bring about a significant difference in behaviour. Therefore, they are more likely to cause a noticeable effect – either positive or negative.

But radical testing does not come without drawbacks. Changing more than one variable means you can't pinpoint cause and effect. One of the variables might in fact be pulling the overall result down, and you'd be none the wiser.

Making radical changes also demands more time and resources. If it delivers a positive uplift, the investment pays off. If it bombs out, not only do you not have an uplift but it's also more difficult to learn from it.

One problem is that 'incremental testing' is often misinterpreted as running pointless experiments, like changing button colours. That's not what we are referring to here.

Making the choice

There is a trade-off between potential effect (from radical testing) and more precise learning (incremental testing). With incremental testing, you can create layers of insight with every iteration, which gradually build up to a big win.

Amazon's Jeff Bezos has a clear view on this, which is supported by our direct experience. The few big wins from bold tests will more than compensate for the ones that didn't win: 'Outsized returns often come from betting against conventional wisdom, and conventional wisdom is usually right. Given a 10 per cent chance of a 100 times payoff, you should take that bet every time. But you're still going to be wrong 9 times out of 10... Big winners pay for so many experiments.'[15]

Our advice is to strive for a balance, leaning towards the more innovative end of the spectrum. Experimentation allows you to do precisely that: push the envelope. Mark Zuckerberg of Facebook understands this too. He says many of his decisions are based on this question: 'Okay, is this going to destroy the company? Because if not, then let them test it.'[16]

You need the learnings from small tests to inform the bigger ideas, though. If you only do big tests, it will slow down your roadmap. So you need both.

At the start of your programme, things are also different. Naturally you'd want to start with the list of ideas in the High Value, Low Effort quadrant of Figure 7.1, but usually that's a short list. If you find it hard to move the dial with sensible incremental improvements, it's time to be bolder.

If the design or structure of the current template is too limiting for the changes that you want to make, it's a clear sign that you need to take a more radical approach. Equally, if you reach a point of diminishing returns after making good incremental gains at first, it's time to go big. Once you've found a new template that works, you can continue optimizing it with incremental testing.

This is known as the 'local maximum'. It means that, relative to the tests you have been running, you have reached the maximum, but not relative to all the potential gains if you started from a different base. It's like climbing up the small hill in Figure 9.3, whereas in fact there's a higher hill with a bigger upside a short distance away.

Figure 9.3 Local and global maxima

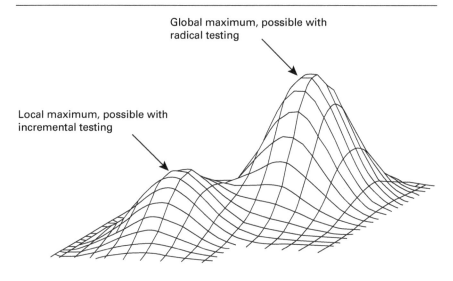

Global maximum, possible with
radical testing

Local maximum, possible with
incremental testing

Figure 9.4 Strategic theme exploration

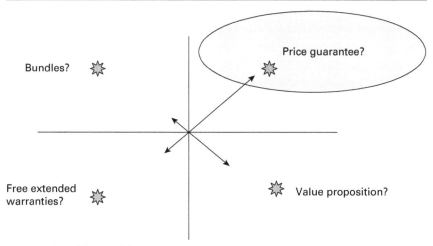

Bundles?

Price guarantee?

Free extended
warranties?

Value proposition?

SOURCE Adapted from Daniel Lee

Analyst Daniel Lee talks about 'getting close to your superior point of optimization, and then iterating around this point'.[17] You find your optimal position
in the grid (Figure 9.4) by incrementally testing towards each area.[18] In this
illustration, visitors react better to the price guarantee than to the other value
claims. The oval represents the area where you would iterate around this winning theme. Future experiments might iteratively test different attributes of

the same theme, for example location on the page or in the funnel, messaging and creative.

Exclusion testing

Also called an existence test, exclusion testing hides an element on a page to quantify the effect of a given page element. It's a good way to identify conversion levers.

Especially at the start of your optimization programme, when your purpose is accelerating insight generation, there's no risk of small 'learning tests' hijacking valuable testing slots.

The purpose of this type of test is not to get a win. If it shows an uplift, you can replace this component with something more valuable – white space, even. The results can be surprising, counter-intuitive.

If the test is negative, it's an indication that the element you hid in the test is an important conversion lever. Can you do more with it? What does it teach you about user behaviour and preferences?

If results are inconclusive, it could be a sign that the element can work harder for you or, conversely, that the space it takes up can be put to better use.

Here's an interesting example. It's a truism that money-back guarantees and friendly returns policies give people the reassurance they need to buy, so they bump up sales. And most of the time, that's what happens.

So it was a surprise when we took a guarantee off the website of one of our clients and saw an increase in revenue. Why? The site sold gifts for children. When we investigated, we found out that many sales were to grandparents buying for their grandchildren. The last thing a grandfather wants to contemplate when buying a gift for his grandson is that things will go wrong and, heaven forbid, the gift has to be returned. The money-back guarantee planted a seed of doubt.

With this type of experiment, always test only one variable at a time so that you can isolate the value of that particular thing being tested.

Statistics for optimizers

When you interpret test results, you are making inferences about the wider population based on what you've observed from a sample. This is where statistics enters the frame. They can help you answer questions like these:

- How confident can you be about those extrapolations?
- Is a reported win really a win?
- Can you expect to see the same uplifts once the change goes live on the site?

To improve your ability to interpret test results and pick the real winners, it is time to gain a basic understanding of the relevant principles. It's a complex area beyond the scope of this book, but our aim here is to give you a reasonable working knowledge.

Statistical significance

First, let's clear up a common misconception. Statistical significance does not tell you that one variation is better or worse than the other. Nor is it an indication that a test is ready to be called.

Statistical significance tells you whether there really is a difference between the control and variation, or whether the result may be down to random chance. As Daniel Kahneman explains in *Thinking, Fast and Slow*: 'We are prone to overestimate how much we understand about the world and to underestimate the role of chance in events.'[19]

Optimizely defines statistical significance as an answer to this question, which gets straight to the point: 'How likely is it that my experiment results will say I have a winner when I actually don't?'[20]

Standard industry practice is to use 95 per cent statistical significance as a threshold. It means there is a 5 per cent chance of being a fluke. So, 1 out of 20 'confident' wins will be false.

Statistical significance is used by many as a comfort blanket, but there are dangers in relying on this alone. It should always be seen in the context of other factors discussed below.

Moreover, *Harvard Business Review* points out that statistical significance does not equate to business relevance. The insistence on 95 per cent statistical significance has been inherited from science, but many business decisions don't require this level of confidence.[21]

Statistical power

A few years ago, a PhD wrote a hard-hitting paper claiming that most winning A/B test results were 'illusory'.[22] Though they may have been statistically significant, those tests were 'under-powered'.

Statistical power is the ability to detect an effect, if there really is an effect to be detected in the first place.

To understand it better, consider this scenario: Tossing a fair coin, there's a 50/50 chance of landing either heads or tails. If the first dozen or so flicks skew one way, you'd probably expect it to settle down at around 50 per cent after enough flips. Intuitively, you want to increase the sample (number of flips) before accepting the result.

Sample size is an important factor in determining whether an experiment has sufficient statistical power. As we saw in Chapter 7, sample size is in part determined by desired minimum detectable effect (MDE).

So to increase the power of a test, to avoid it being 'under-powered', you could increase sample size or increase effect size. Practically, the former is more within your control. You can let more visitors into the test by running it for longer, for example.

An under-powered test holds the risk of declaring a 'confident' winner when it isn't a win in reality. This is known as a *false positive*, or Type I error in statistical jargon. Fortunately, modern experimentation platforms will only declare a win if both statistical significance and statistical power thresholds are met (Figure 9.5).

To avoid the frustration of under-powered tests clogging up your testing slots, or declaring false positives, calculate the minimum required sample size upfront. Refer back to Chapter 7 for details on how to do this.

Confidence intervals

The nature of making inferences is that we can never be 100 per cent certain about it. The *confidence interval* is a measure of that certainty.

Your experimentation platform may report a range of values in addition to the stated uplift. That is the range within which the reported lift can fluctuate at 95 per cent statistical significance. For example, it may report 10 per cent (± 2 per cent) where the bit in brackets reflects the *margin of error*. As more data are gathered by the experiment, this margin should shrink to increase the level of certainty.

In Figure 9.5, you can see that Qubit is reporting RPV at £1.35. It is flanked by values of £1.27 and £1.43, representing the lower and upper limits of the confidence interval at that point in time.

Figure 9.5 A dashboard of Qubit's Digital Experience Platform shows the tension between statistical power and statistical significance. Despite observing a high probability (99.86 per cent) of a strong lift, the experiment 'needs more data' to say that there really is an effect

The test brief

Before launching a test, create a test-brief document to communicate all relevant details. This can take any form, but we find that a deck works well. It should contain the following:

- Name of the test
- Testing slot
- Screenshot of control
- Screenshot of variation(s)
- List of changes
- Data and insights
- Hypothesis
- Primary metric
- Secondary metrics
- Target segment(s)
- estimated test duration.

When to stop a test

When a test is confidently winning or losing, the decision to stop is relatively easy – simply follow the recommendations made by the testing platform. Just a few years ago, that would not have been our advice, but models constantly evolve and have become more intelligent.

But what do you do if a test has been running for a while and a recommendation has still not been made by the software?

If you stop too soon, you might never know if you made the wrong decision. Keeping it live for too long bears an opportunity cost, an argument in favour of stopping the test and moving on. Then again, preparing the next test also has a cost associated with it, so under certain conditions the better decision must be to extend.

In these situations, it's helpful to have clear stopping rules.

Start by calculating minimum required sample size, and work backwards from there to test duration. This was explained in Chapter 7. On the given day, review test performance and make a judgement call.

If the required sample has been reached, with neither control nor variation taking a clear lead, the test should be stopped and declared **inconclusive**. Even if the variation looked as if it was going to win at some point, the only thing that matters is what the picture looks like now.

The RPV graph in Figure 9.6 shows a common pattern. The top line is the variation and the bottom line the control. It starts off looking promising for the variation. After a few days of the variation taking the lead, it may be tempting to stop the test. It might even reach 95 per cent statistical significance – but remember, that's not an indication that one variation is better than the other.

After two weeks the winning variation has lost all that initial shine. Should you remain hopeful about the prospect of a win and keep it going? No. The most plausible explanation is that there never was any real difference between the two. What we observed initially were fluctuations which normalized over time as the proverbial coin was flipped more times. This is known as **regression to mean** (Figure 9.6).

If the variation has consistently outperformed control, there may be a case to extend its run – or even **declare a win**.

First, check that the required sample has indeed been reached. If it has, it would suggest that the difference between the two variations is not big enough (yet?) to be statistically significant.

The testing platform may be holding out for the 95 per cent threshold to be achieved, but you know that it's not the only factor or even the most important one. If it's close to 95 per cent, it may be worth making the trade-off. How close? There is no answer, but definitely closer to 95 than 50.

Confidence interval is another important clue. If the margin of error is shrinking while the variation maintains the lead, this is a bullish indicator. If the overlap between the two sets of confidence intervals is still large, **extend test duration** by a week or two to allow more data in. If confidence intervals continue to shrink, consider calling it a win. However, if confidence intervals do not shrink, or if statistical significance starts to slip, consider it inconclusive and move on.

We usually run A/B tests for at least 14 days. Buying behaviour could fluctuate significantly depending on the day of the week, so we want to observe at least two full weeks and weekends. If there's reason to extend, this is done in increments of 7 days.

If your business is characterized by longer purchase cycles, 14 days may not be enough. Customers don't always make up their mind immediately and often visit the site multiple times before buying. A visitor can enter the test on Day 1 but delay the purchase until Day 20. If the test ended after 14 days, that conversion would not have been taken into account at all.

Figure 9.6 A screenshot from a test result in Optimizely, illustrating regression to mean. This is a common pattern, so be careful of jumping to conclusions before the test has run its course

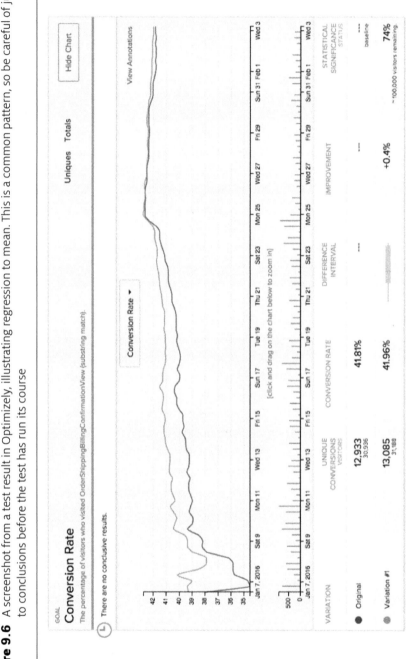

GOAL

Conversion Rate

The percentage of visitors who visited OrderShippingBillingConfirmationView (substring match).

Uniques Totals **Hide Chart**

ⓘ There are no conclusive results.

Conversion Rate ▾

View Annotations

[click and drag on the chart below to zoom in]

VARIATION	UNIQUE CONVERSIONS VISITORS	CONVERSION RATE	IMPROVEMENT	DIFFERENCE INTERVAL	STATISTICAL SIGNIFICANCE STATUS
● Original	12,933 / 30,936	41.81%	---	---	baseline
● Variation #1	13,085 / 31,188	41.96%	+0.4%		74%

~100,000 visitors remaining.

To get a steer on this, consult the *Time to Purchase* report in Google Analytics.

Relying on micro conversion metrics

Micro conversion metrics usually reach statistical significance before macro conversion metrics. This is because there are always more visitors higher up the funnel, and more micro conversion activity, which forms the basis of significance calculations.

If that happens, it may be tempting to declare a win based on a micro conversion metric. Avoid this as far as possible. Though a micro conversion might be positively correlated to a macro conversion, that does not imply causality. The only way to verify that your change in Variation B has a direct impact on the macro conversion is to monitor the effect on the macro conversion.

To explain the difference: In summer months, ice cream sales go up. The number of people drowning in swimming pools also increases, unfortunately. Both variables – ice cream sales and deaths by drowning – rise together, so there is positive **correlation**. However, there is no **causality**: ice cream sales do not cause people to drown. Warmer weather makes people more inclined to buy ice cream, and also more inclined to visit swimming pools. With more people in the water, there are more drownings compared to cooler months.

Testing on low-traffic sites

With all this talk about sample size, it may sound as if only big websites can benefit from experimentation. Without a doubt, higher traffic volumes are more suitable testing grounds.

What qualifies as a 'low traffic' site? I was hoping you wouldn't ask that question. There are views on this – some will say 100,000 monthly unique visitors, others have called it at 30,000 monthly unique visitors and fewer. Fundamentally, it's about how many visitors you can get into a test, but as you've already seen, it also depends on the size of effect.

It's not at all impossible to experiment on smaller sites. Before jumping into testing, invest in thorough explorative analysis. This will help you to focus the roadmap on things that matter. Arrange a few usability testing sessions to identify potential roadblocks. Review session recordings. Speak to recent customers, fine-tune the value proposition.

Then, when you are ready to start testing, follow the suggestions below.

Go big

As you know by now, greater magnitudes of uplift can be detected on smaller sample sizes. Low-traffic sites should exploit this and shoot for bigger impact.

What this means for smaller sites is doing radical testing rather than incremental improvements. Bundle a number of ideas around the same hypothesis into one test. Draw on insights that have come from your users, and rely less on the usual traps of copying competitors and going with instinct.

Use an MDE calculator to balance detectable effect and achieving reasonable time frames. If it's difficult to get to a desired time frame on the basis of sales conversion rate, you can plug in conversion rates of micro events instead.

Target high-traffic areas

To make optimal use of low-traffic volumes, prioritize pages that see the highest number of visitors. Clustering pages together and testing at template level (see Chapter 7 for details) will give the test better exposure.

You can even ramp up PPC and social advertising in this period. If you do that, it's best to send that traffic directly to the page(s) being tested. One caveat is that bought traffic often behaves differently from the rest, so have a look at the traffic mix on that page.

The further you move down the funnel of your customer journey, the lower traffic volume is likely to be. Typically, checkout pages see a fraction of the traffic of a product detail page.

Balanced against this is the fact that when you're closer to the entrance of the funnel, the lower the purchase conversion rate will be. To overcome this challenge, use micro conversion metrics.

Track micro conversions

We've stressed the importance of RPV as the primary metric as far as possible. We've said that micro conversion events should be used only as secondary metrics. On sites with low traffic and sales activity, however, this is not feasible, and using micro conversion metrics may be your best option.

Use sales conversion rate where you can measure it directly, such as in the checkout and on the basket page. Beyond that, track micro conversion metrics. If you're testing on the PDP, instead of tracking conversion rate you might track clicks on the 'Add to Cart' button or even the percentage of visitors who scroll down far enough to even see the button.

The idea is to track whatever user activity you can measure to see if your variation has changed user behaviour. If significantly more PDP viewers clicked on the 'Add to Cart' button, that would suggest that the sales conversation is more persuasive. If more of those visitors proceed to the basket page, it could be an indication that purchase intent is higher.

Those metrics do not automatically translate into more revenue, but you are still able to make more informed decisions. And you're nudging visitors closer to the end goal.

Avoid multiple variations

The more variations in your test, the more your traffic pie is cut into little slices. You'll be surprised at how many more visitors you'd need to power the test adequately by adding just one variation.

Test one variation at a time.

Dial down statistical significance

As we saw earlier, there is no absolute requirement for business decisions to be based on 95 per cent statistical significance.

It's important in science, but in a business context it's not such an important signal according to Thomas Redman, author of *Data Driven: Profiting from your most important business asset.*[23]

Decide on a time frame for the test, say a month or so. At that point, make a decision even if statistical significance is not where the purists would want to see it. It's better than making a guess if your alternative is not testing at all.

How to avoid common pitfalls

After all this effort, the last thing you want is for test results to be rendered invalid owing to technical glitches, or for an experiment to cause your site to break.

The advice below can help you avoid some common traps.

Implement the testing platform correctly

Make sure the vendor's implementation instructions have been followed to the letter. Apologies if it sounds a bit like IT asking you to check if the computer is switched on, but seriously.

Check that the software is correctly deployed and that it's the latest updated version of the code. We saw a case where a retailer could not get any test to run properly. Changes would display inconsistently and pages would load blank. It was a simple matter of the wrong version of the testing platform code being on the site.

We've seen things go wrong because the code had not been placed in exactly the right position on the page. Avoid placement via a tag management tool like GTM (Google Tag Manager).

Do thorough QA

Don't ever make any test live without solid QA (quality assurance). Bugs and technical errors go hand in hand with software development. Therefore, each test has to be thoroughly checked after it's been coded. We have caught issues during QA that could have been detrimental to sales had the test gone live.

Most experimentation platforms let you generate a preview link that can be distributed among the team for QA purposes. Only people with that link can access the test, so there is no risk of your live audience being exposed to it.

As an agency, we have to be even more careful before rolling out tests on our clients' websites. Our developers append query parameters to the target URL in the experimentation platform. So if the test is destined to run on *awa-digital.com/* – the URL of our agency homepage – we would temporarily target it to *awa-digital.com/?q= 1*. What that enables us to do is make the test live, but only to users who follow this special link with query parameters appended. We prefer this to a preview link, because it's 'the real thing'. It allows you to test exactly what a user will see once the query parameter is removed.

Just because it looks fine on your new iMac on a fibre connection, that doesn't mean it looks the same to a user on a laptop and mobile connection. Check that everything is working properly in all major browsers, across devices. Use the device and browser reports in GA to determine which combinations to use for QA. Use a browser emulator to review on platforms that you don't have direct access to.

It's not only bugs you're looking for. The code may be completely error-free, but there might be usability issues. Is it displaying as expected or does anything look out of place? If you interact with it, does it behave as it should?

Go beyond the page targeted by the experiment. For example, if the test runs on the PDP, go through the entire process of adding a product to cart and advancing to the basket page.

Minimize flicker

Flicker is a brief but noticeable delay before the variation displays in the browser. The user gets a fleeting glimpse of the original page, before seeing it change to the variation. Depending on the severity, it can be rather disconcerting. More importantly, it can skew your test results if the user experience is adversely affected.

The number one way of preventing this is to place the code on the page exactly as directed by the vendor. Some experimentation platforms also offer an additional anti-flicker script that you can install.

Should you still encounter flicker, ask your developers to find ways to optimize the test code. The fewer lines of code in a test, the less room for things to go wrong.

They can also try using progressive loading. This is a way to ensure your test code runs as early as possible, and have the variation progressively load over the top of the page. The downside to this is the extra logic needed to poll for various elements, which takes longer and complicates the code.

Avoid code changes during an experiment

Avoid making changes to a test while it's in progress. Best practice would be to pause it, make the adjustment, and then clone to start it afresh.

Any changes to the site code while experiments are in progress may cause a test variation to break. The variation code could have dependencies on seemingly unimportant elements on a page. If you can't avoid making changes to the back end, check each live test afterwards to ensure it hasn't been impacted.

Running concurrent experiments

Is it okay to run experiments in parallel? It depends on who you ask. It's the subject of much debate. In one camp there's a strong argument that you should run no more than one experiment at a time, since there is a risk of cross-contamination.

We assess it on a case-by-case basis, taking into consideration the trade-off with velocity, that is, the number of tests launched in a given period. Limiting yourself to one test at any given time is like crawling when you could be running.

You don't have to rule out concurrent tests to mitigate risk. Instead, set up rules for governing concurrent tests. First, never run two or more tests in the same area of the site. Before placing two tests in the same funnel, review the changes side by side to see if one test may impact the other. Run the combinations with minimum risk. Make the trade-off rather than being slowed down by a purist mindset.

A watertight option, assuming you have loads of visitors, is to make parallel tests mutually exclusive. That means a visitor can only be bucketed into one at a time.

Should you run an A/A test?

The short answer is no. In an A/A test, there is no difference between the two variations. Essentially, you're testing the control against itself in an attempt to surface any anomalies. The theory is that an A/A test should show no difference, and if it does then something is wrong with the setup.

The reality is different for a number of reasons, so this could send you in the wrong direction. It's a waste of time that should be spent running a real test.

Seasonal effects

Seasonal effects can cause your customers to behave differently. For example, motivation to buy is higher over Black Friday. A winning concept in the run-up to Christmas may not have the same impact in January, when the reality of empty wallets has set in.

Clearly, if most of your revenue is generated over those peak periods, it would be unwise to turn off the test during those times. If you have concerns about the potential impact of seasonality, you could run a follow-on test at a later time. Under ideal conditions, you could also leave a stub of the test running by setting the winning variation to 95 per cent of traffic, with the remaining 5 per cent still seeing the control. This will show the effect over time, as explained later in this chapter.

Don't shy away from testing during these times. If large portions of your annual revenue are attributable to certain peak periods, you should be optimizing for those. Because of increased traffic, it's also possible to get more accurate results faster.

Post-test analysis

There are three possible outcomes to an experiment, as measured against the primary metric:

- **Win:** The variation performed significantly better than the control; colloquially we say the test was 'positive'.

- **Loss:** The variation was significantly weaker than the control, so the test was 'negative'.

- **Inconclusive:** There is no clear difference in performance.

Whatever the result, it is not the end of the road. It's vital to analyse test data for a more comprehensive understanding than the headline win, loss or inconclusive. This is an opportunity to get unique insights, and it's a great source of new ideas for the testing roadmap.

Review the hypothesis

Recall from Chapter 8 that the hypothesis is a prediction about how you intend to improve a metric, based on what you believe to be true. Expect the majority of tests to be negative. As you know by now, we don't see negative tests as failures but as opportunities to learn and edge towards a win.

When a hypothesis is refuted, this doesn't make the data-driven observations that led to the hypothesis any less relevant (part 1 of the formula in Chapter 8). It can bring you a step closer to solving the original problem by adjusting the hypothesis. At times, it might bring a new perspective to the original insights that formed the basis of your hypothesis. Either way, you have made progress.

Say you've observed that visitors who use site search convert at a much higher rate than non-searchers. You hypothesize that increasing search-box prominence will push more visitors into the search funnel. Since that funnel converts so much better, you expect to see revenue benefit from that knock-on effect. However, test data show that even though the number of searches increased, revenue went down.

Asking *why* leads to new emergent knowledge and new avenues to explore. Some suggestions could be:

- Site search is 'bad' and needs to be fixed. But if that's the case, why do site searchers in general perform so much better? Not the most plausible explanation for now.

- Browsing and discovery are more important for your visitors than you realized. Test this hypothesis.

- Site searchers tend to know what they want; they are further along the purchase decision cycle (Chapter 4) and therefore have stronger intent to buy. Simply pushing more visitors into the search funnel won't change motivation to purchase. To them, site search is the wrong path since they don't know exactly what they want yet, hence the drop in revenue. How do we optimize the journey for those users?

A good habit is to consider what you will learn from a negative result *before* starting a test. Not only does it help you frame the hypothesis for maximum insight generation, you also remind yourself and others that experimentation is not a way of proving that you were right.

Secondary metrics

While secondary metrics should not be used to decide the outcome of an experiment (if it can be avoided), they are indispensable when it comes to making sense of a test result. The primary metric tells you whether the hypothesis is valid or not. Secondary metrics can tell you why.

They let you construct a narrative of how the change introduced in your variation impacted user behaviour. What did those who saw the variation do more of compared to those who saw the control? Did the variation see more or fewer clicks on key calls to action? Was there a difference in scrolling behaviour? How was the broader journey different for users who had been exposed to the variation?

Segment the results

We all know that people are not the same, and it's likely that different groups of visitors behave differently. It's even possible that what looks like a losing test might in fact be a win in one segment, although it's too early to get excited about that.

Post-test segmentation can usually be done within the experimentation platform, but an even better way is integrating each test with Google Analytics. This enables you to do thorough analysis with all the richness that GA offers.

Just some examples of segments you could look at:

- Desktop vs mobile
- Paid vs non-paid traffic
- New vs returning visitors
- First-time buyers vs loyal customers
- Country or region
- browser or operating system.

As you compare the performance of different segments, try to explain any differences in behaviour. Why did particular segments respond as they did? If there's any difference in performance, what could be behind that? What does it tell you about preferences or behavioural differences between the various user groups? Does it give you any new insight into a persona?

Don't jump to conclusions based on segmented reporting, as it increases your chance of finding a *false positive* or fluke win. Disregard any interesting results based on small sample sizes. Also bear in mind that one segment in isolation is just one part of the full picture.

CASE STUDY   Thompson & Morgan

Thompson & Morgan is a brand leader in plants, seeds and fruit trees. Customers love Thompson & Morgan for its wide variety of merchandise, and many of them spend hours browsing the site. We found that shoppers were heavily influenced by images.

Product listing pages (PLPs) are a vital part of how they discover Thompson & Morgan's full range of merchandise. We hypothesized that showing more products on the PLP, and using larger images, would better show off the breadth of offering, and would improve the buying experience. This meant changing the PLP from a list view to a grid layout.

The experiment was negative. As to why this could have been the case, we identified a few possibilities:

- The hypothesis that a bigger variety of images on the PLP would improve the buying experience was refuted.

- Basic product information, which was present in the list view but removed from the grid view, is vital in the customer's purchase decision.

- Showing the breadth of offering actually made it more difficult to make a choice, a concept known as the 'paradox of choice'.

Each of these possible explanations gives rise to new ideas, so it led to a few more experiments in this area. We subsequently found that larger images were in fact better, but showing basic product information at this point in the journey was equally important. That was the insight we needed to have in order to generate decent wins on this page. The only way to get to this learning was by testing it, and working with the negative result.

Make the winning experience live

Clearly you want to lock in the win as soon as possible. Yet, you'd be surprised how many times this fails to happen. The only thing worse than not testing at all is to sit on winning variations without committing the changes live on the site in order to start realizing the gains.

There are a number of options for rolling out the winning changes on your site. Here are the most common approaches in our experience.

1 Hard-code the winning variation, to make it a permanent feature of the site.

2 Serve the winning variation to 100 per cent of visitors, rather than 50 per cent as before.

3 Put the winning code live on the site via a tag manager.

4 Run a stub, where 5 per cent of website visitors continue to see the control.

Table 9.1 summarizes the pros and cons of each of these approaches.

When asking your web development team or agency to hard-code a win, give them a good brief, covering the following:

- Screenshots of the control and variation(s)
- Outline of differences introduced by the variation(s)
- Any changes to business logic
- Results achieved during the test
- Code created for the variation in the testing tool's code engine
- any special events that require additional QA/checking in development.

As with any change to your site, review this implementation before it goes live. Make sure it's a fair copy of the winning variation, that it looks and functions exactly the same. It sounds like an obvious thing, but ignoring it means disregarding the test results.

Document test results

A test is not done until everything has been recorded and insights have been shared with the team. Diligent documentation is an inseparable part of the experimentation programme. It also loops back into your experimentation roadmap, so you can build on the learnings.

Table 9.1 Options to integrate a winning test result into the live site. Number 1 is the preferred route

#	Approach	Advantages	Disadvantages	Recommendation
1	Hard-code the winning variation	The winning variation becomes part of the permanent code of the website. The most reliable option. Experimentation can help to prioritize your development backlog. It is a good way to ensure that your developers are working on features that will have a positive impact.	Integrating this version into the website's code will require backend development resourcing.	If you have development resource available this is most sensible option.
2	Test platform serves winning variation to 100% of website visitors	All visitors will see the winning variation, and instead of getting only 50% of the uplift, you get all of it. It is immediate; you save development costs in the short term.	While this practice is common, most platforms are not built to be serving winning variations on a continuous basis. It's standard for the number of test participants to be capped by the experimentation platform. Serving tests at 100% will erode your allocation and may have commercial implications. If the page targeted by the experiment is updated on the server, the variation running at 100% might break. Google's guidelines are to serve variations only as long as is necessary, in other words until the experiment is concluded.[24]	

(continued)

Table 9.1 (Continued)

#	Approach	Advantages	Disadvantages	Recommendation
3	Make the code live via a tag manager	Usually an interim solution to lock in the win until the back-end resources are available to hard-code it. We've seen commercial tag managers do a good job of serving several winners simultaneously over a prolonged period, without any noticeable adverse impact.	Tag management mechanisms are not designed for this purpose. There is a risk that site performance may be impacted by this.	This is the right option if you have treated a relatively static part of the website and want to see what uplift the winning variation continues to produce on an ongoing basis.
4	Show the winning variation to 95% of the audience, and let 5% of them still see the control	You can validate the win on an ongoing basis, and check for seasonal and perishability effects. Perishability is when an uplift gradually fades out, which can happen for many reasons. This option will be useful if you're likely to need external validation at a later time.	Unless you have huge volumes of traffic, you can't read much into a 5% segment. If regular changes are made to your website, this could cause the variation to 'break'.	

Knowledge base

Set up a knowledge base where results and insights are captured. This is a detailed record of every split test. It doesn't have to be anything fancy. We've seen it done effectively using a spreadsheet in the cloud, an internal wiki and bespoke software.

What's more important is that it's done and accessible throughout the organization. It is an inventory of hypotheses, insights and conclusions from all tests. It quickly becomes a huge institutional asset with benefits way beyond website optimization.

After each split-test result, update your knowledge base in the following areas:

- unique ID;
- Descriptive title
- Number of variations
- Audience or segments targeted
- Number of visitors per variation
- Hypothesis
- Area of website treated
- Source(s) of insight
- Start and end date of test
- Cost to create and run test
- Cost to implement test
- Screenshots of the control and variations
- Screenshot of test results
- Outline of the changes introduced
- Primary metric and uplift
- Statistical significance
- Annualized revenue impact on the business
- Key segments
- Key learnings
- next steps.

Test conclusion report

Send a summary of each concluded experiment to stakeholders. This can simply be an extension of the test-brief document. Below is a recommended structure:

- Overview:
  - Summary of insights leading to the test
  - Hypothesis
  - Result
- Details:
  - Screenshots of the control and variation(s)
  - Outline of the changes introduced
  - Pages or area of the site targeted
  - Audience or segments targeted
- Results:
  - Primary metric
  - Statistical significance
  - Number of visitors per variation
  - Test duration and dates
  - Screenshot of the results
  - Annualized revenue impact on the business
  - Key learnings
  - Next steps

There are many benefits in distributing the results to your colleagues, including:

- They can learn about the value of experimentation and see evidence triumphing over opinion.
- What you learn from the test results, which is effectively how your online customers behave, can be shared and often used in other forms of marketing, such as stores, catalogues or direct marketing campaigns.
- It shows you are open and willing to share what you have learnt about the behaviour of your website visitors – whether or not the test is positive.
- It's great to celebrate wins when your optimization efforts pay off.

Summary

An experiment enables you to test hypotheses and to establish causality. That makes it one of the best inputs for data-backed decision-making.

A/B tests are the most common type of online experiment. Half of your visitors see the control and the rest see the variation, which contains the changes being tested.

A primary metric is used to measure the impact of these newly introduced changes on a business KPI. In e-commerce optimization, the most typical KPIs are revenue per visitor, average order value and conversion rate.

As long as the difference between the control and the variation is the only change, any movement in the primary metric must have come about as a result of that change. This is how cause and effect can be determined.

In choosing a primary metric, try to get as close to revenue as possible. When the site does not have a lot of traffic, it may be difficult to use revenue goals. In this situation, it is better to opt for conversion rate instead.

It is equally important to track a broad range of secondary metrics as part of the test. The main purpose of these metrics is to give context to any observed change in the primary metric. It helps you to build a narrative about how user behaviour was altered and how that contributed to the result. All of this can help you understand where to focus efforts in the future.

Basic understanding of a few statistical principles will help you interpret test results. Avoid the common and misguided over-reliance on statistical significance and use other equally important data points to get a comprehensive and robust picture. In a business context, statistical significance should not be the primary consideration.

Once a test is concluded, you should conduct post-test analysis. This is an opportunity to tap unique insights from the test results. It is especially important to analyse negative test results to understand why the hypothesis has been refuted. It will bring you one step closer to a winning solution to the problem being addressed in the hypothesis.

An experiment is not finished until results and discoveries have been documented. Finally, have a process in place to make winning variations live on the site so that you can bank the gains.

Notes

1   Price, C (2015) *Vitamania: Our obsessive quest for nutritional perfection*, Penguin Press, London

2   Worrall, S (2017) [Accessed 7 August 2020] A nightmare disease haunted ships during Age of Discovery, *National Geographic* [Online] www.nationalgeographic.com/news/2017/01/scurvy-disease-discovery-jonathan-lamb/ (archived at https://perma.cc/7RGX-A8ZW)

3   Hughes R E (1975) James Lind and the cure of scurvy: An experimental approach, *Medical History*, 19 (4), pp 342–51

4   Tull, D and Hawkins, D (1984) *Marketing Research: Measurement and method*, 3rd edn, Macmillan, New York

5   McFarland, C (2012) *Experiment! Website conversion rate optimization with A/B and multivariate testing*, New Riders, Berkeley, CA

6   Bauer, K (2004) KPIs – the metrics that drive performance management, *Information Management*, 14 (9), p 63

7   Bladt, J and Filbin, B (2013) [Accessed 7 August 2020] Know the difference between your data and your metrics, *Harvard Business Review* [Online] https://hbr.org/2013/03/know-the-difference-between-yo (archived at https://perma.cc/B3KA-68MM)

8   Kohavi, R and Thomke, S (2017) The surprising power of online experiments, *Harvard Business Review*, September–October, pp 74–82

9   Weiss, C H (1997) *Evaluation: Methods for studying programs and policies*, 2nd edn, Prentice Hall, Upper Saddle River, NJ

10 Jewkes, H, Stuart, T and Aijaz, A (2018) *Understanding Experimentation Platforms*, O'Reilly Media, Farnham, Surrey

11 Kohavi, R and Thomke, S (2017) The surprising power of online experiments, *Harvard Business Review*, September–October, pp 74–82

12 Optimizely (nd) [Accessed 7 August 2020] Multivariate testing, *Optimizely* [Online] www.optimizely.com/optimization-glossary/multivariate-testing/ (archived at https://perma.cc/C6AV-CBZ4)

13 Gu, J (2018) Continuous experiment framework at Uber, Presentation at the Open Data Science Conference, California

14 Kohavi, R *et al* (2013) Online controlled experiments at large scale, in *KDD '13: Proceedings of the 19th ACM SIGKDD international conference on knowledge discovery and data mining*, ed R Ghani *et al*, pp 1168–76, ACM, New York

15 Mac, R (2016) [Accessed 7 August 2020] Jeff Bezos calls Amazon 'best place in the world to fail' in shareholder letter, *Forbes* [Online] www.forbes.com/sites/ryanmac/2016/04/05/jeff-bezos-calls-amazon-best-place-in-the-world-to-fail-in-shareholder-letter/#4a69c5587bc5 (archived at https://perma.cc/R8X7-5978)

16 Hoffman, R (2017) [Accessed 7 August 2020] Facebook's Mark Zuckerberg: 'Is this going to destroy the company? If not, let them test it', *Masters of Scale podcast* [Online] www.linkedin.com/pulse/going-destroy-company-let-them-test-reid-hoffman/ (archived at https://perma.cc/ESN3-92HX)

17 Conversation at Which Test Won, Berlin, October 2015

18 Lee, D (2015) [Accessed 7 August 2020] AB testing: Test big to find your strategic optimal, *LinkedIn* [Online] www.linkedin.com/pulse/ab-testing-test-big-find-your-strategic-optimal-daniel-analytics (archived at https://perma.cc/4XP7-N45E)

19 Kahneman, D (2011) *Thinking, Fast and Slow*, Farrar, Straus and Giroux, New York

20 Optimizely (2020) [Accessed 7 August 2020] How long to run an experiment, *Optimizely* [Online] https://help.optimizely.com/Analyze_Results/How_long_to_run_an_experiment (archived at https://perma.cc/4LB7-QJVC)

21 Gallo, A (2016) [Accessed 7 August 2020] A refresher on statistical significance, *Harvard Business Review* [Online] https://hbr.org/2016/02/a-refresher-on-statistical-significance (archived at https://perma.cc/9Y49-JZFK)

22 Goodson, M (2014) [Accessed 7 August 2020] Most winning A/B test results are illusory, *Qubit* [Online] www.qubit.com /research/most-winning-ab-test-results-are-illusory/ (archived at https://perma.cc/ET7V-2L2F)

23 Gallo, A (2016) A refresher on statistical significance, *Harvard Business Review* [Online] https://hbr.org/2016/02/a-refresher-on-statistical-significance (archived at https://perma.cc/9Y49-JZFK)

24 Moskwa, S (2012) Website testing and Google search, *Google Webmaster Central Blog* [Online] https://googlewebmastercentral.blogspot.co.uk/2012/08/website-testing-google-search.html (archived at https://perma.cc/7EV4-3NGS)

Personalization 10

Statistician's humour alert: You and I sit at the bar. In walks Bill Gates and joins us for a drink. Our average salary shoots up exponentially.

That is the problem with averages. The average user doesn't exist, and yet our websites are created for them. Even when doing optimization, many of the improvements may be targeting that non-existent average user.

Personalization fixes that by tailoring the experience, based on what we know about a visitor. It is the online equivalent of walking into a hotel, being recognized by the concierge and having the barman ask if you would like the 'usual'.

Adoption of personalization is increasing as tools and resources become more accessible. An impressive 90 per cent of organizations reported uplifts from personalization, with 58 per cent seeing more than 10 per cent in their KPIs.[1]

The ultimate personalized experience is truly unique to each visitor, but that's not the only approach, or even the best one. You may already have started putting together personas, as recommended in Chapter 5. That forms the perfect foundation for personalization, because it identifies the most valuable segments based on shared characteristics.

Personalization is not a substitute for optimization; it is part of it. That said, data requirements and resourcing needs are more demanding, and execution has proved to be tough for some. If you're just starting out with experimentation, personalization is perhaps a distraction. If you're already enjoying the fruits of an active testing roadmap, personalization is the next step in the evolution of your programme.

Data and segments

Data are the backbone of personalization campaigns. To give your visitors a tailored experience, you act on what you know about them. So before you can do any form of personalization, you have to put measures in place to start collecting relevant data. Useful types of information include:

- Declared or discovered preferences
- Demographics
- Behaviour
- Context.

Data allow you to split the audience into various **segments**. The data can be collected in a number of ways. On one side of the spectrum, it can be fully automated, with advanced algorithms constantly digging for segments. Specialist personalization platforms employ machine learning and predictive modelling to do that. It's more common, however, to create segments manually, especially in the beginning.

Some information can be obtained directly from the user through surveys, and through self-selection mechanisms on the site. We worked with a specialist retailer of baby goods, who had identified three broad personas – expectant parents, parents and gifters. Each one had different needs. First-time visitors to the site were presented with a box, giving them the option to self-select one of these segments. That information was then stored in a cookie against their profile, along with other data. Over time, the journey and experience of those users would become increasingly targeted and relevant.

Not all personalization data are linked directly to the individual; relevance also depends on their context. This includes information such as where they are (country, region, town, on the move, in the store etc), what device they are using, time of day and even the weather in their current location.

Where data are linked to an individual, they can be classified into *who* they are and *what* they do, as well as whether they are anonymous or identified:

Anonymous: The information stored is either cookie based or session based. For example, is it a new or returning visitor (who)? Which product or category have they visited (what)? Since the data are anonymous, this is useful for building segments.

Identified: This can be information they have given you, or that you know about them from other data sources. It might include their name and demographics (who), and previous purchase history (what). This can be used for hyper-personalized campaigns, tied back to the individual visitor.

Table 10.1 shows a framework for viewing different types of data for personalization.

Table 10.1 Framework for viewing different types of data for personalization.

	Anonymous	Identified
Visitor	Returning visitor On their 10th visit Has converted Referred by Facebook	Name Age Income Address
Behaviour	Viewed 'sofas' category Signed up for e-mail newsletter Logged in to view previous orders Abandoned their basket	Bought four times in the last 12 months, spending a total of £512 Shops both in-store and online Typically orders two items and returns one
Context	Mobile device user Browsing from Canada Cold weather, snowing	Interested in windsurfing

Research by Econsultancy revealed that organizations are using mainly the following data sources for personalization, in order of popularity:[2]

- Pages and categories visited
- Transaction data
- Products browsed
- Geographic information
- Demographics
- Customer engagement
- Acquisition channel
- Contextual (device, weather etc)
- RFM (recency, frequency, monetary)
- Preferences, interests, hobbies.

One of the best-known examples of personalization is a product recommendation engine (PRE). These are algorithms to generate suggestions when a visitor is looking at a product. They show up on the site as images and messages such as 'People who bought this also bought that'.

PREs can also be used to give the customer recommendations based on what they have bought in the past, to the extent of creating a personalized homepage for them based on previous buying behaviour.

You can develop a PRE yourself or use one of the many commercially available engines from companies like Rich Relevance, Attraqt, Peerius and Barilliance. In 2012 Amazon reported a 29 per cent increase in sales after introducing their own recommendation system.[3]

To offer deeply personalized experiences requires investment in a personalization platform that can drill down to the level of the individual, marrying its own behavioural data layer with contextual and external data sources.

These experiments tend to be harder and more expensive to implement.[4] Not only do they require sophisticated technology, but they also need considerable thought about the data layer's components and how the algorithm will work to ensure that the correct experiment is served to the right individual. Companies like Qubit, Optimizely, Monetate, Maxymiser and Insider GMP offer advanced personalization capabilities that make this more accessible.

However, there are other ways to do personalization, without the use of complex algorithms and expensive technology. Here are some examples.

Location targeting

Some sites have reported an uplift in sales by showing images of local landmarks on their homepage, such as the Eiffel Tower for users in Paris and the Statue of Liberty for users in New York.

Taking it one step further, it is possible to incorporate the weather in the visitor's location. Leading men's clothing retailer, Burton, used this technique on their homepage by showing a different image whenever the temperature dropped below a certain level (Figure 10.1). A selection of warm clothing would appear alongside the symbol for snow as well as the name of the town and the local temperature.

New visitor

Basic anonymous data powered an effective project for Boyle Sports. Anyone visiting the site for the first time was given a personalized offer to encourage them to create an account (Figure 10.2).

Figure 10.1 Personalizing the Burton homepage to show weather data to users in cold locations achieved an 11.6% increase in conversion rate

SOURCE Qubit

Figure 10.2 Boyle achieved a 5 per cent increase in new account creation by showing a personalized offer tailored specifically to new visitors

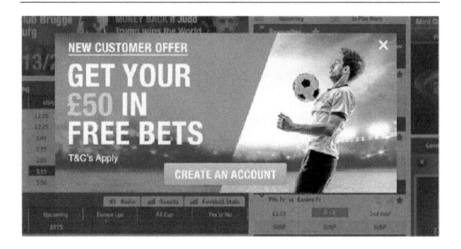

When to do personalization

Success stories like these mean that many companies are keen to do personalization, and there is now a host of technologies available to do this quickly and cheaply. Here are three indicators that tell you when to put personalization high up on your shortlist of opportunities:

1 **Research uncovers segmentation opportunities**: You discover that there are one or more valuable segments, or they seem to behave in a significantly different way, or they are underperforming.

2 **Experimentation reveals segmentation opportunities**: Post-test analysis reveals markedly different results among different visitor segments.

3 **Results from A/B tests start to plateau**: Optimization is geared towards increasing sales for all visitors, so in a sense you are always optimizing for the 'average visitor'. This one-size-fits-all approach does the job very well, but there may come a time when personalization is the logical next step.

Indicator 1: Research-led segmentation opportunities

Imagine you discover that a high proportion of first-time visitors are unfamiliar with your brand and have some concerns about your products. Many of these first-time visitors land on your homepage. From this insight you might hypothesize that you need to give new visitors a personalized experience to educate them and reassure them.

Your chosen creative solution is to show a video of your CEO talking about why they started the business, the customer problems they wanted to solve, and interviews with the committed customer service team. The video has been specifically made to allay fears and increase trust in your brand. This is an example of where you have discovered a personalization opportunity through research.

Indicator 2: Experiment-led segmentation opportunities

Post-test segmentation lets you examine how different segments reacted differently to changes introduced in a test. Integrate GA with the test to identify segments that might respond to a personalized approach.

For established enterprises a substantial segment could represent just 5 per cent of your revenue; if you are a start-up it could be as high as 75 per cent of your revenue.

To show you how this works, Table 10.2 shows test data around all visitors, not just a segment. Say the hypothesis was related to the product detail page, and the experiment tested a revised layout. Separately, you have calculated the size of your segments for both new and returning visitors and are aware that both are substantial.

The data show that while uplift in RPV as a whole was only 1 per cent, there is a marked difference in the two segments of new visitors and returning visitors. The revenue uplift from new visitors who saw the experiment was much higher than from returning visitors. Armed with this knowledge, it may well be worth creating a personalized experience just for new visitors.

Indicator 3: Revitalizing a plateauing testing programme

When you reach the point where optimizing for the average visitor is becoming less effective, personalization could get you good uplifts once again. As always, it's preferable that your experiments are grounded in objective research and analysis.

Designing a personalized experience

The creative possibilities are endless and the technology to make it happen gets cheaper and easier all the time. There are a huge number of solutions, so your biggest problem could be not the mechanics of personalization but deciding what unique experience to offer visitors.

Before you invest a lot of time and effort in a personalization programme, bring some clarity to your decision making by asking yourself these three questions:[5]

- Who will see the experiment?
- What are they going to see?
- Where in the journey will they see it?

Table 10.2 Example of results from a product detail page (PDP) experiment showing differences in behaviour for new and returning visitors

	TOTAL All visitors	SEGMENT New visitors	SEGMENT Returning visitors
Unique visitors	995,000	497,500	497,500
Total revenue	£6,209,950	£1,813,950	£4,396,000
RPV – control	£6.21	£3.31	£9.12
RPV – experiment	£6.27	£3.99	£8.55
Uplift in RPV	1%	21%	−6%

In the scenario above, where you have created a video especially for new visitors, the answer to the three W questions would be:

Q. Who is going to see this experiment?

A. New visitors

Q. What are they going to see?

A. A video about your business and your commitment to customer service

Q. Where in the visitor journey is this going to be shown?

A. At the beginning, on the homepage

If you can give clear, satisfactory answers to all three W questions, there is a good chance that a personalized experience will have a positive impact and improve your website.

Technical options for personalization

Of companies doing personalization, 61 per cent are using their A/B testing tools and only 27 per cent are using a specialist personalization platform.[6]

Existing experimentation platform: Choose from native segments in the platform, or create custom segments by planting cookies. For a high street retailer, we ran an experiment targeting visitors who had not purchased before. To create this segment, one of the things we did was to set up a campaign registering a visitor once they reached the transaction confirmation page, and let it run for a few months to build the audience. Those visitors were excluded from our test.

Many A/B testing platforms now offer some personalization capabilities, for example Convert, A/B Tasty and VWO.

Specialist personalization platform: For more sophisticated personalization, invest in a dedicated personalization platform. Vendors include Optimizely, Qubit, Maxymiser, Monetate, Adobe and Insider GMP. These platforms will also auto-suggest segments for which it may be profitable to run experiments.

Although it is possible to run exciting, highly personalized web experiences, they can be expensive, so have the right resources in place to ensure a return on investment. It may be a good idea to involve a specialist agency in the initial stages, as many vendors have noticed agencies consistently delivering superior results to internal teams.

Our recommended approach is to start with basic personalization, using your current A/B testing platform to build a business case for future investment.

Personalization vs A/B testing

There are big similarities between personalization and testing. Both test a hypothesis, which could be validated or refuted. Both involve two versions and, in both, each version is shown to a particular set of users. When the test period has ended, both are reported using a metric such as RPV.

Where personalization experiments are different is when they use a data layer to deliver a bespoke experience borne from information held on that individual. Advanced personalization campaigns are continuously served by the platform, whereas A/B tests are stopped and hard-coded into code base.

The majority of organizations (84 per cent) see an increase in conversion rates when they combine A/B testing with web personalization, according to various research reports.[7]

Summary

Personalization is a natural evolution of your website optimization strategy. It offers you the opportunity to make the web experience more relevant to segments of your visitors, even down to individual users.

The more relevant you make the experience, the better your website is able to convert visitors into customers.

Personalization relies on data to define segments. This includes what you know about who your website visitor is, how they behave on your site and their context. Those data can come from various sources, including information provided by the user as well as behavioural information stored in cookies. It's wise to start setting up data channels as early as possible to be ready for personalization in the future.

Many companies have seen healthy uplifts from running simple personalization experiments based on variables such as new and returning visitors, user location and visits to particular product categories. The opportunities can be discovered through research and post-test segmentation, as well as machine learning algorithms.

If you see the results from optimizing your website for all visitors starting to wane, consider using personalization to revitalize your website optimization efforts.

To design and launch a personalized experiment, answer three questions – who will see the experiment, what will they see and where in the customer journey will they see it.

You can use your A/B testing platform to serve simple personalization experiments. In fact, this is what the majority of companies are doing. Once you want to integrate customer information, external data and machine learning, look at investing in a personalization platform.

Notes

1 Sweet, K (2019) [Accessed 7 August 2020] Personalization trends: 2019 survey results [Blog], *Evergage* [Online] www.evergage.com/blog/personalization-trends-2019-survey-results/ (archived at https://perma.cc/2NFB-C83D)

2 Econsultancy (2018) [Accessed 7 August 2020] 2018 optimization report, *Econsultancy* [Online] https://econsultancy.com/reports/2018-optimization-report/ (archived at https://perma.cc/QU9L-SDVP)

3 Mangalindan, J (2012) [Accessed 7 August 2020] Amazon's recommendation secret, *Fortune* [Online] fortune.com/2012/07/30/amazons-recommendation-secret (archived at https://perma.cc/LQ9P-NB2A)

4 Econsultancy (2016) [Accessed 17 August 2020] Website personalisation buyer's guide, *Econsultancy* [Online] https://econsultancy.com/website-personalisation-buyer-s-guide-showcases-a-complex-technology-marketplace/ (archived at https://perma.cc/R9CE-YN8P)

5 Marketo (2016) [Accessed 7 August 2020] The 3 W's of personalization, *Marketo* [Online] www.marketo.com/slides-and-templates/the-3-ws-of-personalization/ (archived at https://perma.cc/3SU2-2CB9)

6 Evergage (2019) [Accessed 7 August 2020] Trends in personalization survey report, *Evergage* [Online] www.evergage.com/resources/ebooks/trends-in-personalization-survey-report/ (archived at https://perma.cc/UR97-XVLB)

7 Econsultancy (2015) *Conversion Rate Optimisation Report 2015*, Econsultancy, London

Optimizing the optimization

Kaizen is an approach to continuous improvement, where small changes are constantly introduced to improve quality and efficiency. You can apply the Kaizen mindset to optimize your own optimization process.

One way to assess overall performance of the optimization programme is compounded annual uplift. This takes into account the effect of all your winning tests over the course of a year. You can leverage big gains in your annual results by making small changes to three key levers. These power metrics hold the key to exponentially improve the ROI of your entire optimization programme.

The three power metrics are:

1 **Test velocity**: How many experiments launched in a given period, usually measured as tests per year.

2 **Win rate**: The number of tests that generated a positive uplift, expressed as a percentage of the total.

3 **Average uplift**: The average size of uplifts of winning tests, in terms of RPV or another KPI.

Here's how it works in practice. Let's say this is your baseline performance:

Test velocity over the last 12 months	24 tests
Win rate	29% (7 tests were positive, 17 negative)
Average uplift per test	5.9%

Compounding the effects of the seven positive tests, averaging 5.9 per cent RPV uplift, generates a total compounded site-wide uplift, over the last 12 months, of 49 per cent.

However, don't fall into the trap of thinking that this means a 49 per cent increase in sales. Extrapolating split-test results into predictable sales increases is notoriously difficult. For one, you have to calculate the impact of that uplift on site-wide revenue, covered in Chapters 7 and 9. We also saw that 95 per cent statistical significance means that 1 in 20 wins is a fluke.

A test measures short-term changes in user behaviour. Your test may run for a few weeks, reflecting a certain level of increase in RPV. After you have coded the experiment to be a permanent part of your site, the gain may not be exactly the same as that observed during the test. There are other factors at play, including long-term changes in customer behaviour, competitor actions and even the economy. This may cause fluctuations.

To be clear: you will have the benefit of a win after it's gone live on the site. What you can't be certain about is the precise effect on an ongoing basis, without running a holdback set. A holdback set is when you continue to serve the control to a small segment, typically 5 per cent, while 95 per cent of your visitor base will see the winning variation. You can only do this if you have huge volumes of traffic and a platform designed to work this way. Even then, the value in this practice is debatable (see Chapter 9 for more).

These factors don't take anything away from the fact that you are growing online revenue in demonstrable ways. Referring to the **ROI of experimentation programmes,** Harvard Business School Professor Stefan Thomke says: 'What's the cost of NOT doing it?'[1]

So the value of the compounded annual uplift lies in being a robust benchmark of your optimization programme. To improve it, focus on those three power metrics:

- Run more tests.
- Get more of those tests to win.
- Increase your average magnitude of lift per winning test.

Table 11.1 illustrates the impact of an increase of just 10 per cent in each area.

Table 11.1 Thirty-two per cent improvement in total uplift from just a 10 per cent increase in each of your three power metrics

	Benchmark	10% improvement
Test velocity in 12 months	24	26
Win rate	29%	32%
Average uplift	5.86%	6.44%
Compounded uplift over 12 months	49%	64%

You can see that those tiny changes in each area have had a profound effect on the compounded annual uplift, which has gone up from 49 per cent to 64 per cent. This is a healthy indicator that your optimization programme is benefiting from being optimized itself.

Below are some ways in which you can improve the three metrics.

Power metric 1: How to increase test velocity

The truth is, you have very little to no control over win rate and average uplift. However, velocity is almost completely within your control. Therefore, this should be your main lever. In terms of experimentation programme success metrics, this is the one that matters.

However, it does not mean simply increasing the number of tests for the sake of it, throwing spaghetti at the ceiling to see what sticks. Indulging in random acts of testing (RATs) to increase velocity will depress your win rate and average uplift, and ultimately reduce the ROI on your optimization programme.

Five strategies you can use, without sacrificing the quality of your testing programme, are:

1 Keep filling your bucket of new ideas from the pipeline, so there's never a time when you are searching around for a hypothesis to test. This can be done by continuously mining relevant data sources, for example running regular small batches of usability testing. New ideas and hypotheses also come from post-test analysis, covered in Chapter 9.

2 Work out your testing capacity and how many testing slots you have on your website. As explained in Chapter 7, these may include:

  o Homepage
  o Category page
  o Product listing page (PLP)
  o Product detail page (PDP)
  o Search results page
  o Basket page
  o Checkout pages
  o Site-wide (header, navigation etc).

Think of your tests like spaces in a car park. If you have a test running on one area, that is one of your car park spaces occupied. You won't be able to run another test on this area until the first one has been declared.

3 For each testing slot, have one waiting in the wings, queued up and ready to go. To minimize the risk of cross-contamination, avoid running concurrent tests that might have an effect on each other.

4 Executing complex tests takes time and money. At the same time, bolder tests are more likely to result in big swings that are easier to detect. Try to find a balance between the two on your roadmap. If there are already tests in progress, leaving your developer with spare capacity, it's time to tackle something with more complexity.

5 Run your tests only for the required amount of time. Don't extend test duration without good reason. If you leave them running longer than necessary, you are occupying one of your car parking spaces, and reducing the efficiency of your optimization programme. As discussed in Chapter 9, the industry standard 95 per cent statistical significance is not an absolute requirement. Watch the other signals and, if necessary, settle on a lower level in exchange for moving faster.

Calculate in advance how long a test should run, adjusting the minimum detectable effect (MDE) as explained in Chapters 7 and 9. Increasing the MDE will reduce the length of time required to reach significance. For example, if an MDE of 3 per cent will take too long, increase it to 5 per cent or higher. This means you won't detect results that are less than 5 per cent and means you can make the best use of your available traffic and testing slots.

Power metric 2: How to increase your win rate

If 100 per cent of your split tests are winning, you either had a very poor website to begin with, or you are misinterpreting test results and declaring false positives. False positives look like wins, but on closer inspection there is unlikely to be any real change to visitor behaviour. In fact, sometimes it could even have a have a damaging impact on sales.

Likewise, if only a tiny percentage of your tests are beating the control, then you also have a problem. Don't obsess over what that number should be. The most important thing is to get your overall win rate increasing from its baseline.

The fact is, every test has a 50/50 chance of winning or losing. In a famous letter to Amazon shareholders, Jeff Bezos wrote 'if you know in advance that it's going to work, it's not an experiment'.[2]

That said, here are approaches to increase your chances of seeing a higher win rate:

1 Make sure your hypothesis development is informed by data and research, so that you avoid RATs.

2 Prioritize your hypotheses diligently – if you prioritize dumb tests, then however good your creative execution is, win rate will be less than you could have achieved.

3 Have more than one variation per test – this increases the number of false positives, but it's a small price to pay for increasing discovery rate, quality of insights and more real wins too. The only caveat is that it will extend test duration, so use this tactic wisely if you have enough traffic.

To avoid any misunderstanding, a higher velocity is more important than a higher win rate. If for no other reason, you have more control over the number of tests.

Power metric 3: How to increase your average uplift

You can't predict the outcome of an experiment, let alone the potential size of uplift. By observing these best practices, you can give yourself the best chance:

1 Test bolder ideas. Moving the needle is easier when you test noticeable changes. Remember, it can swing both ways – up or down. It also requires more development time. That doesn't matter. One win can pay for all those losses, as we explained in Chapter 9.

2 Review the results from previous tests. This will help you to identify areas where you are consistently getting high-impact results, or areas with significant potential.

3 Refine your approach to prioritization. Examine which tests produced healthy uplifts and see if there are any patterns. Also look at tests that didn't produce a positive result and consider what you can learn about how this should shape your prioritization.

Summary

The process of optimization is itself a target for optimization. You can improve your experimentation programme exponentially by focusing on three key metrics. An increase in any one of these areas will improve your annual compounded uplift:

1 Test velocity – the number of tests you run over the period, usually a year

2 Win rate – the number of tests that show a positive uplift

3 Average uplift

The one metric that matters is velocity, because it is the one most within your control. Ensure that you are testing on as many areas of the website as possible and that you have a new test ready to go as soon as each split test is declared. Don't extend the run of a test in the hope of it 'turning around'. The industry standard 95 per cent statistical significance is not an absolute requirement, so you may accept a lower level in exchange for moving faster.

You have very little to no control over win rate and average uplift, but best practices will improve your chances. Most of them are rooted in diligent research, analysis and prioritization, as well as careful planning of logistics.

An increase in all three will optimize your optimization exponentially. This is not a measure of how much your revenue will increase, but a robust way to benchmark the fundamental effectiveness of your CRO programme.

Notes

1 Optimizely (2018) [Accessed 7 August 2020] Optimizely partner story: HBS Professor Stefan Thomke on Experimentation [Video interview], *YouTube* [Online] https://youtu.be/5sklu7J5r90 (archived at https://perma.cc/L5ZP-UGZQ)

2 Bezos, J (1997) [Accessed 7 August 2020] Amazon.com letter to shareholders, *US Securities and Exchange Commission* [Online] www.sec.gov/Archives/edgar/data/1018724/000119312516530910/d168744dex991.htm (archived at https://perma.cc/4M4X-UNHN)

Optimization people and culture 12

This book is intended as a guide for anyone wanting to do website optimization themselves.

It can also be used if you want to know more about the nuts and bolts of website optimization, so that you can understand better what your team does and how to help them deliver the best results.

How to find, select and motivate in-house optimizers

An in-house website optimization champion may need to fulfil a number of roles:

1 researcher – using a variety of data sources to build a rich picture of visitors and customers

2 data analyst – analysing data from the website, and interpreting the results of split tests

3 project manager – managing a team of specialists; utilizing a structured data-driven process as well as engaging with stakeholders and presenting results

Skills and traits of talented optimizers

A key skill these people have is the ability to switch comfortably between left- and right-brain thinking (Figure 12.1).

Figure 12.1   Left- and right-brain thinking

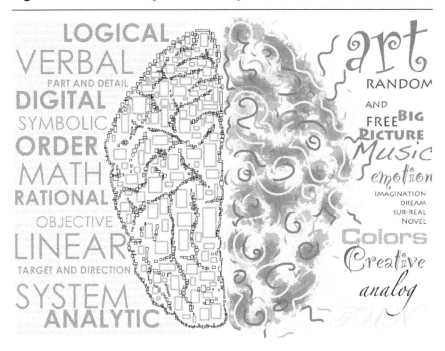

Left-brain thinking

Left-brain thinking is concerned with logic, rationality and working with numbers. Analytical skills are a huge part of what an optimizer needs to have in their toolkit. For a recent client, one of our optimizers:

- analysed 20 million Google Analytics and IBM Digital Analytics sessions;

- observed website visitors for 20+ hours during usability testing;

- examined the click pattern from 175,000 sessions using heatmaps, scroll maps, confetti maps and others;

- read and analysed 20,000 survey responses;

- performed 443 navigation tasks using specialized tools;

- read numerous live chat transcripts;

- conducted five store visits, interviewing store managers and shop floor staff;

- interviewed the customer service team and the live chat operators.

To cope with this amount of data, an optimizer needs advanced information processing and number-crunching skills. The process of prioritizing large numbers of possible website improvements to create an optimization plan requires focus and independent thought. To accurately interpret a completed test, the optimizer needs both analytics skills and a thorough grounding in statistics.

Right-brain thinking

Contrast this attention to detail with the thought processes dominant in right-brain thinking.

First is the ability to build relationships with the broader internal team (developers, copywriters, managers, co-workers, business leaders, etc). They also need to be able to quickly establish rapport and show empathy with people when using research methods like moderated usability testing. This should be allied with creative skills; coming up with imaginative but relevant solutions to the identified opportunities. It's one thing to identify a conversion killer, but it takes a leap of imagination to understand how to translate this problem into a new, improved version:

- What will the wireframe look like?
- What copy is required?
- How will someone navigate this new page?

These are examples of creative questions the optimizer will deal with. Understanding the fundamentals of consumer psychology, covered in Chapter 13, plays an important part here.

Presenting the results of research and tests also requires creativity; to put oneself in the position of your audience and tailor the presentation to their needs. Here the focus is on condensing vast amounts of research into a few powerful ideas that have been tested scientifically, and then presenting the results in non-technical language that illuminates the insight gained.

To bring left- and right-brain thinking together, an effective optimizer has to be obsessed with detail and familiar with the minutiae of the visitor experience, while at the same time holding onto the bigger picture. They understand that buying online is a complex process involving your offer and how it's positioned in the market, user experience, persuasion techniques and a number of psychological factors.

Other traits include a passion for website optimization, zealot-like determination to be continually improving and a drive to translate optimization into hard cash for the business. Overwhelmingly, talented optimizers are both curious and humble; they know what they don't know and are always looking to learn more.

Being an attractive employer

The competition for optimizers is intense, so think about this question, which your ideal candidate will be asking him or herself: 'Given the competition for my talents, why would I join your company?'

If this sounds similar to the principles of creating a strong value proposition that we discussed in Chapter 5, then you're right. The technique works just as well for recruiting your team as it does for recruiting customers.

Find out what optimizers are looking for in an employer. Reach out to communities in relevant LinkedIn groups and the blogosphere. Study how other companies looking for the same sort of person are defining their value proposition. Is yours clear and compelling?

Ask your existing team why they enjoy working for your business, and use that in your job ad. Being specific when communicating your value proposition adds credibility. For example, instead of 'We are committed to your professional development', consider: 'Last year each member of our team received on average 112 hours of training, that's nearly 4 weeks of solid investment in you – we are committed to your development.'

Remote working

Chances are that your ideal optimizer is not living nearby. They may be located in a different country, a different time zone even. If you want to employ the best, consider the adaptations you might need to make – technology, team and processes – to allow a remote worker to be an effective team player. If your setup supports this way of working, better to get the most talented optimizer to work for you and make the necessary adjustments than to choose someone on the basis of their proximity.

Finding the right person

Simply advertising the role might not attract enough experienced individuals. Another option is to approach people directly. Website optimization covers many disciplines and talented optimizers are always soaking up new knowledge and sharing what they have learnt, so look out for people who are active in public forums, commenting and sharing their knowledge.

- Many conversion agencies publish blogs with an active comments section – eg ConversionXL, Widerfunnel, Unbounce, Conversion Sciences, Occam's Razor, Get Elastic and Marketing Experiments. Testing platform providers – Qubit, Maxymiser, Monetate, Optimizely, Convert, VWO and Adobe – provide similar forums.
- LinkedIn groups for CRO and website optimization.
- Slack channel on CRO/website optimization.

Before approaching candidates, create a survey for interested individuals to complete as part of the selection process. Questions could include:

- Please provide 2–3 examples of how you have created impressive results for online businesses.
- Tell us about your experience of:
  - direct response marketing and copywriting;
  - designing/wireframing high-converting webpages.
- Tell us about the level of experience (extensive, some or none) you have with the tools used in our organization: eg analytics packages, testing platforms, voice-of-customer tools, statistics, JavaScript and facilitation of usability sessions.

To form a richer picture about a candidate, we set up a voicemail account and ask candidates to phone in after they have completed the survey. For us, this part of the process is as important as their responses to the survey. On the voicemail the prospective candidates are asked a number of questions:

1 Why are you applying for this role?

2 What has been your greatest achievement to date?

3 Tell us about a time when you overcame a difficulty; what was it and how did you overcome it?

Listening to a candidate's tone of voice, and how they handle these questions with little time to prepare, will tell you a lot about them.

Having defined your value proposition, and set up your survey and voicemail account, you can now start approaching possible candidates. Create a shortlist of those who responded to your contact, completed your survey and left you a voicemail. The next stage is to hold individual interviews and talk through the answers they gave in their survey response.

Focus particularly on the metrics that applicants are using to explain the results they have created – is this site-wide revenue uplift, or is it just progression to the next step in the customer journey, reducing bounce rate on a landing page or increasing e-mail sign-up rates? We have had some experience of applicants exaggerating the significance of the results they have created.

If relevant, explore how a remote working environment could fit in with your business. What experience do they have of building relationships remotely? What challenges do they face working remotely? Could they come and spend a week in the office, at least initially?

Try to discover what effort they make to stay up to date; what was the last new tool or research technique they used? Do they have a clear sense of what they don't know, and what plans have they got to address this?

If you feel confident about their track record, how they would work with you and their commitment to keeping at the top of their game, the next stage is a practical test. We ask candidates to review a particular web page. Along with it we provide some basic data. We ask them to come up with a wireframe, explain their thinking and the data on which they have based these recommendations.

You can develop your own criteria for evaluating applications, but we pay particular attention to:

- Demonstration of analytical thinking

- The logic of their arguments

- Ability to communicate clearly

Then hold a group interview with individuals who make the practical test stage. We have done this successfully on Google Hangouts, with four interviewers and a similar number of candidates. It can be telling to see how candidates react to a competitive selection process.

How to keep your in-house optimizer motivated

For a single in-house optimizer, the job could be lonely and isolating, with no one to bat around ideas and refine hypotheses. At the same time, talented optimizers value autonomy. Motivation and retention require you to manage their need for community and independence simultaneously. They also have an insatiable thirst for knowledge, and knowing what they are doing is making a difference to the bottom line. To keep them motivated, ensure there are processes in place that allow them to:

- spend time acquiring knowledge and being part of the conversion community;

- go on training courses, subscribe to paid-for courses and attend events;
- present your company's results at conferences and spark debate and interaction with their peers;
- work flexibly – from home, from remote locations and from the office when the need is there;
- allocate a proportion of their time to work on their own project, as companies like 3M and Google do.

Having spoken to many optimizers, as well as those who recruit for these roles, one of the most common criticisms of employers is that firms do not fully understand what optimization is and what it can do for the business. Consequently, optimizers are directed to work on parts of the site where there is little evidence of it being a real opportunity. Or there is a lack of support for testing controversial areas where an opportunity has been identified. Before hiring an optimizer, you and your management should agree on the scope of the role.

Obstacles to a culture of optimization

Finding and motivating a talented optimizer is one factor in the success of your programme; another is to build and reinforce a culture of optimization. Some of the benefits of having a culture of optimization:

- You grow your business more quickly.
- You spend less time in endless internal debates.
- You learn continuously.
- You get focused on what really matters.
- Your developers only work on ideas that have been validated.

A number of obstacles can prevent your organization from becoming data driven and having an optimization mindset, which should be tackled first.[1] In this section we'll examine cognitive biases that can impact the individual, particularly your optimizer, as well the obstacles your organization might face in terms of embedding an optimization culture.

Obstacles faced by individuals

When we are making judgements and decisions about the world around us, we like to think that we are objective and logical. Unfortunately, the reality is that our judgements and decisions are often impaired by errors and influenced by a wide variety of biases. These are called cognitive biases, and can have a detrimental impact on an optimization process reliant on making judgements on huge quantities of data. By being aware of them, you have a better chance of reducing their impact. Here are 11 biases we believe are most relevant to website optimization:

- **Belief bias** – We often accept invalid data to support a judgement based on our own beliefs. Believing something to be the case doesn't make it true. As much as possible, be aware of the role of your own beliefs in reaching a decision.

- **Certainty bias** – In a perfectly rational world, we would value equally a change of probability going from 0 per cent to 10 per cent as we would from, say, 45 per cent to 55 per cent. In fact we don't; we value certainty differently, depending on the starting point. This often results in us being more risk averse as we experience more disquiet as certainty diminishes, even if the less probable situation could benefit us more.

- **Confirmation bias** – Sometimes one theory, or hypothesis, dominates our thoughts so strongly that it becomes a preconception, so much so that we don't even realize there are alternatives – or even look for them. This means we could easily overlook data or conclusions that fly in the face of this preconception.

- **Congruence bias** – Though similar to confirmation bias, congruence bias is concerned with the risk in optimization that we only split test one possible hypothesis, when in fact there are other possible hypotheses that may have been more valid and worthy of testing.

- **Dunning–Kruger bias** – This is where people who are 'incompetent' are more likely to be confident in their actions because they don't know what they don't know. When recruiting for an optimizer, ask them about areas where they feel less competent and be cautious of people who claim expertise in every area.

- **Framing bias** – We will often react to choice based on whether the outcome has been presented or 'framed' as a loss or a gain. Even small changes to how these outcomes are framed can have a profound impact on the choices we make and the risk we will tolerate.

- **Fundamental attribution error (FAE)** – This is where we give undue impor-tance to people's character and intention, rather than unconnected external factors. For example, if your checkout is causing users frustration, some might blame their 'stupidity' rather than accept how difficult the site is to use.

- **Hindsight bias** – Sometimes called the 'knew it all along' effect, this is the tendency to see an event, after it has occurred, as predictable. This bias can often be seen in the analysis of medical experiments, judicial systems and historians writing about past events. For website optimization, this might mean that positive tests are less carefully scrutinized than negative tests, because the result, in 'hindsight', was predictable and therefore less worthy of analysis and challenge.

- **Information bias** – Sometimes we continue to collect more and more in-formation on the basis that more is better, and the additional data will lead to a more informed decision. When you are investing more time in collecting larger data sets, be clear as to exactly what question you are trying to answer and whether these new data will help you achieve this.

- **Narrative fallacy** – A common tendency many of us have is to try to ex-plain why something has occurred; we seek to provide a 'logical' link between two facts. Explanations bind facts together, and yet this explana-tion may be incorrect. For example, in the case of a split test, the only datum that is known is the split-test result; providing a narrative is just conjecture.

- **Self-serving bias** – This tendency arises out of a need to bolster our self-esteem by claiming 'success' to be down to our own qualities or traits, With 'failure' we are more likely to blame this on external factors. To work effectively in website optimization, divorce yourself from your need for self-esteem and avoid being emotionally invested in the results of your split tests.

Whenever we are presented with information, we are prone to cognitive bias – and more than one at a time. Think about how you can counter these biases. Remember data are neutral, but it is the way we process information that can have a significant impact on the validity of our decisions.

Obstacles faced by organizations

Three of the most powerful obstacles you may face in embedding a culture of optimization in your organization include:

1 the impact of a top-down organizational hierarchy;

2 internal competition;

3 lack of understanding about data and statistics and reliance on gut instinct.

Top-down organizational hierarchies

As senior managers climb the organizational hierarchy, they tend to spend more time managing those with direct contact with the customer, and less time with customers themselves. While power rests with the manager, insight about the customer's needs and motivations are further down the organization. Rigid organizational hierarchies, where there is little sharing of knowledge between those leading the business and those interacting with customers, represents an obstacle to optimization. Decisions about the way to treat customers can be disconnected from what customers need. We have seen e-commerce teams 'hide' controversial tests from the rest of the organization in case senior managers, unfamiliar with the reasons behind the test, choose to stop the test prematurely.

Internal competition

Competition can arise between departments when objectives, measures and incentives do not align. This lack of alignment can turn friends into foes as well as undermine efforts to collaborate.[2] Often this lack of cooperation goes hand in hand with departments not sharing valuable information with others. As an agency we have seen many departmental battles over what should appear on the homepage, each department determined to fight for their right for equal prominence. We have also seen store managers reluctant to direct in-store customers to the website as this online purchase wouldn't be reflected in store sales.

Lack of understanding about data and statistics

As more organizations aspire to be 'data driven' and the volume of available data increases exponentially, research indicates that managers' data literacy has not kept pace.[3] Even when they believe they are making decisions based on data, the interpretation is flawed. When reviewing new clients' previous test results, we often find that wins have been declared prematurely. In some cases, a senior manager had intervened and stopped the test, based on his or her opinion that the test had produced a 'good result'.

Successful optimization cultures

Successful optimization cultures share seven things in common:[4]

1 **Sharing culture – are shared, and shared widely,** rather than being 'owned' by departments. Without a commitment to data-sharing practices, data hoarding results, a richer picture fails to be grasped and opportunities are missed.

2 **Broad data literacy** – In order for a data-informed culture to flourish, senior managers need training to understand the nuances, terminology and inferences of statistical analysis. There are courses available on Coursera, Udacity, Khan Academy and others.

3 **Goals-first culture** – Optimization is for a purpose, an overarching mission. A strategic vision allows the optimization process to work towards this goal.

4 **Inquisitive, questioning culture** – Frank and open discussion about the data, rather than the personalities or layers of hierarchies involved, allows a far more scientific evaluation of the experiments and the results. This experimentation mindset can help to eliminate the egos often present in organizational improvement projects.

5 **Iterative, learning culture** – Using the language of 'learning' rather than 'failure' or 'success' allows you to focus on what you can learn from each experiment, and to continue the process of iterating and optimizing.

6 **Anti-HIPPO culture** – Senior managers who continue to adopt a decision-making style that is based on their experience, preconceived notions and their gut, without regard to the available data, will undermine successful data-informed cultures.

7 **Data leadership** – Successful businesses 'compete on analytics' and leaders set an example in their use and promotion of data-informed decision making. This means providing the tools and training, but most importantly, recruiting other senior managers through celebrating wins – however small they may appear at first.

CASE STUDY   Culture of optimization

This 350-year-old bank, which serves over 24 million customers across the globe, adopted a unique approach to how they embedded a culture of optimization. Each conversion manager is responsible for one of the 38 key customer journeys important to the bank. The bank labelled these conversion managers as 'Superstar DJs'. Weekly updates to the organization, as well as announcements of wins and learnings, were peppered with dodgy puns and suggested soundtracks.

The optimization team went on roadshows to different bank locations to talk about their successes, wearing 'on tour' t-shirts, complete with venues and dates – just like the real thing. To promote competitions between the 'DJs', a 'chart' was published showing the best-performing split test. Stakeholders from outside the team were 'given' tests as their own, with access to the testing platform so they could easily monitor their performance. Senior managers, from outside the digital and analytics team, were able to grasp the importance of a testing culture to the bank – and get the chance to briefly join the troop of Superstar DJs.

'The way you are bringing this to life is nothing short of brilliant', one senior manager commented.

Embedding an optimization culture is about recognizing the obstacles that affect the individual, such as cognitive biases, as well as the organization – the negative impact of hierarchies, internal competition and lack of understanding about data. This case study shows how such an optimization culture can be both exciting and creative.

When to outsource

Sometimes it is not possible to recruit an in-house optimizer because of obstacles such as headcount budget, inflexibility about remote working or inability to find the right candidate. An external resource or agency can help in a number of different ways:

- You are growing rapidly, website traffic is growing quickly and you realize you have the financial resources but not the time to invest in optimization. A third party can start working alongside you to turn this burgeoning traffic into correspondingly higher online sales. Also, high-growth companies are often focused on growth and may overlook some conversion issues that no one else has had time to address.

- Your digital team is young and, although enthusiastic, is inexperienced with website optimization. This might be the time to consider an agency that will help you get off to a flying start, and over time transfer knowledge to your team as they see how the agency does what it does. Make sure the agency you choose has experience of knowledge transfer and is able to provide mentoring or coaching services as your need for direct assistance starts to taper. Doing the work well is not the same as teaching and mentoring others to do it equally well.

- You might have been optimizing your website for quite some time, and starting to see your results plateau. This is the time to engage an agency that can provide a fresh perspective and develop a completely new roadmap, so have a number of new sets of optimization opportunities on which your in-house team can focus.

- You may be expanding into new, international territories, where the culture is different and the needs of these website visitors and customers will not match those from your domestic market. Many companies have simply localized their current website into an international version, without fully understanding the differences between cultures and approaches to online buying. Agencies with international optimization experience would be a good use of resources in leveraging the investment you are making in these new markets.

- Likewise, if you are creating a new customer journey, as in creating a new range of products or services, then it makes sense to bring in an agency to do the research as to how a new set of visitors might respond to your new merchandise or services.

- Finally, if you are based in a rural location, it is going to be challenging to find sufficiently experienced talent on your doorstep. In this case, bringing in an agency on a monthly retainer basis is the best opportunity for getting an optimization programme in place.

Summary

Talented optimizers are skilled at using both left-brain (analytical and data-driven) and right-brain (creative and empathetic) thinking styles. They are marked out with traits such as humility, curiosity, persuasiveness, being process oriented and detail obsessed. As people, they are determined, passionate and have a thorough grounding in consumer psychology and web technologies. The competition for their talent is, unsurprisingly, intense.

To compete for this talent, focus your attention on what makes you stand out as an employer. Use online forums to discover what it takes to be an employer for which optimizers want to work. Compare the proposition offered by other companies looking for this resource and be specific as to why you would be an ideal fit. Use a structured selection process to evaluate the claims made by your candidates, as well as offer the chance to show how they would optimize a real site.

Being data driven and embedding a culture of optimization poses challenges for both individuals and organizations. Cognitive biases can sway an individual's understanding of what the data really are communicating. Organizations are often faced with issues around top-down hierarchies, internal competition and a lack of data literacy at senior level. We proposed a seven-point model of a successful optimization culture, and showed how an international bank repositioned optimization team members as Superstar DJs.

Finally, there may be times when it makes sense to outsource optimization to a third party. This may be because the business is in a high-growth phase, you are based in a talent-starved location, you have an inexperienced optimization team, your current results have started to plateau or you may be expanding into a new territory or building new customer journeys.

Notes

1 Lewin, K (1964) *Field Theory in Social Science: Selected theoretical papers*, Harper & Row, Washington, DC

2 Pfeffer, J and Sutton, R (2000) *The Knowing–Doing Gap: How smart companies turn knowledge into action*, Harvard Business Press, Boston, MA

3 Croll, A and Yoskovitz, B (2012) *Lean Analytics*, O'Reilly, Sebastopol, CA

4 Anderson, C (2015) *Creating a Data-Driven Organization*, O'Reilly, Sebastopol, CA

The science of 13
buying

Joe Girard, in a wonderful rags-to-riches tale, became the world's greatest salesperson against all odds. The title was officially bestowed on him by the *Guinness Book of World Records* for selling more cars than anyone else.[1]

After retiring from car sales, he became a prolific writer and shared his mainly self-taught wisdom. From reading his books, it's evident that he understood – and applied in practice – fundamental principles of the science of buying, despite having no formal education.

He would construct a **sales conversation**, not around the product, but around the wants and needs of the customer.

In our own work with clients, we like to spend time with their call centre agents (more on this in Chapter 5). Analysing the sales scripts of successful agents can be revealing for many reasons, but one stands out. The top salespeople would never use the language, phrases and words plastered on their company's website.

This disconnect happens because the site is viewed through the wrong lens – pages, user interface, navigation, design elements, copy, images and so on. In website optimization, those things become the focus, so they optimize pages and funnels.

But your site can be viewed through a different lens – a sales agent, conducting sales conversations with prospects. Your website visitors don't care much about the site UI and all the rest, as long as it works. They care about themselves, their needs and whether you can help them without ripping them off.

In the process, they may have questions about the product, concerns about the transaction, anxieties about the delivery process and other thoughts running through their mind. In a store, they would pick up an item from the shelf, feel the weight, read the description on the box and ask the assistant a few questions. Online, your website has to do all of that. Seen through that lens, website optimization looks very different.

Conversion rate is black and white. A user has either purchased, or not. The reality is not that clear-cut. Half-brewed decisions and 'almost bought' moments are strewn along the way; hurdles and interruptions trip the buying brain before making that final decision. To improve your conversion rate, you have to knock down these brain hurdles, which means aligning your website with the way the buying brain works.

That is the purpose of this chapter.

Why do people buy?

The terms 'shopping' and 'buying' are used interchangeably in everyday conversation, but consumer psychologists make a distinction between the two.

Shopping refers to the entire process of going to the store, and its online equivalent – but this doesn't always lead to buying. In fact, 'going shopping' is one of the world's most popular leisure activities, enjoyed for its own sake, regardless of whether anything is purchased.[2] People love shopping so much that it's sometimes known as retail therapy, and studies have shown that shopping genuinely does help lift the spirits.

One might think that consuming – that is, using the things that we buy – is what drives us to make a purchase. In reality it's much more complex than that. Author of *Why We Buy* Paco Underhill once said, 'If we went into stores only when we needed to buy something, and if once there we bought only what we needed, the economy would collapse – boom.'[3] In other words, we may shop in order to buy stuff, but we shop for many other reasons too.

Don't think this is limited to shopping malls and the high street. From our own research done on behalf of many retailers, we have seen that a large portion of mobile phone shopping takes place purely because people are trying to find diversion from everyday tasks such as cooking dinner and even having work meetings.

What this means for optimization is that your site is likely to have far more visitors who are there to browse than buy. Your objective is to turn more of them into buyers, more frequently, and get them to spend more when they do buy. Understanding the influences that make them purchase during their shopping activity is therefore a central piece in the puzzle.

What makes people buy?

So we know that people shop for different reasons, and that shopping does not always lead to buying. Then what makes them buy?

Often, it is not what it appears to be on the surface; in other words, their goal is not directly related to consuming the purchased product.[4] Someone doesn't buy slimming tablets because they want to be taking more pills. Nor even is it to lose weight. No, their goal is seated far deeper – to feel better about themselves.

It's the difference between what you are selling and what your customer is buying. A retailer of outdoor clothing for kids may be selling waterproof coats, but what the mum is buying is the rosy-cheeked smile of her child playing happily in the rain.

Later on in the process, if you have identified that core goal you will be able to adjust the sales messages to resonate with your prospective customer. This is about more than just content; it covers every touch point between your 'online sales team' (your website) and the visitor.

One of our clients is a high-end furniture retailer. When we spoke to their customers about why they bought from this company, no one really mentioned the quality of workmanship, the dovetail joints or the flawless paint finishes. It turns out the reason they bought was because it made them feel special. 'My guests always comment on things I buy from here,' a happy customer said. Their core goal was purely emotional, to be admired for their uniquely stylish taste.

That's why it's so important in e-commerce optimization to be aware of the true reasons why your customers buy and how the decision-making process works. In the situation above, it would be easy to fall into the trap of thinking that people would be keen to own these particular homewares for the sake of practical utility. That would lead you to follow a feature-driven hard-sell approach, which would miss out on so many opportunities to get your site performing to its full potential.

Are you selling to 5 per cent of the brain?

Our brains have two different modes of processing information, known as System 1 (the ancient, unconscious brain) and System 2 (the modern, conscious brain).

One of the best explanations of this is by Nobel Prize winner Daniel Kahneman in his book, *Thinking, Fast and Slow*.[5] He colourfully describes how when we buy anything, these two systems can create internal tension.

Every thought enters the brain via the subconscious System 1, which deals with things automatically and rapidly. Thus the overwhelming majority of thoughts, including purchase decisions, are processed subconsciously. It happens on autopilot, in a flash.

Only about 5 per cent of our decisions and behaviours are escalated to the rational and analytical System 2. This implies that 95 per cent of the time, your customers have made their buying decision before they're even aware of it. When conscious thinking takes over, everything gets more complex and nailing a decision becomes difficult. Clearly this is something you want to avoid, because it makes people less likely to buy.

If you understand how System 1 and System 2 work, you can use this information to your advantage. At every stage of the optimization process, remember that by the time the conscious mind gets involved, the decision has already been made.[6] When you create treatments to test, check if they appeal to System 1 thinking. By the time System 2 thinking kicks in, its job is to justify the purchase, rather than putting up intellectual barriers that rationalize against buying.

You will almost certainly have lots of System 2 reasons already to hand as to why your customers should buy from you. The optimization process will help you uncover 'System 1' motivations that you can incorporate into your website.

Roger Dooley, a world-leading neuroscientist who specializes in retail, strongly advocates leading with content that appeals to System 1's emotional and subconscious needs. That means presenting benefits rather than features. The difference is that features are what a product is or does, while benefits are what it does for the user. Features describe what you are selling – benefits are what the user is really buying.

Sales messages that are dominated by prices, discounts and features tend to tip the balance towards System 2 brain activity.

There is also a difference between the benefit *per se* and how it is dramatized creatively. Table 13.1 lists three examples to illustrate this.

One retailer that does this well is Zappos, the online shoe store. They use large images on the product detail pages, which trigger an emotional response from System 1. Factual data are placed behind a link, where System 2 can access it to rationalize the purchase decision, but where it's less likely to get in the way of that initial decision.[7]

Six principles of influence

One of the best-known experts on persuasive psychology is Dr Robert Cialdini, author of the chart-topping book, *Influence: The psychology of*

Table 13.1 The difference between features and benefits, and how it could be expressed

Feature	Benefit	Creative expression
A gadget that grips the lid of a jar to give extra leverage to remove it	Tight jar lids can be removed more easily even by people with a weak grip	Open tight jars in a flash
Spanish learning course	Speaking Spanish quickly and easily	Learn Spanish in your sleep
A doormat that collects dirt from shoes	Floors stay cleaner for longer	Life's too short to mop floors

persuasion. Having studied how to appeal to the subconscious over decades, he offers six ways of getting people 'to say "yes" without thinking first'.[8]

Reciprocation

A client of ours discovered one of their most effective customer acquisition methods with a very interesting experiment. They sent out printed catalogues, half of which included a unique free gift. The response rate to those catalogues, with the free gift, is 3 × 4 higher than the standard package.

Imagine trekking through London's shopping district. It's cold, and you're tired from walking around. A store in Regent Street catches your attention. On arrival, the assistant offers you a cup of delicious warm herbal tea. An innocent, generous gesture? Maybe, but there's more to it. That cup is likely to create a feeling of indebtedness towards the shop assistant, easily settled by, well, buying something. This is because the rule of reciprocation asserts that any favour or gift has to be returned. The free unexpected gift is also used by some e-commerce retailers.

The rule of reciprocation is so fundamental to the human make-up that it applies to all cultures all over the world.

An interesting variation of this rule is what Cialdini calls rejection-then-retreat. I recently experienced this when buying a new jacket. The store manager first showed me an enormously expensive jacket. When I made it clear that this was way beyond my budget, he didn't skip a beat and quickly emerged with a similar item about half the price. What a deal! Psychologically, because the second price appears to be small in comparison with the first one, the shopper reacts favourably – a principle known as price anchoring.

Commitment and consistency

Once we've committed to doing something, we face internal and societal tension if we don't see it through. To avoid that, we have an innate drive to be consistent with earlier actions and decisions.

You can use this to your advantage in surprisingly subtle ways. For example, if you want someone to fill in an online form, initially you may just ask for some small piece of information such as a name or e-mail address. The theory is that, once they've started the process by giving you those data, they've made a commitment and will be more willing to give much larger information later.

Another example is requesting a catalogue on a retailer's website, which leads to the expectation of buying something from that catalogue.

Social proof

We tend to look at the actions of others for clues on how we should behave. In situations where there's any uncertainty, we are especially likely to copy their behaviour.

So powerful is this mechanism that it has been employed to cure a fear of dogs in children. Cialdini explains how researchers showed them clips of other kids playing with dogs. Within four days of watching the videos, two-thirds of them were petting the same dogs they were previously scared of.

This is one of the most commonly applied techniques in e-commerce. Examples include testimonials, highlighting best sellers and showing the number of Facebook likes. We find comfort in the knowledge that others are there with us, or have trodden the path before us. Hence the saying: 'safety in numbers'.

This principle came into play in one project we ran for a large website selling flowers. Adding a simple banner stating 'Over 10 Million Bouquets Delivered' produced an increase of 6 per cent in revenue per visitor (Figure 13.1). Our research had pointed to a lack of familiarity with the brand being a barrier to buying. The banner gave people the social proof they needed that many others trust the brand, and thus made them feel it was a legitimate site and safe to order.

Liking

We are more likely to buy from those we like. One perhaps slightly controversial method cited by Cialdini is showing photographs of attractive people. Only if it's relevant to your product, I should add.

The world's best salesperson understood this instinctively. Joe Girard, whom you met at the start of this chapter, wrote in his book *How to Sell Anything to Anybody*: 'One of the most important determining factors of a sale is: Does the prospect like, trust and believe me?'[9]

You can invoke liking by creating the suggestion of similarity. We want to associate with people like us. Girard tried to dress like his customers. Online, you could do this by using the same language as your customers. What you often find, instead, is platitudinal corporate speak and marketing waffle.

Another example is using carefully selected testimonials to align with your target personas. Some e-commerce sites have even used the old, boring About Us page to introduce liking, by depicting the team as friendly, honest people – just like you and me.

Girard would approve.

Authority

We are easily influenced by authority figures, especially those with credentials such as 'doctor', 'professor' and so on. This can also be achieved by quoting from authoritative sources, for example citing studies, showing

Figure 13.1 The social proof message that led to a 6 per cent increase in revenue per visitor

Over
10 Million
Bouquets
Delivered

excerpts from academic journals or even just a photograph of someone in a white coat.

In Chapter 5, you saw an example of this technique in Figure 5.2. The well-known avian veterinary surgeon is a trusted figure among target customers.

Scarcity

Value tends to increase as supply comes under pressure, so we are more likely to buy something if stock is low. Daily deals sites are designed to exploit this principle.

Bonus: The rule of material self-interest

People want to maximize gains and minimize cost; in other words, they want to get the most for the lowest possible price. This seventh principle is given only scant attention by Cialdini in his foreword, explaining that it is such an obvious factor that it was deliberately omitted from the official list.

Lowest price does not always mean cheapest and it's not always monetary value alone that's important, but the whole experience. The perception of a good deal often counts for more than the actual price.

In fact, when we spot something we want for a lot less than expected, our brains light up with pleasure in exactly the same place as when people take heroin, according to research by Dr David Lewis.[10] When it comes to snapping up a bargain, it seems we just can't resist.

The buying decision-making process

An e-commerce transaction doesn't start, or end for that matter, with a purchase. The purchase is the only visible link in a chain of events that starts much earlier, and continues beyond the point where the transaction is concluded. The buying decision-making process[11] is a well-known framework that shows the mental stages consumers pass through when buying products:

- Need recognition
- Information search
- Evaluation of alternatives

- Purchase of product
- Post-purchase evaluation

Need recognition

Without a need, there can't be a purchase. Not only that, but it influences everything around the purchase decision, and even satisfaction levels after purchase.

To quote Joe Girard again: 'The more you understand about their needs and wants, the better equipped you'll be to provide them with the right solution.'[12]

This is why it's so crucial to really understand your customer's core need, which is what Chapter 5 is devoted to.

Information search

Once the need is recognized, consumers search for information about potential solutions. They might do a Google search, ask friends for recommendations or look at customer reviews. Purchases of everyday goods also pass through this step, but we tend to use memory recall or previous experience to find the information.

With tools like Google Analytics, it's possible to see what search terms visitors used to find your site. You may observe that some phrases relate to early exploratory stages, while others are closer to the next step of evaluating alternatives.

Evaluation

Having completed their information search, your potential customer now has a range of possibilities. It may amount to nothing but price comparison, which is so easy online. In that case, you have to justify your prices, if you aren't the lowest in the market. Key here is your value proposition, which we discuss in Chapter 5.

One of our clients is a famous electronic goods brand. The major sales objection on their website is that the same products can be bought at prices up to 20 per cent less from popular retail outlets. Our research revealed that their customers were prepared to pay more for the promise of global warranties, availability of the full product range and a fear of buying inferior 'grey' imports from department stores. That knowledge enabled us to mirror it back at visitors, boosting their perception of value.

Other factors that can help consumers narrow down options include product attributes and brand perception. Different attributes appeal to different people. You may think you know what matters to customers, but it's always worth checking this with surveys. Brand perception is a subjective judgement based on things like the look and feel of your site, and the content and tone of your messages (Figure 13.2). Be sensitive to that when creating alternative designs to test.

Purchase

Finally, we get to the source of that metric so keenly tracked, conversion rate. Hopefully this discussion helps to put it in context, and underscores the

Figure 13.2 Our client, a famous retail chain, makes the evaluation of alternatives easier by offering a great variety of product images. This invokes System 1 thinking by subtly answering key questions that a customer may have. What is the shape? How thick is it? How large is it? What is the texture like? These can all be answered subconsciously by looking at this collection of images. By the time the user examines product copy, it may be just a matter of System 2 rationalizing the decision, already made subconsciously by then

importance of investigating what happens 'upstream'. However, just because a potential customer made a choice in the Evaluation stage, there is no guarantee they will conclude the transaction. Some evidence of this can be seen in the high percentage of baskets that get abandoned – an average of 69.57 per cent across the board at the time of writing.[13]

Post-purchase behaviour

After making the purchase, your customer evaluates to what extent the product meets their original need. Whether or not those expectations are met determines customer satisfaction. In some cases the consumer will do another round of information search, this time to confirm that they've made the right decision. In behavioural psychology this is known as an attempt to reduce post-purchase cognitive dissonance, or buyer's remorse, which is surprisingly common. What they experience at this point can influence future sales.

FBM model of behaviour

Now that we've examined the decision-making process that precedes action, it's time to take a closer look at the action component itself. What makes people take a desired action, such as buying a product from your site?

Dr B J Fogg of Stanford University sheds light on this question with the Fogg Behavioural Model (FBM). It does a great job of capturing the fundamentals of complex human behaviour. For any given behaviour to occur, three things need to fall into place at the same time: motivation, ability and trigger (Figure 13.3).

What this means for e-commerce optimization:

- Understand the customer's core motivation:
  - Motivation refers to how strongly the individual is driven to act. Ability relates to how easy it is for that individual to take the desired action – this is usability in our context.
  - Throughout this book, we emphasize the importance of understanding your customer's core motivation. One of the best ways to do that is with the qualitative research methods discussed in Chapter 5.
  - Studies have shown that highly motivated users actually underestimate usability difficulties.[14] Therefore, someone with high motivation may be influenced to act by improving usability. It's one of the most effective interventions. A good way to identify these opportunities is by doing remote moderated usability testing, covered in Chapter 4.

Figure 13.3 The Fogg Behavioural Model shows how different factors come together to make target behaviour occur

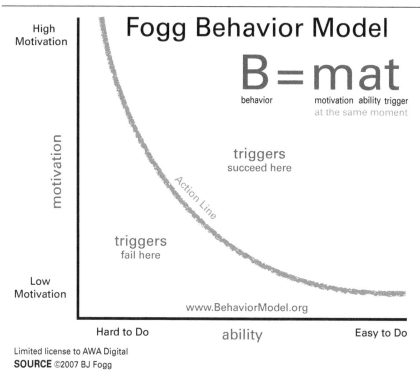

Limited license to AWA Digital
SOURCE ©2007 BJ Fogg

- Align your sales conversation with their needs and wants:
  - Your visitor will not take action without a trigger, even when motivation and ability are both high. Consequently, this is an area you want to be paying attention to. If the need is strong enough, it could act as a trigger. But you can create triggers too, for example e-mails with discount codes, and the offer of free delivery above a certain basket value. How about your calls to action? Is the button visible? Does the copy resonate with the user's need? Are you infusing triggers with benefits and features, when an appeal to System 1 thinking would be more appropriate?
  - Timing is everything, says Fogg. A trigger at a time when either motivation or ability is low will not result in a sale. All three ingredients have to come together, at the same time, for the credit card number to be punched in.
- Improve the usability of the website.

FBM in practice

Cox & Cox has very loyal customers, highly motivated. They love the unique and eclectic mix of furniture and homeware. These pieces are a form of self-expression for target customers, they are not just functional.

On the mobile page shown in Figure 13.4, motivation is high and ability is there to click through. However, the trigger is weak. The thumbnails in the control (left) are small and the text is hard to read. The variation on the right was 17 per cent more effective in sending traffic to PDPs, which is a key objective of this page, and led to an increase in revenue of 6 per cent.

Figure 13.4   This winning test intensified the trigger force on the Cox & Cox mobile site. In the control, on the left, each category is represented by an image. Our variation, on the right, removed the images and simply replaced it with tabs

 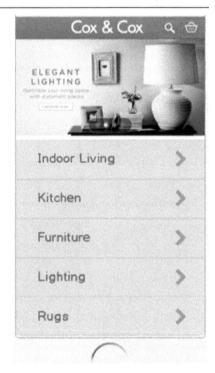

Summary

The job of your website is to conduct a sales conversation with the prospect. That should be the focus of your optimization efforts, rather than pages and funnels.

To influence behaviour, you have to recognize and understand it. Being familiar with the basic principles covered in this chapter will serve you well. It will shape your analysis, help you formulate better hypotheses and improve your ability to make sense of experiments.

We tend to view buying as a simple yes/no decision. In fact, it's not black and white, but several shades of grey. About 95 per cent of all decisions happen subconsciously. This means that we tend to purchase with emotion more than rational deliberation – even if we think we don't.

As a consequence, throughout your optimization process, you should be trying to identify the core needs and motivations of your target customers so that you can align your approach with that.

The FBM model explains that motivation alone is not enough to make someone buy. There must also be a trigger and ability. In the context of optimization, this means aligning the sales conversation with customer needs as well as improving the usability of the website.

Notes

1 Mello, T (2017) Quality over quantity: How to focus on your most valuable customers, *Forbes* [Online] www.forbes.com/sites/theyec/2017/11/30/quality-over-quantity-how-to-focus-on-your-most-valuable-customers/ (archived at https://perma.cc/P7DN-MB6U)

2 Lewis, D (2013) *The Brain Sell: When science meets shopping*, Nicholas Brealey Publishing, London

3 Underhill, P (2008) *Why We Buy: The science of shopping*, Simon & Schuster, New York

4 Ratneshwar, S, Mick, D and Huffman, C (2000) *The Why of Consumption: Contemporary perspectives on consumer motives, goals and desires*, Routledge, New York

5 Kahneman, D (2012) *Thinking, Fast and Slow*, Penguin, London

6 Lewis, D (2013) *The Brain Sell: When science meets shopping*, Nicholas Brealey Publishing, London

7 Dooley, R (2012) *Brainfluence: 100 ways to persuade and convince consumers with neuromarketing*, John Wiley & Sons, Hoboken, NJ

8 Cialdini, R (2007) *Influence: The psychology of persuasion*, p xiv, Harper Collins, New York

9 Girard, J (1977) *How to Sell Anything to Anybody*, p 37, Warner Books, New York

10 Lewis, D (2013) *The Brain Sell: When science meets shopping*, Nicholas Brealey Publishing, London

11 Blackwell, R D, Miniard, P W and Engel, J F (2005) *Consumer Behavior*, 10th edn, South-Western College Publishing, Mason, OH

12 Girard, J (2013) *Joe Girard's 13 Essential Rules of Selling: How to be a top achiever and lead a great life*, McGraw-Hill, New York

13 Baymard Institute (2016) [Accessed 11 August 2020] 41 cart abandonment rate statistics, *Baymard Institute* [Online] http://baymard.com/lists/cart-abandonment-rate (archived at https://perma.cc/2ANU-XKZP)

14 Venkatesh, V (2000) Determinants of perceived ease of use: Integrating control, intrinsic motivation, and emotion into the technology acceptance model, *Information Systems Research*, **11** (4), pp 342–65

Launching a new website   14

'We need a better website' is often where it starts.

Switching to a new website, or migrating to a new e-commerce platform, is likely to be one of the biggest capital expenses any 21st-century online business could make. Typically, it's a huge investment of time, management resources and money.

It's exciting, and naturally comes with high expectations that the effort and expense will be worth it, with improved efficiencies and sales.

All too often though, the reality is somewhat different. Things do go wrong and there are endless ways for the changes to lead to reduced revenue and a poorer customer experience.

What problems are typically encountered? How do you prevent them happening and get the website you're hoping for? And if, despite your best efforts, the website fails to give you higher sales when you launch, what can you do to put it right?

Do you need a new website?

Before you start on a major replatform or redesign, the first question is whether a new website is required in the first place. Have you fully considered the other option of keeping the current site and investing the resources you might have spent on a new website on optimizing it? It's less exciting, but it's a way to de-risk the migration.

A brand new website that replaces your existing one with another, which often bears little resemblance to the old website's look and feel, navigation and/or functionality, is called a 'radical redesign'.

The opposite is 'evolutionary site redesign', which comes about naturally as part of the experimentation process. Evolutionary site design (ESR) gives you continual improvements and increasing online sales in a controlled way.

By contrast, radical redesign is typically undertaken every five years or so, costing large amounts of money and time. The hope is that it will achieve a substantial increase in sales immediately, although this is by no means guaranteed. Figures 14.1 and 14.2 illustrate why you make just as much money, if not more, with evolutionary changes, without any of the risks and uncertainties of a brand new expensive design.

In ESR, gains are made each year. Any improvements made in Year 1 carry on over the following four years, so revenue growth is cumulative and exponential. To achieve ESR requires a systematic programme of continuous learning, testing and optimization. Since you are verifying each incremental improvement, the extra sales are predictable before they go live on the website.

Radical redesigns are risky. Often there has not been a process of learning and discovery, so revenue uplifts are not as predictable. Second, there is often not a clear line of sight between changes to the website and the result they may generate. As we've seen in Chapter 9, this cause and effect can be established by way of running experiments.

Once the decision to invest in a radical redesign has been taken, there remains a significant question mark as to whether this investment will be

Figure 14.1 Evolutionary site redesign

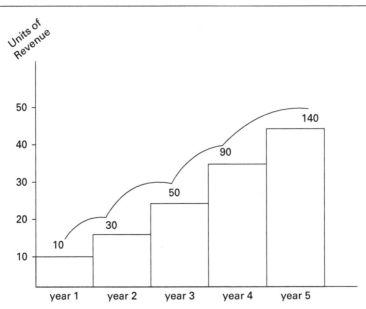

Figure 14.2 Radical redesign

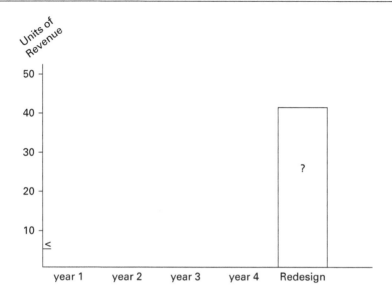

repaid. Worse, you will only find out after the investment has been made and the new site is live.

While we recommend the evolutionary approach, there may be times when a radical redesign will be justified:

- The website's underlying technology is severely outdated, eg the website is not responsive or the website has been patched so frequently that simple updates become slow and costly to implement.

- The third party providing website development services on their proprietary platform is slow and expensive and you need to replatform and start a new relationship with a different supplier.

- The overall design of the website is so outdated that it has a negative impact on the standing of the brand.

- Results from your optimization efforts show diminishing returns and you have hit your local maxima (first mentioned in Chapter 9).

However, almost certainly for you an ESR would be not only possible but desirable. This is the current practice of most of today's internet giants. The likes of Facebook, Google, Amazon and eBay continually evolve their current design and functionality:

1 Still get the new 'look and feel' and lift conversion at the same time.

2 Get real-time feedback on whether a change is delivering the desired impact or not. If not, you can easily retrace your steps.

3 Focus on key business metrics rather than a design that may look aesthetically pleasing but does not perform or offer a good user experience.

4 Avoid the financial risks and loss of competitiveness associated with the radical redesign approach.

5 Mitigate the risks that your existing customers will be confused by the new radical design and start spending less.

6 Works at a faster pace and is a more effective form of optimization than a radical redesign.

7 Offers your customers and visitors a website that is continually evolving rather than waiting for the typical 3–5-year gaps between radical redesigns.

However, you may not be in a position to adopt an evolutionary approach to site design, either because of the four reasons listed earlier, or for political reasons management has simply proclaimed 'We need a better website'. It may also be that the business is used to managing projects using the waterfall approach of radical redesign, rather than the modern agile approach.

But what is the impact of the e-commerce website project that goes badly off the rails? To answer this question we commissioned our own research, surveying those with extensive experience of working on these types of project. The study revealed more than half (55 per cent) of respondents experienced problems working on 'new website and/or functionality' projects.

What is clear from our investigation and the M&S example was that launching a new e-commerce website often generates significant problems for the business. The investigation showed that the most common problems when launching a new e-commerce website were:

- Loss of sales/revenue
- Disgruntled visitors
- Management time wasted

These were not isolated incidents, but experienced by over 70 per cent of our respondents.

It is possible to avoid or mitigate these pitfalls by careful management of a radical redesign project. What follows is a step-by-step guide to protect your online sales when you create a new e-commerce website, and avoid a conversion rate disaster when it's launched.

Five stages of a new website

Our research revealed that the development of an e-commerce website comprises five key stages. Whether you are right at the start and have just got the business case signed off, or whether you are about to go live, there are clear, concrete actions you can take to improve your chances of success after launch.

---

1 Strategy stage: Development of a business case.

2 Early stage: Production of functional specification and identification of suppliers.

3 Middle stage: Design and development has started.

4 Final stage: The run-up to launch.

5 Live stage: The website has launched.

Each stage is different, with a range of beliefs and pitfalls. At any one of these stages, decisions will be taken that could seriously harm sales when the new site is launched.

Conversely, there are concrete actions you can take at each stage, to protect your existing conversion rate and make sure the new site performs as well as or better than the current one. And if you have just launched a new site and the worst has happened, there are methods to revive your sales quickly and effectively.

Strategy stage

What happens at the strategy stage?

Typically, at the strategy stage there is an awareness that the website is becoming out of date, while newer website platforms offer exciting features. Competitors' websites are pored over and sometimes copied wholesale (of course, with no knowledge of exactly how well their website is performing).

A financial case may be developed to weigh up the cost of updating and optimizing your current website versus commissioning a new one – especially if updates are currently slow and costly to make and/or there are no other companies that could take over the maintenance of the website.

Right now though, this analysis is unlikely to be well documented, and the process of deciding whether to replace the current website has just begun.

Beliefs at the strategy stage

- While the decision to replace your current website requires a good deal of thought, it is expected that your new website will convert visitors into customers at a much higher rate – why else would this much money be spent?

- Expectations are that the new website build, if it happens, will be on time, within budget and deliver substantial ROI.

Pitfalls at the strategy stage

Most of the pitfalls at this stage are around the quality of information available and the assumptions that are being made.

It is common at this stage for there to be little investigation into the cheaper (but less exciting) solution of optimizing the current website. This could be a cost-effective way of replacing the current site. In reality, though, once the decision has been made to commission a new website, any expenditure on the current one is often perceived as 'dead money'.

There is a good deal of excitement around the project, and looking forward to the greener grass on the other side that the new website will offer.

Finally, despite all the nightmare stories that surround new website projects going horribly wrong, there is an overwhelming belief that disasters only happen to others.

Conversion rate protection at the strategy stage

This early stage may be your best opportunity to gain a high-performing 'new' website at a fraction of the cost of replatforming or redesigning, so optimization should be given serious consideration.

What factors should influence your decision? It's all down to how much money is being left on the table versus how much could be gained by launching a new website.

What you know is the cost of the new website and, by extrapolating from previous years' revenue, you could forecast likely sales. What you don't know and is hard to predict is the increase you may gain from optimizing the current website. What you can do is conduct a review of the website's weaknesses.

As a recap, here are some of the tools and techniques used to do this kind of evaluation:

- **a conversion funnel** to reliably show where visitors are dropping off;
- **heatmaps** to understand exactly what your visitors click on, what they don't click on and how they really navigate your pages;
- **usability testing** with testers recruited directly from the website to understand their experience of the current website in the most revealing way;
- **asking your website visitors and customers** why they abandon/don't buy more from your website (either personally, or with a survey);
- **asking customers** why they choose to buy from you and not your competitors;
- **compiling a list** of how you can strengthen your value proposition to your visitors and customers;
- **benchmarking** your website against your competitors' websites in terms of the strengths and weaknesses of your value proposition versus theirs.

For more detail on how to research your website and identify conversion killers, reread Chapters 3 to 6.

Having completed this evaluation, you will be far more informed about how the current website can be optimized, without the need to invest in a new website. You can then present a detailed analysis of the costs associated with the new website along with the untapped opportunities still on the current site.

Early-stage protection measures

What happens at the early stage?

This is the stage when the business case for a new e-commerce website/platform has been made and the investment has been agreed in principle. The functional specification is being written, web development partners are being appointed and project plans are being finalized.

Although it may seem unthinkable at this point that sales might be lower than at present, it could happen. Here's how you can protect the conversion rate of your website at the early stage.

Beliefs at the early stage

- It is tacitly expected that the new website will generate positive ROI and convert at a higher rate than the current one.
- It is anticipated that the website will be delivered on time – there are months to go before the specified delivery date.
- Changes to the functional specification can easily be made. At this stage, it's just a document, with little set in stone.

Pitfalls at the early stage

These are some of the practices and assumptions we have seen at first hand that can cause problems later on:

- Businesses are overly influenced by competitors' websites that they believe give their competitors an advantage. However, this can be misleading. The way to stay ahead is to focus on your customers' needs, not on what others are doing.
- The functional specification may be based on industry 'best practice' (there are many guides and resources offering this kind of advice). However, these 'one-size-fits-all' techniques may not be right for your website. Websites' visitors are unique to the business, and high-converting websites are designed with their needs at the forefront.
- Sometimes a functional specification is based on what the business 'believes' about its website visitors and what they want, rather than based on rigorous research. So often these hunches and opinions turn out to be simply wrong – or at best do okay, but not as well as a specification based on knowledge of what your real visitors are looking for.

Conversion rate protection at the early stage

The key question to focus on at this stage is: 'How can I be sure that the functional specification for the new website is based on the needs of my website users?'

Answering this central question, using similar tools and approaches as deployed in the strategy stage, will help you clearly state what needs to be fixed on your next website.

You can use all of this evidence to create a specification review, which will minimize the risk that the website you are about to commission will fail to deliver. This is because you are cross-checking the functional specification with what you now know about your website customers and visitors.

Middle-stage protection measures

What happens at the middle stage?

The board has signed off the business case and the project is well under way. The functional specification has been written and approved and now design and development have started.

Wireframes have been developed and may already be signed off, together with the look and feel of the template pages and the user flow through the checkout.

Beliefs at the middle stage

- This exciting new e-commerce project is well under way, and is set to deliver a new website jam-packed with features and hooks that it is hoped the visitors are going to love.

- There is excitement to see how different the new website will be from your current one, and the design is much crisper and more modern – all the ideas the business had are now crystallized into one perfectly designed website.

- The new website will be launched in time for your peak season and you are sure to capitalize on its extra pulling power, turning visitors into customers at a far higher rate.

Pitfalls at the middle stage

Our research shows that these are some of the common issues at this stage:

- Designers and developers are now running the show and, with a strict deadline, many decisions are being taken without much regard to the users of this new website. Making a website look good is not the same as building one that converts well.

- Insufficient thought is being given to the taxonomy of the product categories and subcategories. The assumption is that this hierarchy is easy to change.

- Copy for products, categories and general static copy is being left until last – just words to fill up the space rather than integral to the customer journey.

The project is now clearly in the delivery phase. The time to make large-scale changes has passed, so anything that was not properly thought through in the early stages can't be put right. Any attempt to do so will affect the launch date.

Conversion rate protection in the middle stage

At this point the central question is 'How can I be sure that this website is going to deliver, without holding up the go-live date?'

In answering this central question, you should consider performing the following quick and easy checks as a mid-launch audit:

- Get the wireframes and mocked-up pages reviewed by actual users of your website. This is quick and inexpensive, but will give invaluable feedback. True, you may get one or two red warning lights – but if they are going to seriously affect conversion rate when the site goes live, it's much easier and cheaper to know now.

- Make sure that the copy is professionally written, with the website visitor in mind (not search engine spiders).

- Review the wording around the value proposition of the new website. While the proposition itself should remain constant, there may be a more compelling way of expressing it. Test the new messaging with your customers if you're not sure.

- Analyse the sales performance of categories and subcategories to ensure that they are in the correct position within the new navigation.

- Perform a look-to-book ratio analysis to see which products require more attention to make them as compelling as others.

Final-stage protection measures

What happens in the final stage?

The live date is fast approaching

Light years seem to have elapsed since the business case and functional specification were being written. Chances are it's taken longer than everyone expected – for a myriad of reasons that are nobody's fault. (We have yet to hear about a new website that launches on time.)

With the live date quickly approaching, relationships may be fraught, tensions running high and team members can't agree on the priorities.

Beliefs at the final stage

- The website is a few days away from being live and although a number of compromises on all sorts of things have had to be made, it's just a matter of time before you can flick the switch.

- Everyone is excited to see how the new website will perform. There is huge expectation that online sales are going to shoot through the roof in the very near future.

Pitfalls at the final stage

The main danger at this point is that compromises the business has been forced to make have affected what the website offers to visitors in terms of frictionless usability and a persuasive experience.

Of course, some of those compromises were necessary, as they could have jeopardized the whole project. But some may actually cause the new website to perform at far lower levels of conversion than before.

We have seen this many times over – the challenge of keeping to a deadline has meant that some companies have inadvertently thrown out the baby with the bathwater. Even worse, they are really not sure which was the baby and which the bathwater.

Conversion rate protection at the final stage

At this stage, there's no more time left to make changes for launch day. The main focus now should be to ensure funnels are correctly configured so that the customer journey can be analysed. These funnel reports allow you to make revealing comparisons between the current and new websites.

Useful metrics for benchmarking include:

- Revenue per visitor (RPV)
- Bounce rate for key landing pages (BR)
- Exit rate (ER)
- Basket abandonment rate (AR)
- Add-to-basket ratios for your bestsellers (A2B)
- Conversion rate (CR)

Segment these metrics by new and returning visitors, by your five most popular traffic sources and by device type.

We very much hope your conversion will not drop when the new site goes live. But we've seen it happen many times. If you are unlucky enough that it happens to you, you'll be one step ahead, because you'll know exactly where your customers are dropping out compared to the old site.

Also do some usability testing with your website visitors. You won't be able to use their input to make changes to the new site, but it will mean you have a good idea of which elements of the new website are the most important ones to fix as soon as you go live – elements that matter to your website visitors, not you.

Live-stage protection measures

If you have jumped straight to this section, it is probably because you have got a conversion disaster on your hands – and you're really not sure what to do.

What happens in the live stage?

If conversion and sales are going up, there is jubilation. But if the numbers are all heading south, it's a real anti-climax. Everyone is disappointed that their months of work have not paid off and morale is low. The finance team may be looking at the money spent and wondering how it was justified for a website that is, seemingly, worse than the one it replaced.

If this has happened, despite all best efforts and smart planning, what can be done?

Sometimes the answer is obvious – the funnel tells you that a lot of visitors are dropping out at checkout stage or there is an issue with page load speed.

At other times it's not clear. The site loads quickly, looks great and performs functionally, but visitors are just not buying like they used to.

Beliefs at the live stage

Plunging sales create an urgent requirement to do something to address the issue – and to do it quickly. Everyone is looking for leadership and a sensible course of action that will attack the issue at its core – where the problem is and what we are going to do about it. The time for guesswork has passed and everyone is expecting the way forward to be based on data and evidence.

Pitfalls at the live stage

As with any crisis, the biggest problem is likely to be the blame game, blind panic and grasping at straws. Every minute needs to be focused on understanding the conversion problem and its root causes.

Figure 14.3 Conversion disaster recovery programme

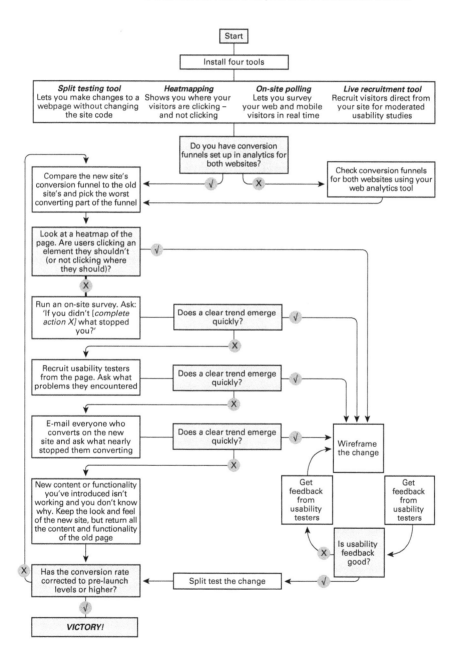

Website disaster programme

Use this conversion disaster recovery programme to identify the conversion killers on your new e-commerce website

Your analytics reports will tell you where the problems exist between the new and old sites but they won't tell you why these problems exist. By using voice-of-customer tools, like surveys and usability testing with real visitors, you can develop valid hypotheses to test to fix the problems.

Conversion rate protection at the live stage

The right approach at this stage is to have a plan – and to stick to it. Figure 14.3 shows a step-by-step guide to rescuing a poorly performing new website, sensibly and systematically.

Just like an effective optimization programme, you install tools on your site for research and analysis, as well as split-testing tools to test your hypotheses.

But why put yourself in this situation? Why risk everything, when you can simply optimize the site you've got, make your customers happy and reap the rewards? We've shared with you everything you need to put your own programme in place. Follow what we've told you and it will work. The future is in your hands, and we hope you enjoy the exciting and prosperous journey ahead.

Summary

Our experience is that in the majority of cases you will gain a greater and quicker return on investment by continuously optimizing your e-commerce website, and going for evolutionary redesign rather than the radical redesign of a brand new website. Of course, there are times when a radical redesign is unavoidable, but it is always worth investigating whether a redesign will bring higher rewards than an evolutionary approach.

There are five stages to launching a new website, and there are pitfalls at each one. You can mitigate the risks by taking protective actions. These actions split into two main approaches.

At the strategy, early and middle stages, focus is on understanding your website visitors and customers and ensuring that their needs will be delivered by the new website.

Later on, at the final and live stages, focus on checking whether there are any negative effects caused by the new website. Research why these pages are causing visitor dropout and then launch split tests to test fixes that will reverse the decline in sales.

A new website always carries risks, which you can remove entirely by adopting a test and validate approach. Throughout this book, we have aimed to give you the tools to do just that.

We wish you every success.

Note

1 Wood, Z (2014) [Accessed 11 August 2020] Shareholders attack Marks & Spencer as website revamp loses customers, *Guardian* [Online] www. theguardian.com/business/2014/jul/08/marks-and-spencer-shareholders-attack-website-online-sales-fall (archived at https://perma.cc/WPU6-93TL)

INDEX

CPSIA information can be obtained
at www.ICGtesting.com
Printed in the USA
JSHW051409091220
10133JS00008B/96